The Mexican Revolution in Chicago

D1526635

LATINOS IN CHICAGO AND THE MIDWEST

Series Editors
Frances R. Aparicio, Northwestern University
Juan Mora-Torres, DePaul University
María de los Angeles Torres, University of Illinois at Chicago

A list of books in the series appears at the end of this book.

The Mexican Revolution in Chicago

Immigration Politics from the Early Twentieth Century to the Cold War

JOHN H. FLORES

UNIVERSITY OF
ILLINOIS PRESS
Urbana, Chicago, and Springfield

The companion website is located at
https://www.press.uillinois.edu/
books/flores/mexican_revolution_in_chicago

Cataloging-in-Publication Data available from the
Library of Congress
ISBN 978-0-252-04180-8 (cloth: alk.)
ISBN 978-0-252-08342-6 (paper: alk)
ISBN 978-0-252-05047-3 (ebook)

This book is dedicated to my father, a Mexican immigrant who taught me to work; to my mother, a Mexican immigrant who taught me to study; and to my brothers, who taught me to share.

Contents

Acknowledgments

I could not have written this book without the support of a community of scholars, friends, and family members. My community read chapters of this book, recommended ways to improve them, pointed me toward specific sources, and, at times, reminded me of the values that led me into this profession in the first place.

As a graduate student in the History of Work, Race, and Gender in the Urban World program at the University of Illinois at Chicago (UIC), I was privileged to have been advised by Leon Fink, the director of the program. Leon mentored me throughout my graduate education. He shared his expertise and experiences with me, always assessed my work thoroughly, and always offered me critical and valuable advice. Eric Arnesen also mentored me at UIC. Eric provided me with extremely helpful and caring guidance at pivotal moments during my graduate education. I cannot thank him enough for his commitment to me and my future. Juan Mora Torres at DePaul University took an interest in my research early on and expanded my professional network in Chicago, providing me with opportunities to share my findings with the public. Juan, along with Susan Levine and Perry Duis, worked closely with me to refine my early research, which served as the starting point for this book. I thank them all for their help, patience, and key recommendations.

In its current form, this book came into being through the support and encouragement of the Department of History, the Social Justice Institute (SJI), and the College of Arts and Sciences at Case Western Reserve University (CWRU). My colleague in the Department of History and the director of the Social Justice Institute, Rhonda Williams, helped place me in the position to contribute to the field of immigration history and to the development of the department and the institute. I am incredibly fortunate to work with Rhonda and the faculty and staff of an institute that reflects my core values and consistently demonstrates that another world is necessary and possible.

Within the Department of History, David Hammack has served as my faculty mentor, and he has been invaluable to me. I have benefited tremendously from David's vast experience, his keen recommendations, and his consistent encouragement. I am fortunate to have been mentored by David Hammack. Ken Ledford and Jonathan Sadowsky have also served as my de facto advisors, providing me with guidance and fellowship over the course of many years. Ken is truly exceptional in his support of junior faculty members, and I routinely drew on him for advice and assistance. All the while, Ted Steinberg has been a true friend. Working at any university can be challenging, but caring and genuine people like Ted remind you that you are not alone. Outside the department, Marilyn Mobley has been a strong advocate of my work and a kind friend. I always felt empowered after talking to Maril, and for that, I thank her tremendously. More recently, Ananya Dasgupta and Tim Black have bolstered my morale as I labored away on the final aspects of this manuscript. They are insightful and wonderful people, and I thank them for their friendship and encouragement.

Notably, the research for this book could not have been completed without the vital support of Dean Cyrus Taylor of the College of Arts and Sciences and Provost William Baeslack. Soon after I began my appointment, I was awarded the Climo Junior Chair, which provided me with resources to expand the research for this book. Through this research, I was able to create a census of Hispanic naturalization in Chicago, which distinguishes my work from other projects on Mexican Chicago in a number of fundamental ways. Working with several graduate students, including Nathan Delaney, Elizabeth Salem, John Baden, Corey Hazlett, Eric Miller, and Ryan Chamberlain, I was able to organize and aggregate data from more than three thousand naturalization records. Nathan Delaney, in particular, was instrumental in the data collection and in the creation of the historical maps of Latino Chicago that appear in the companion website to this book. Elizabeth Salem, meanwhile, helped me track down numerous sources and worked with me on managing various aspects of the project. I thank all of these graduate students for their assistance.

The immigration records I worked with were collected through the considerable work of many archivists and administrators. In particular, Martin Tuohy and the staff at the National Archives and Records Administration worked patiently with me as they retrieved tens of thousands of naturalization documents for my use. In this same vein, Licenciado Alejandro Rivera and the staff at the Archivo Histórico de la Secretaria de Relaciones Exteriores in Mexico City worked closely with me to access records that reshaped my understanding of the transnational activism of Mexican immigrants. Licenciado Rivera is a true gentleman. He not only expedited my research at the archive but also offered me his friendship and taught me much about his incredible city.

As the book took form, I was delighted to learn that it would be published by the University of Illinois Press and, in particular, within a series on the Midwest and Chicago, the city of my birth, which will always hold a special place in my heart. At the University of Illinois Press, I would especially like to thank Francis R. Aparicio for her commitment to the project. I cannot thank her enough. I would also like to thank my patient editor, Dawn M. Durante, whose enthusiasm has been incredibly encouraging. Finally, I wish to express my sincerest appreciation to the copyeditor, Mary M. Hill, and to the two anonymous outside readers who helped me produce a better book.

There are many wonderful people who also helped make this book possible in direct and indirect ways. Among those whom I wish to thank for their advice, assistance, and friendship are José Angel Hernández; Lorrell Kilpatrick; Sam Mitrani; Joseph Lipari; John Rosen; Juanita Del Toro; Sarah Koning; Marc Rodriguez; Josh Fennell; Dan Harper; Jaime Pensado; Cat Jacquet; Theresa Christensen-Caballero; Lunaire Ford; José Perales; Francisco Piña; Kathy Tobin; James Lane; Alan Spector; Gene Defelice; Victor Holden; Lupe Ramirez and Jaime Salazar; Agustina, Enrique, and Sylvia Lizcano; Mat Chico; and Martha, Juan, Steven, Bryan, Logan, Bianca, and Nana Flores. I thank each of you for your unique contributions.

As an undergraduate I was mentored by Professor Joseph Biggott. Joe inspired me and guided me into the academy. I owe him a debt that cannot be repaid.

Earlier iterations of sections of chapters 1, 4, and 6 were published in "A Migrating Revolution: Mexican Political Organizers and Their Rejection of American Assimilation, 1920–1940," in *Workers across the Americas: The Transnational Turn in Labor History*, edited by Leon Fink (New York: Oxford University Press, 2011) and in "Deporting Dissidence: Examining Transnational Mexican Politics, US Naturalization, and American Unions through the Life of a Mexican Immigrant, 1920–1954," *Aztlan: A Journal of Chicano Studies* 38 (Spring 2013): 95–126.

The Mexican Revolution in Chicago

Introduction

There is very little published on the Mexicans in Chicago . . . and [they] are perhaps the least understood people in the community.
—Mexican Relations Committee of Chicago, 1925

Nearly 100,000 Mexicans constitute what is probably the Chicago area's least understood minority group.
—Tom Littlewood, *Chicago Sun-Times*, October 19, 1953

On a warm summer day in August 1927, Mexican immigrants Juana and Valentin Guevara and their two small children walked down Laflin Street on their way to their apartment in the Back of the Yards neighborhood of Chicago.[1] Like other ethnic neighborhoods in the city, the Back of the Yards was undergoing a profound demographic transition. Over the preceding years, Irish, Polish, and Italian Americans had witnessed a surge in the Mexican population of Chicago. While only a few hundred Mexicans had lived in the city in 1900, more than thirty thousand now resided throughout Chicagoland. White ethnic Americans held ambivalent attitudes about their new Mexican neighbors.[2] Decent jobs were difficult to secure, and many white ethnics had invested what little wealth they had into their homes. Although the sentiment varied, white ethnics often regarded Mexicans as competitors for jobs, apartments, houses, and city resources, and they consequently resisted Mexican encroachment into their communities.[3]

Most recently, a Mexican had killed a Pole during a fistfight in the Back of the Yards, and Mexicans were now being assaulted in retaliation. As the temperature in Chicago rose, a Polish teenager named Joseph Jopek spotted the Guevaras as they bustled along his block. Acting rambunctiously, Jopek decided to pedal his bicycle into the Guevaras' ten-year-old son. After the boys collided, Juana Guevara began scolding Jopek, and in the heat of the moment, she slapped Jopek across the face. By chance, a former police sheriff named Paul Grabinsky happened to be driving by and caught sight of Juana just as she struck Jopek. Infuriated, Grabinsky jumped out of his vehicle, ran at Juana, and shouted, "You wretched Mexican woman, you are a . . ."—but he never finished his tirade. As Grabinsky rushed Juana, she reached into a pocket in her dress, withdrew a .32 caliber pistol, and quickly fired three rounds, striking Grabinsky in the throat. Hearing the gunshots, Polish Americans and Mexican immigrants ran toward the commotion, and an all-out riot ensued. Several hours later, Chicago police officers arrived at the Guevaras' home, found Juana and her pistol, and arrested her for homicide.[4]

As news of Juana Guevara's arrest spread, Mexican and Hispanic immigrants went into action, mobilizing all of their resources in Guevara's defense. Leading the charge, the Spanish-language press of Chicago, founded by Mexican, Puerto Rican, and Nicaraguan journalists, published articles that lamented that Grabinsky had died during the altercation but maintained that "Juanita" had "legitimately defended her honor," her body, and the lives of her children in a city that sanctioned discrimination against Mexicans. For years, Hispanic journalists had written articles condemning racially motivated attacks on Mexicans. In their current editorials in support of Juanita, Mexican newspapermen defined her as their "compatriot," their fellow Mexican citizen, who required the assistance of all "honorable" Mexicans if she was going to persevere through this ordeal. Concurrently, Mexican journalists characterized Paul Grabinsky as a "gratuitously offensive Pole" when they referenced the incident and other conflicts between white ethnics and Mexicans. Through their control of the Spanish-language press, Mexican and Hispanic journalists constructed a narrative that justified why a Mexican immigrant like Juanita carried a loaded firearm in Chicago and why she had shot Grabinsky when he had made the ill-fated decision to charge at her.[5]

Over the proceeding months, Hispanic activists used their networks to defend Guevara successfully. Mexican journalists such as Julián Mondragón, an immigrant from Mexico City, joined with the Mexican vice consul of Chicago, Luis Lupian, to apply community and political pressure on the police department and city prosecutor. They ensured that Juanita was treated humanely while in custody, they demanded that she be tried fairly, and they vetted defense attorneys before settling on a lawyer who appears to have been well connected in Chicago. Juanita Guevara could never have afforded to hire such an attorney, but she and her husband were members of immigrant societies such as Club Cultural Latino Americano and the Sociedad Feminil Mexicana, which organized fund-raisers and collected donations to pay for Juanita's expensive legal fees. While the Sociedad Feminil disseminated information about Juanita, Mexican playwrights and performers then sojourning in the city lent their names to the cause, and they staged elaborate productions to raise awareness and revenue for the Guevaras. Mexican small businessmen also offered their assistance. They donated money and provided community activists with the use of their restaurants and halls to serve as meeting and fund-raising spaces.[6]

Some Mexican immigrants, however, were less supportive of Guevara. Within the Hispanic community, some were critical of their own country-men, arguing that poor and uneducated Mexicans behaved rudely in public, drank too much liquor, and engaged in criminal activities, and it was sug-gested that these types of Mexicans became involved in the neighborhood brawls that exacerbated racial tensions. The Mexicans who expressed these views were often critical of violence and were therefore wary of supporting Juanita, because she had shot Grabinsky. He had died, after all, while she was still alive.[7]

Within four months of Guevara's arrest, the front page of *La Noticia Mun-dial* celebrated, "Juanita de Guevara Has Been Released!" Guevara escaped a life-long jail sentence because of the crucial support she received from the most influential Mexican and Hispanic immigrants in Chicago in the 1920s. The majority of Spanish-language newspapers, the Mexican consulate, and a coalition of Mexican societies had thrown their collective weight behind Guevara. The talented lawyer who was hired to defend Juanita argued that she believed her life was in grave danger when Grabinsky rushed at her. Guevara's attorney selected a jury of white Americans who sympathized with Juanita and were open to discussing violence against Mexicans. During the trial, Guevara's lawyer secured testimonies from white doctors and city officials who discussed in detail the beatings that Mexicans could receive during racial attacks. Mexican community activists followed the trial from start to finish, and some attended the proceedings. Their presence must have conveyed an image of a unified Hispanic community committed to a positive outcome for Guevara. In the end, Hispanic immigrant activists were victorious, for Guevara was only fined and placed on probation. She was released from jail, to the exhilaration of the Mexicans who defended her.[8]

This book is about the Mexican immigrants who fought for Juanita Gue-vara, and it is about those who refused to support her. This book examines the political beliefs and social activism of Mexican immigrants in Chica-goland, a region that included Chicago and the cities of East Chicago and Gary in Northwest Indiana. Beginning in the mid-1920s and extending into the years of the Great Depression, the New Deal, and the Cold War, Mexi-can immigrants engaged in a wide range of political activities. Middle-class Mexican immigrants carried out liberal reform projects, providing poorer immigrants with social welfare services, educational programs, and criminal justice assistance. These liberals were passionate Mexican nationalists who were critical of U.S. interventions in Latin America and U.S. race relations. By comparison, working-class Mexican radicals, some of whom were skilled craftsmen, "organic intellectuals," and affiliates of the Partido Comunista Mexicano (Mexican Communist Party), organized Mexican workers to support anti-imperialist, "socialist education," and workers' rights initiatives. All the while, conservative Mexican immigrants, professionals and laborers alike, stressed the importance of religion, family values, and mutual aid endeavors, and they pointed migrants to politically moderate labor unions that eschewed radical politics. These Mexicans rejected the politics of the liberals and radicals and recruited migrants to establish Spanish-language parochial schools and Mexican Catholic parishes in the United States.

As diverse and divided as these Mexican immigrants were, I characterize them all as members of a "revolutionary generation" because their political beliefs were defined by their experiences and understandings of the Mexican Revolution (1910–20), a civil war fought by distinct factions. The liberal, radical, and conservative factions of the revolution that migrated to Chicagoland competed with each other to win recruits and to mold the identity and political perspective of the broader Mexican population. Initially, all three revolutionary factions defined themselves as Mexican patriots loyal to the Mexican state. Over the course of the 1920s and 1930s, however, major political events in Mexico led the conservatives (or traditionalists, as I call them) to become the most critical of the Mexican state and the most amenable to U.S. naturalization. Then, during the Cold War years of the 1940s and 1950s, the U.S. government took aim at the radical faction of the revolutionary generation and disciplined them through deportation. Recently naturalized traditionalists and young U.S.-born Mexican Americans were largely passed over by the U.S. government during the Cold War deportations. These remaining Mexican Americans formed their own organizations, led the Mexican community in new directions, and left the politics of the liberal and radical Mexican nationalists behind them.

Beginning in the 1920s, Mexican immigrant liberals, radicals, and traditionalists established transnational social movements in Chicagoland that promoted their distinct brands of Mexican nationalism, recruited other immigrants to their particular causes, and initially discouraged their supporters from becoming U.S. citizens. Each revolutionary faction (the liberals, radicals, and traditionalists) organized societies and coalitions; held meetings, events, and fund-raisers; delivered statements to the Mexican public through the Spanish-language press; and stressed the dignity of their constituencies.[9] These Mexican movements were transnational in that they involved "processes by which immigrants forge and sustain multistranded social relations that link together societies of origin and settlement," and these movements were made possible by the organizations Mexicans created in Chicagoland.[10] The "political, religious, and civic organizations" that transnational immigrants create, Peggy Levitt has explained, "arise or are reorganized to meet the needs of their newly transnational members, enabling migrants to continue to participate in both settings [societies of origin and settlement] and encouraging community perpetuation."[11] Through this organizational process of community formation, Mexican liberals and radicals were able to secure the support of the Mexican government, while traditionalists obtained the assistance of a well-established international institution in the United States, the Catholic Church.

Mexican immigrants in Chicagoland lived transnational lives, and as immigration scholars have long noted, Italian, Slavic, and Jewish immigrants, among others, have also lived transnationally. In search of remunerative opportunities, between 1880 and 1930 these Europeans immigrated to the United States, Canada, Argentina, Brazil, Colombia, Uruguay, Venezuela, Libya, and other nation-states, where they worked and lived but maintained familial, cultural, political, and economic ties to their homelands. Globally, millions of European immigrants eventually returned to Europe, many stayed in the nation-states that received them, and a smaller but significant number continued to cyclically migrate. Between 1880 and 1930 one-quarter to one-third of all the Europeans who immigrated to the United States eventually returned to Europe, and between 1900 and 1920 return rates increased: for every one hundred immigrants who entered the United States, thirty-six returned. Among certain nationalities, the return rates were much higher. Between 1820 and 1921 roughly 60 percent of southern Italians, 57 percent of Slovaks, 46 percent of Greeks, and 40 percent of Poles eventually went back to Europe. It is commonly believed that European immigrants quickly became American citizens after arriving in the United States, but that was hardly the case. In 1920 only 31 percent of the foreign-born men who had been in the United States for ten to fifteen years had naturalized as U.S. citizens. As late as 1930 about half of the Italians and Poles in the United States had not yet naturalized, while slightly more than half of all Greeks had not yet become American citizens.[12]

Until recently, the political ideas and activities of these European immigrants—who lived neither in Europe nor in the United States exclusively—remained lost in the limbo of international space. Years ago, the historian Mark Wyman urged scholars to produce a new historiography that would recover the stories of the Europeans who worked and struggled in the United States but continued to migrate to and from Europe.[13] Immigration historians have since adopted a transnational framework to assess European immigrants. They no longer focus solely on the Europeans who became Americans, and they have started to revise what we thought we knew about the European immigrant experience. The new history of southern Italians is especially informative. Jennifer Guglielmo and Michael Miller Top reveal the considerable differences between the Italian immigrant communities of the United States prior to and after the First World War. Before the war, Italians had high rates of cyclical migration and low rates of naturalization. Anarchism was a political force in Italian communities, and Italian women and men were critical of capitalism, imperialism, and U.S. race relations. During the war and after the First Red Scare in 1919, Italian anarchists and other European radicals were arrested, jailed, and sometimes deported by the U.S. government. In the wake of the Red Scare, the Italian community became more conservative and more assimilationist, and many Italians became American citizens. Guglielmo's and Top's monographs bring into sharp relief the largely forgotten radical history of Italians before 1919 and underscore the ways the U.S. government helped determine which Italians would become Americans, a process that involved the threat of deportation.[14]

The scholarship on transnational immigration has compared the experiences of Europeans and Mexicans and has yielded insights, but what the literature often fails to acknowledge is the way deportation has distinctly shaped the lives of Mexicans.[15] While hundreds of European radicals were deported during the First Red Scare, Mexicans were expelled from the United States by the tens of thousands between 1920 and 1921 and by the hundreds of thousands during the Great Depression, the Cold War, and other political and economic crises.[16] Moreover, while Europeans were at times recruited to work in the United States by U.S. companies, Mexicans have been incorporated into the United States by the hundreds of thousands through state-sponsored contract-labor programs. The Mexican people have a truly exceptional history in the United States in that they alone have been both recruited to and deported from the United States by the hundreds of thousands.[17]

This book contributes to the scholarship on transnational immigration and engages the pioneering studies that have examined Mexican immigrants' international politics, their forced removal from the United States, and their history of naturalization, assimilation, and Americanization.[18] In *The World of the Mexican Worker in Texas*, Emilio Zamora uncovered a rich history of Mexican self-organization and mobilization in South Texas during the early 1900s. Mexican immigrants and U.S.-born Mexicans worked together to challenge exploitative labor conditions by forming unions, organizing strikes, and joining political groups such as the Partido Liberal Mexicano and the Texas Socialist Party, organizations that operated on both sides of the U.S.-Mexico border. Ethnic Mexicans (Mexico- and U.S.-born Mexican people) in South Texas, Zamora argues, subscribed to an "all-inclusive Mexicanist identity" and expressed "a broad concern for the condition of the entire Mexican community."[19]

Building on Zamora's work and studies that examine the "sin fronteras" (without borders) activism of Mexicans in the Southwest, this book extends this literature's scope to the industrial and multiethnic Midwest and reveals that a far more diverse body of Mexican immigrants settled in Chicagoland during the early twentieth century.[20] In the Midwest, diverse cohorts of Mexican immigrants subscribed to contradictory liberal, radical, and traditionalist brands of Mexican nationalism that were not all-inclusive and were, in fact, often incompatible.

Assessing Mexican Los Angeles between 1900 and 1940, Douglas Monroy found that working- and middle-class Mexican immigrants were divided political partisans who nevertheless created a "México de afuera" in L.A., a community outside of but connected to the Mexican nation-state.[21] According to Monroy, a "tiny [Mexican immigrant] middle-class, including the intelligentsia," were the key actors in creating this community. Middle-class Mexicans were in tune with revolutionary politics. They supported the ratification of the Mexican Constitution of 1917 during the revolution and paid tribute to it by referring to themselves as Constitutionalists when they rallied other Mexicans to support the Mexican presidencies of Venustiano Carranza (in office 1917–20) and Álvaro Obregón (in office 1920–24). Middle-class Mexicans organized patriotic assemblies throughout Los Angeles and, at times, attempted to "uplift" or "morally and materially elevate the rest of the raza [the race / the people]." When measuring the influence of the Mexican immigrant middle class in Los Angeles, Monroy concluded that they were too elitist to form genuine coalitions with working-class migrants and therefore had a limited impact on the broader Mexican population.[22]

Little has been written about the Mexican immigrant middle class of Chicagoland, but the extant scholarship suggests that it was much larger than that of Mexican Detroit or Mexican St. Paul.[23] By 1928 there were more than two hundred Mexican-owned businesses in Chicagoland, and U.S. corporations had recruited more than four hundred Mexican professionals to work in the city.[24] Mexican immigrant proprietors and professionals often appear in the backgrounds of the history of Mexican Chicago, and they are typically dismissed as arrogant, disconnected, light-skinned Mexicans who, we are told, distanced themselves from their working-class compatriots.[25]

This book challenges the standard account of the Mexican immigrant middle class, fully incorporates middling Mexicans into the history of Chicago, and demonstrates that many middle-class liberals and traditionalists were social reformers who shaped the political beliefs of the broader working-class Mexican population. Chapter 1 recovers the history of the liberal wing of the revolutionary generation, which migrated to Chicago in the 1920s. These Mexicans were formally educated immigrants who found white-collar occupations in Chicago or arrived in the city with enough capital to start a small business. Middle-class liberals were Mexican nationalists, and many subscribed to anticlerical and social reform ideologies that became influential in Mexico during the revolution. In the Chicago area, Mexican liberals started community projects that provided poor and working-class migrants with social services and with educational courses that refined migrants' Spanish-language skills, celebrated the Mexican nation-state, and encouraged migrants to honor their Mexican citizenship. The Mexican liberal community reinforced the nationalist sentiments of the larger, predominantly working-class Mexican population, and as the liberal movement grew, it dissuaded many migrants from becoming U.S. citizens. During the Great Depression, liberals lost their businesses and occupations, many self-repatriated, some were deported, and those who remained in Chicago were now challenged by Mexican traditionalists.

Chapter 2 examines the formation of a Mexican traditionalist community in Chicagoland with a focus on El Círculo de Obreros Católicos San José (Círculo), a Catholic society founded by Mexican immigrants in East Chicago, Indiana, in 1925. The leaders of the Círculo were also middle-class Mexicans, but they were faithful Catholics who united with devout working-class migrants to create a large and vibrant Catholic community. Middle- and working-class traditionalists were critical of the liberals' anticlericalism, elitism, and what they called "secular" or amoral liberal politics. These Mexicans established a Catholic community that offered migrants social services and a parochial education program that rebuked the anticlerical aspects of the Mexican Revolution and advanced a Catholic interpretation of Mexican identity.

In 1926 conflicts in Mexico between anticlerical liberals and Catholics erupted into the bloody Cristero Rebellion, which lasted for three years and resulted in more than one hundred thousand casualties. The rebellion transformed Mexican Chicagoland in several ways. First, it exacerbated the political and cultural divide between the liberals and traditionalists. The anticlerical liberals in Chicago were often from Mexico City and other cities in Mexico, while the majority of Catholic traditionalists were from the rural Bajío region of Mexico from the states of Guanajuato, Jalisco, Michoacán, and Querétaro. The Bajío was the heartland of militant Catholicism in Mexico in the 1920s and was the stronghold of the Cristero movement. Over the course of the rebellion, Mexican bishops, priests, and nuns fled Mexico and entered the United States, and they were accompanied by thousands of Bajío immigrants. In both Chicago and Northwest Indiana, traditionalist societies such as the Círculo grew in size and influence, endorsed the Cristeros, received the backing of the Catholic Church, and then aggressively challenged the anticlerical liberals in Mexico and Chicagoland. With the onset of the Depression, the large traditionalist community was now subjected to an intense deportation campaign that led some traditionalists to question the value of their Mexican citizenship, a citizenship that could cost them the Catholic community and freedom of worship they had found in the United States.

As chapters 1 and 2 demonstrate, Mexican immigrants cannot be described as a monolithic mass: Mexican liberals and traditionalists defined themselves as Mexican nationals, but they were fundamentally divided by their political beliefs. Chapter 3 focuses on explaining why Mexican liberals frequently declined U.S. citizenship and why traditionalists became more open to U.S. naturalization through a comparison of liberal and traditionalist understandings of empire, race, and gender. In Chicago, Mexican liberals formed coalitions with liberal Puerto Ricans, Nicaraguans, and other Latin Americans, and they created "Hispanic" alliances that protested "the imperialism of the United States."[26] The Mexicans who joined in these protests embraced an interpretation of Mexican identity, developed during the revolution, that affirmed Mexico's indigenous and *mestizaje* (mixed-race) heritage. Anti-imperialist Mexican liberals in Chicago asserted themselves as proud "bronze" mestizos. These Mexicans rebuffed U.S. citizenship because they were put off by U.S. imperialism and a U.S. society they argued was too racially exclusive and too gender egalitarian. By contrast, Mexican traditionalists seldom entertained discussions about U.S. imperialism, racial discrimination, or gender equality. These Mexicans were less interested in U.S. interventions abroad and far more concerned with the Mexican government's anticlerical policies, which engendered the violent Cristero Rebellion. In their determination to challenge the anticlerical liberal mestizos, the traditionalists exalted all that was Catholic and thus Spanish in Mexican national history and contemporary society. In so doing, the traditionalists created an intellectual culture that was more open to a U.S. understanding of race, naturalization, and citizenship. Into the 1930s Mexican liberals were still championing Mexico's liberal and mestizaje roots, while traditionalists were becoming advocates of U.S. naturalization.

The history of Mexican assimilation in Chicago thus differs from that of Los Angeles and other cities in the Southwest in several significant ways. In *Becoming Mexican American*, George Sanchez examined the process by which Mexican immigrants became Mexican Americans in Los Angeles, and he found that the "struggle which forged a Mexican American identity was powerfully rooted in the decade of the 1930s." The Great Depression, Sanchez explained, destabilized Mexican Los Angeles. Approximately one-third of the Mexican population either self-repatriated or was deported during the Depression, and the Mexicans who remained in L.A. became "keenly aware of the fragility of their social position." They consequently "became more active in American unions and struggles for civil rights," which "created the context for a new identity" as Mexican Americans.[27] The Depression, the election of Franklin Delano Roosevelt (in office 1933–45), the New Deal, and even the influence of the Communist Party of the United States (CPUSA) all contributed to the assimilation and Americanization of the Mexican immigrants of Los Angeles.

The CPUSA, a complex and influential organization in the 1930s, helped assimilate immigrants through its involvement in unionization campaigns. As Zaragosa Vargas, Nelson Lichtenstein, Robin D. G. Kelley, Lizabeth Cohen, Michael Honey, Robert Korstad, and others have shown, during the Depression the CPUSA recruited and empowered many working-class Americans and immigrants who were coping with poverty, unemployment, evictions, racial discrimination, and nativism. All the while, a dedicated cadre of CPUSA activists strove to unionize all working people, regardless of their racial or immigration status, through the labor union federation the Congress of Industrial Organizations (CIO).[28] Elaborating on the relationship between the CPUSA and Mexican immigrants in L.A., Sanchez explains that American Communists helped "transform the radical tradition Mexican laborers derived from the Mexican Revolution into a new 'American' form of radicalism" oriented toward building the CIO: "Communist organizers and New Deal labor activists may have played a more important role in 'Americanizing' the Mexican working-class population than [the U.S.] government simply by characterizing the labor union and ethnic political organizing of the 1930s as a quintessential American activity."[29]

In *Labor Rights Are Civil Rights*, Vargas reconstructs the history of the Mexican Americans who joined the CIO.[30] Focusing on the Southwest, Vargas demonstrates that Mexican Americans contributed significantly to the growth of the CIO, which established the first permanent industrial unions in the United States, helped defeat Fascism during the Second World War, advanced the early civil rights movement, and supported postwar government policies that increased the standard of living of thousands of Americans.[31] When assessing the role of Mexican immigrants in this process, however, Vargas argues that one of the many "threat[s] to Mexican American economic and social advancement came from across the border: the steady arrival of documented and undocumented Mexican workers in the United States." Centering his analysis on Texas, Vargas asserts that Mexican immigrants "displaced local labor, depressed wages and working conditions, and more important, made labor organizing in the region extremely difficult." "The huge alien presence," Vargas stresses, "not only retarded social and economic advancement but also redefined Mexican American identity for years to come, because the surge of Anglo nativism branded all Mexicans as undesirable foreigners."[32]

The history of Mexican naturalization, assimilation, and CIO participation in Chicagoland diverges from what occurred in Los Angeles and in cities in Texas and the Southwest. First, as chapters 2 and 3 explain, the anticlerical policies of the postrevolutionary Mexican government and the Cristero Rebellion in the 1920s primed the Mexican traditionalists of Chicagoland for U.S. naturalization. In the context of the rebellion, traditionalists distanced themselves from the extremely anticlerical presidency of Plutarco Elías Calles (in office 1924–28). Many traditionalists began to characterize themselves more often as devout Catholics than as Mexican citizens, and the intelligentsia within the traditionalist community started offering Mexican Catholics a supranational understanding of Mexican identity that emphasized the ways the Catholic faith bonded Mexicans as a people irrespective of their citizenship. While some traditionalists began to discuss the benefits of U.S. naturalization in the 1930s, Mexican liberals remained Mexican nationalists uninterested in becoming American citizens.

The Depression-era deportations disrupted the lives of all ethnic Mexicans in the United States and largely destroyed the Mexican liberal community of Chicagoland. But a handful of liberals now joined with numerous radical Mexican laborers to form the Frente Popular Mexicano (Frente), a Mexican nationalist and radical transnational affiliate of the Partido Comunista Mexicano that continued to orient many migrants toward Mexico.

Chapter 4 examines the rise of the Mexican nationalist Left in Chicago through the ideas and activities of the Frente. While Mexican laborers in the Southwest were influenced by the Americanizing activities of the CPUSA, Mexican workers in Chicago were inspired by the Frente's brand of Mexican nationalism. The emergence of Fascism in Europe, the international Communist movement's shift toward an anti-Fascist popular front strategy, and, most importantly, the radical Mexican presidency of Lázaro Cárdenas (in office 1934–40) motivated Mexican laborers in Chicago to join the Frente and other newly organized radical and nationalist groups like Club Lázaro Cárdenas and Club Vicente Lombardo Toledano, named after the Marxian leader of the Mexican labor federation, the Confederación de Trabajadores de México (CTM). The Cárdenas and Lombardo clubs merged with the Frente, and the Frente led a radical political movement in Chicago that was anti-Fascist, anti-imperialist, and prounionization. Frente members formed friendships with radical Spaniards, Cubans, and CTM officials and then began supporting the CIO. Galvanized by the Cárdenas presidency and the CTM, Frente activists in Chicago reinforced the nationalism of Mexican immigrant workers, discouraging many from becoming U.S. citizens but encouraging them to become CIO labor leaders.

Frente members were too impoverished during the Depression to secure their own office spaces and facilities, and so they were forced to rely on the resources of the Chicago settlement houses. As Mexican traditionalists learned of the Frente's activities in the settlement houses, they started mobilizing Mexican Catholics against it. Over time, settlement house administrators also grew weary of the Frente's radical politics, and they eventually expelled the Frente from their institutions. The Frente now went into decline, but its radical members continued to join the CIO, and there they encountered working-class Mexican traditionalists who had their own reasons for supporting the CIO.

There are few histories of Mexican immigrant CIO union organizers, which leads specialists and nonspecialists to conclude that Mexican immigrants have been a passive and even antiunion people, toiling away in the fields and factories, only to become change agents after they became U.S. citizens and were influenced by progressive Americans. In the 1930s and 1940s, in the decades when Vargas and Sanchez identify a surge in Mexican American CIO participation in the Southwest, the vast majority of Mexicans in the Midwest were Mexican citizens, and yet they too joined the CIO. Chapter 5 follows working-class Mexican radicals and traditionalists into the CIO and compares their aspirations and accomplishments as they helped build the CIO-affiliated United Packinghouse Workers of America and the United Steelworkers of America.

On a pragmatic level, Mexican radicals and traditionalists joined the CIO because they wanted to expand the social welfare net that immigrant fraternal societies and mutual aid groups had established in Chicagoland in the 1920s. Ideologically, Mexican CIO radicals remained Mexican nationalists committed to building a left-of-center international labor movement. By contrast, working-class traditionalists were open to the CIO because they too desired the benefits of unionization, but they interpreted the CIO as a politically moderate alternative to radical labor groups like the anarcho-syndicalist Industrial Workers of the World and the Magonistas. Mexican traditionalists were already debating the merits of U.S. citizenship when they began participating in CIO activities because they had been put off by the anticlerical and radical policies of the Mexican government in the 1920s and 1930s. As traditionalists applied for U.S. citizenship, they joined the CIO and the Democratic Party, and then they encouraged all Mexicans to follow suit. Mexican traditionalists, however, did not sever their cultural ties to Mexico. By the early 1950s, naturalized Mexican American traditionalists had developed a deterritorialized brand of *mexicanidad* (Mexican national identity) that celebrated Mexican patriotic holidays and selective aspects of Mexican nationalist culture but was devoid of any substantive allegiance to Mexico. Mexican traditionalists were in part motivated to become American citizens by the Depression-era deportations, and the New Deal, but Mexican traditionalists also became Americans because of the anticlerical and radical legacy of the Mexican Revolution, which alienated them from the postrevolutionary Mexican government and set them on course to create new lives for themselves in the United States.

At various points throughout this book, I compare Mexican Chicago to Mexican Los Angeles. A number of historical monographs have examined Mexican Los Angeles because it had the largest Mexican population of any city in the United States before the Depression. I chose Chicago as the site of this study because it received more Mexican immigrants than any other city in the Midwest before the Depression.[33] Today, Chicago is estimated to have the second-largest Mexican population (after Los Angeles) and the third-largest Latino population in the United States (after Los Angeles and New York).[34]

More important still, Mexican Chicagoland is an extraordinary place to examine the politics of Mexican immigrants because, unlike Los Angeles and other cities in the Southwest, the Mexicans who settled in Chicagoland did not have to negotiate their political agendas with an established "native" Mexican American population. As Vargas's work demonstrates, southwestern Mexican Americans, especially those whose families had been in the United States for generations, often competed directly with Mexican immigrants for jobs and scarce resources, and, at times, these Mexican Americans favored policies that would restrict further Mexican immigration into the United States.[35] By contrast, Mexican immigrants established the Mexican communities of Chicago and the Midwest and thus rarely described other immigrants, "legal" or "illegal," as their obstacle to higher wages and better working conditions or to improved relations with white Americans.

To determine which Mexicans in Chicagoland were most likely to become American citizens and to adequately compare Chicago to Los Angeles, I drew, in part, on Sanchez's successful methodology. In *Becoming Mexican American*, Sanchez analyzed the naturalization records of every Mexican immigrant who applied for U.S. citizenship in Los Angeles before 1940—an impressive task that involved surveying all naturalization applications, as these were filed chronologically and not by national origin. For this book, I created a historical census of every Spanish-speaking immigrant who applied for U.S. citizenship in Chicago before 1940 (see the appendix). Like all forms of evidence, there are limitations and advantages to using naturalization records. For example, before the 1940s, the vast majority of Spanish-speaking immigrants who applied for naturalization were men. I tried to address this imbalance by searching through the Spanish-language press, the records of the Mexican consulate, the reports of U.S. social workers, and the field notes of contemporary social scientists for evidence of Mexican women activists, and what I found I incorporated into my analysis and narrative. While naturalization records were limiting in certain respects, they allow us to examine assimilation in a way that no other sources can. As John A. Garcia explains, "[T]he acquisition of citizenship is considered one of the most significant indicators of political integration for an immigrant into the recipient society. It represents a new political and civil rights arrangement, as well as psychological affiliation from the previous mother country to the immigrant's host country."[36] Although some scholars emphasize the importance of cultural markers of assimilation, I stress the significance of naturalization when examining Mexican assimilation because I found that Mexicans could assimilate almost every aspect of American culture (English-language acquisition, clothing styles, food and music tastes, etc.), but if they chose to retain their Mexican citizenship, they would still be targeted for deportation by the U.S. government during economic and political crises. On a final note in regard to sources, naturalization records were essential in recovering the histories of the non-Mexican, Spanish-speaking immigrants of Chicagoland. A number of monographs assess Latino coalitions in our present, but this book demonstrates that Mexicans have formed alliances with Puerto Ricans, Nicaraguans, Spaniards, and Cubans in Chicago since the 1920s, and these alliances oriented the trajectory of the history of Latino Chicago.

As the chapters of this book will reveal, Mexican immigrants have a rich history of political activism in Chicagoland during the interwar years, but since the majority of Mexicans never became U.S. citizens in this period, their activism remains relatively unknown to American scholars. Yet their history has much to teach us about our increasingly international and interconnected world. Imperialism, globalization, and transnationalism are all terms scholars use to talk about processes that Mexicans have been experiencing on a personal level for more than a century. Addressing "what needs to be done" in the field of Mexican studies, the pioneer historian of Mexican Chicago, Louise Año Nuevo Kerr, advised scholars to humanize the Mexican experience through biographies, because "there are great stories to be told . . . [about] seemingly ordinary people who have had extraordinary experiences and who have survived travail in the face of tremendous obstacles, usually unheralded and without fanfare, but with great importance to our collective history."[37] This book took Kerr's advice to heart. Each chapter recovers the histories of individual immigrant activists, liberals like Julián Mondragón and Milla Domínguez, traditionalists like Carlos Figueroa and Rosaura Herrera, and radicals like Nicholas Hernández and Jesús Flores. While chapters 1 through 4 touch on the lives of individuals, chapters 5 and 6 are even more biographical and personal in style.

Chapter 6, the final chapter of this book, examines the demise of the radical wing of the revolutionary generation and the rise of the U.S.-born second generation. During the Cold War and the McCarthy years, the federal government initiated yet another mass deportation campaign against Mexican immigrants. As the U.S. Immigration and Naturalization Service (INS) started deporting thousands of Mexicans, police departments and the Federal Bureau of Investigation (FBI) coordinated with the INS to investigate and deport radical Mexican and Latin American immigrant union organizers. From the Southwest to the Midwest, the INS disciplined Latino labor leaders through deportation. Refugio Roman Martínez was a radical Mexican immigrant who lived through the revolution, migrated to Chicago, and became an active member of the Frente and the CIO; he then was deported as a dissident during the Cold War. Through Martínez's life, chapter 6 argues that the U.S. government settled the contest between the revolutionary factions at the expense of the radicals and in favor of the traditionalists who were passed over by the INS during the Cold War deportations and left in the position to leave the deepest imprint on the young Mexican Americans of Chicagoland.

In one sense, this book is a history of the Mexican Revolution as it unfolded on the streets and in the neighborhoods of Chicago. In his classic study of the revolution, Alan Knight wrote that "when all is said and done, the Revolution was a *national* phenomenon; it stretched from Tijuana to Tapachula, from the Rio Grande to the Rio Hondo; it touched the lives of all Mexicans. It therefore deserved a *national* history. And, without a national history, it is impossible to gauge whether local studies are typical or aberrant."[38] This book demonstrates that the revolution was a truly *transnational* phenomenon that stretched from Mexico City and the Bajío to Los Angeles and Chicago. During the entire first half of the twentieth century, Mexican immigrants remained intellectually, emotionally, and politically connected to revolutionary Mexico.

Scholars of Mexico such as Knight, D. A. Brading, Mary Kay Vaughan, John Mason Hart, Jean A. Meyer, and Claudio Lomnitz have assessed Mexican nationalism and what has been referred to as the consciousness of the campesinos (rural folk) who rose up against the Mexican state during the Cristero Rebellion.[39] *The Mexican Revolution in Chicago* explores the consciousness of the Mexican people who supported the revolution and the rebellion and then immigrated to the United States, where they recommitted themselves to a life of political struggle. This book suggests that there was and perhaps still is an irreconcilable contradiction between the Mexican secular mestizaje state (often symbolized by the Aztec eagle in Mexican nationalist cultural productions) and a Mexican Catholic identity rooted in a Catholic ethic and sense of morality (frequently exemplified by the iconic image of the Virgin of Guadalupe).[40] In Chicagoland, the devout followers of the Virgin concluded that in order to live peaceful lives as Mexican Catholics, they needed to become American citizens free from the tethers of the anticlerical Mexican state and safe from the draconian deportation drives of the United States.

1 The Mexican Revolution Migrates to Chicago

He [the Mexican immigrant] cares nothing about government in his primitive state; government means to him nothing at all except something to eat and [a] place to sleep.

—Carlos Bee (D-TX), 1920, U.S. House of Representatives, House Committee on Immigration and Naturalization, *Temporary Admission of Illiterate Mexican Laborers*

They [Mexican immigrants] don't know who the President of Mexico is.

—John Nance Garner (D-TX), 1921, future vice president, Senate Committee on Immigration, 66th Congress, quoted in David Stafford Weber, "Anglo Views of Mexican Immigrants"

During the early 1920s, Mexican liberals immigrated to Chicago. These were well-educated immigrants who subscribed to a democratic, reformist, anti-clerical, and activist political culture informed by their participation in the Mexican Revolution of 1910. After settling in Chicago, Mexican liberals created a community and a political movement to uplift their immigrant compatriots. Through social welfare, educational, and criminal justice services, liberals encouraged migrants to commemorate the Mexican nation-state, to honor their Mexican citizenship, to safeguard their Spanish language, and to remain loyal to Mexico. Liberals believed that education could empower migrants and facilitate their upward mobility in the United States while allowing them to retain their Mexican citizenship. Mexican liberals were passionate nationalists whose allegiance to Mexico had been bolstered by the promise of the revolution, which they thought would transform Mexico into a more democratic, educated, and prosperous country. As the liberal movement grew in size and influence, it succeeded in discouraging many migrants from becoming U.S. citizens, and it imbued the Mexican population with a more attractive understanding of Mexican nationalism.

The Liberal Mexican Revolution Migrates into the United States

The revolution was led by liberals who desired broad social reforms and the dissolution of the thirty-five-year dictatorship of Porfirio Díaz (the Porfiriato, 1876–1911). Mexican liberals came of age as their country became more densely populated, urban, literate, and middle class, and they believed there was an inherent contradiction between the cosmopolitan way of life they aspired to and the Díaz dictatorship. During the Porfiriato, Mexico's total population grew by 61 percent, to about 13.5 million persons by 1910, and the population of the state capitals grew by 88 percent. Between 1870 and 1900, Mexico City's population increased from 200,000 to 471,000; Monterrey's from 14,000 to 79,000; and Chihuahua City's from 12,000 to 30,000. Schools were established in nearly every major city. Between 1878 and the revolution, the number of primary schools increased from about 5,200 to more than 12,000, which translated into a surge in the student population from 140,000 students to more than 700,000. The national literacy rates from the period obscure the regional realities of literacy and print culture in Mexico. Mexican census figures suggest that only 20 percent of Mexico's population was literate in 1910, but scholars have discovered that literacy rates were much higher in the Distrito Federal, in most cities, and in all of the border states. In the Distrito Federal, the literacy rate was 64 percent in 1910, and in the border state of Sonora, 47 percent of men and women could read and write in this year. The higher literacy rates in cities and in regional pockets throughout Mexico help to explain the expansion of the Mexican press. While only two hundred newspapers were published in Mexico in 1884, more than fifteen hundred circulated throughout the country in 1907.[1]

The growth of Mexico's cities created a more diverse economy and a larger middle class. As Alan Knight has argued, the Mexican middle class during the revolutionary era is best defined by its "measure of property, education, and respectability." Middle-class Mexicans owned small businesses or worked as lawyers, doctors, engineers, state officials, administrators, teachers, and journalists. They dressed in business attire, subscribed to newspapers, and were aware of contemporary global affairs. Scholars estimate that only 8 percent of Mexico's total population was middle class in the 1890s.[2] At first glance, this percentage appears rather minor, but this figure represented the lives of more than one million Mexicans.

The upper- and middle-class liberals who criticized the Porfiriato, such as Camilo Arriaga, Fernando Iglesias Calderón, Juan Sarabia, and Ricardo

Flores Magón, agitated for democratic rights, such as the freedom of assembly, freedom of speech, and freedom of the press, and the right to a universal and secular education. In various cities, liberals founded clubs and presses, or *prensas de combate* (oppositional presses), as they were called, which offered Mexican citizens a constant stream of criticisms of the Porfiriato. By 1901 the Mexican government counted more than 150 liberal clubs in Mexico and estimated that more than twice this number operated clandestinely. In Vera Cruz, Club Literario Liberal published *Excelsior* against the Díaz regime; in San Luis Potosí, Club Ponciano Arriaga (named after an influential nineteenth-century Mexican liberal) distributed *Renacimiento*; and in Mexico City, Mexicans could read several liberal papers, including the *Diario del Hogar*, whose editors were jailed repeatedly by Díaz, and *Regeneración*, started by Jesús, Enrique, and Ricardo Flores Magón. Díaz closed *Regeneración* in 1905, sending the Flores Magón brothers and their allies (the Magonistas) into exile in the United States, where they formed the Junta Organizadora del Partido Liberal Mexicano (PLM). The PLM grew in Texas by recruiting Mexican immigrants and U.S.-born Mexicans, and these ethnic Mexicans formed PLM-affiliated fraternal societies and mutual aid groups, such as the Liga Liberal Benito Juárez and Club Liberal Mexicano. Texas officials, concerned about anti-Díaz revolutionary movements in their state, established an arrest and extradition agreement with the Díaz administration. Fearful of being extradited to Mexico, Magonistas traveled around Texas, disseminating their ideas. They then moved to St. Louis, Missouri, where they relaunched *Regeneración*, and then to California, where they settled in Los Angeles.[3]

The U.S.-Mexico border was porous during the early twentieth century; the United States did not create the Border Patrol until 1924. As Mexicans cyclically migrated to and from the American Southwest they brought the politics of the liberal revolution with them. In Mexico, Catarino Garza worked for an American company and became critical of the preferential treatment Díaz offered foreign corporations. After immigrating to Texas, Garza formed several anti-Díaz clubs and a newspaper. Sara Estela Ramírez also came to despise the Díaz dictatorship. In Saltillo, Coahuila, Ramírez had worked as a journalist and schoolteacher, and after immigrating to Laredo, Texas, she started two anti-Díaz papers, *La Corregidora* and *La Aurora*, and then joined the PLM. Surrounded by working-class Mexicans, Ramírez supported their labor struggles and recruited them to the PLM. From Texas, Ramírez moved to Mexico City and then back again several times, and through her sojourns she helped establish anti-Díaz papers on both sides of the border.

Díaz responded to these émigrés with a vengeance, sending Mexican agents into the United States to suppress their activities. In Brownsville, Texas, Díaz agents caught up with Dr. Ignacio Martínez, the publisher of an anti-Díaz paper. Díaz's men engaged Martínez and his supporters in several gunfights and eventually killed him in 1890. After another renowned anti-Díaz liberal activist was assassinated on the streets of Laredo, Catarino Garza organized an armed band of émigrés to lead raids against the Mexican military in northern Mexico. As hundreds of Mexicans joined up with Garza, the Texas Rangers learned of Garza's exploits, partnered with the U.S. Army, and then pursued Garza across the Southwest, forcing him to flee to the Caribbean.[4]

Back in Mexico, Díaz attempted to crush the liberal movement. His governors and generals raided liberal clubs and presses and conscripted, jailed, and executed liberal activists. As they had in Texas, some liberals in Mexico responded to repression by becoming more militant, while others continued to seek change through parliamentarian methods. Anti-Díaz armed revolts occurred in the states of Tlaxcala and Sinaloa and were aggressively suppressed. In Coahuila, moderate liberals mobilized around Francisco I. Madero's presidential candidacy and his call for "sufragio efectivo, no reelección" (effective suffrage and no reelection). Díaz was serving one consecutive presidential term after another, underscoring the facade of democracy in Mexico. Madero, a wealthy landowner and a moderate liberal, won numerous supporters in the border states, and they established antireelection clubs in his name. When it appeared that Madero was becoming an actual political threat, Díaz shut down Madero's paper, *El Antirreeleccionista* (edited by a young José Vasconcelos); put down antireelection protests in Coahuila, Nuevo León, Zacatecas, San Luis, and Puebla; and jailed intransigent supporters of Madero (Maderistas). Madero was eventually arrested, but after he was released on bail, he escaped to San Antonio, Texas, where he was embraced by the former followers of Catarino Garza. One of Garza's men owned a press in San Antonio, and Madero used it to publish his "Plan de San Luis," which called for a mass revolt against Díaz in November 1910.[5]

Madero's call to arms fed into a broader and diverse movement to depose Díaz. By February 1911 Maderistas and Magonistas were organizing armed rebellions, while campesinos and indigenous tribes, who had grievances against the Díaz regime that predated Madero's plan, led independent insurrections along the mountains of Coahuila, Sonora, Chihuahua, and Durango. Unable to contain these uprisings, Díaz lost towns and cities to revolutionary factions. When Mexican citizens began rioting in Mexico City, Díaz accepted that he had lost control of the country, and under pressure from his generals, he relinquished power and fled to Europe.[6]

Díaz's self-exile galvanized liberal intellectuals, who took the opportunity to call for a new and expanded secular education system. Mexican liberals were typically well-educated individuals who believed in the power of ideas, and they frequently argued that education could reshape Mexican society. The majority of liberals desired a clear separation between church and state, but many liberals were anticlerical, believing that Mexico's educational system and intellectual culture were constrained by the influence of the Catholic Church, which was disparaged as the embodiment of antiquity and as an institution that was more loyal to Rome than to Mexico. During the colonial period, the church had managed the majority of schools in Mexico. In the aftermath of the Mexican American War (1846–48), liberal and conservative conflicts intensified as the liberals sought to create a more unified and powerful country capable of defending itself from the United States. Led by Juan Álvarez, Miguel Lerdo de Tejada, and Benito Juárez, who would eventually be elected president of Mexico, the liberals triumphed over the conservatives during the Wars of Reform (1856–61) and ratified the Constitution of 1857, which established a separation between church and state and banned clerics from political life and from teaching in federally funded public schools.[7]

Seeking to placate conservative Catholics who decried the creation of public "godless schools," liberals allowed the church to continue to manage private Catholic schools. The revolutionary liberals who witnessed the fall of the Porfiriato believed the liberals of the mid-nineteenth century had not gone far enough. Revolutionary liberals wanted to sever the ties between the church and public education. Although the various revolutionary factions fought each other, they typically agreed on the need to secularize the schools. When Francisco "Pancho" Villa, Emiliano Zapata, and the Conventionists, as they are called, controlled Mexico City, a Villista declared, "The school must be kept apart from anything religious. . . . The priests inculcate the child from his first years with lies. . . . We cannot form the national character while the priests control education, for they have made their teaching a means of propaganda." When the capital transitioned into the hands of Venustiano Carranza, Carranza's Constitutionalist faction concurred: "The doctrine of the clergy has been the interests of the Church before the interests of the people. . . . It is necessary to exclude the priests from any part in primary education. . . . If [we] allow the clergy to come in with their outdated and retrogressive ideas, we shall not form new generations of intellectual and cultivated men." Moderate liberals pushed back against the complete secularization of education, arguing that Mexico would never achieve national unity under such a political course. The majority of the schools in Mexico at this time were primary schools, and under pressure from the moderates, the *puros* (the "pure ones," who typically rejected compromise) acquiesced. Primary public schools would be secularized and administered by the state, while the church would be permitted to manage its smaller number of parochial secondary schools.[8]

As revolutionaries and politicians debated educational policies in Mexico City, liberal intellectuals experimented with public education projects. José Vasconcelos, an emerging luminary in Mexican intellectual circles, and other scholars created the Ateneo de la Juventud, which taught the works of Immanuel Kant, Arthur Schopenhauer, and Henri Bergson to challenge the Mexican people's Catholicism and to discredit the positivist philosophies that had been taught during the Porfiriato. Positivism exalted order and progress, which legitimized Díaz's authoritarianism as the means to achieve stability and economic growth in Mexico. For the majority of revolutionary liberals, positivism was a fundamentally undemocratic philosophy that needed to be negated. In 1912 Vasconcelos and other liberals formed the Universidad Popular Mexicana, which operated as a mobile university, taking the curriculum of the Ateneo to the masses through free courses taught in labor shops and factories. In 1920 Álvaro Obregón became the president of Mexico, and he appointed Vasconcelos to serve as his secretary of education. Between 1920 and 1924, Vasconcelos created more than a thousand schools, built nearly two thousand public libraries, and printed and distributed thousands of textbooks that advanced a more liberal interpretation of Mexican history.[9]

The liberal revolution filtered down to all segments of Mexican society, including Mexico's urban workers and campesinos who were immigrating to the United States and to Chicagoland. The case of Tomás Echeverría illustrates this point. In Mexico, Echeverría had worked as a mason. He had been a devout Catholic and at one point even aspired to the priesthood. During the revolution, he read about liberalism and became skeptical of organized religion. Although he possessed what a contemporary described as only a "grammar school" education, Echeverría read Nietzsche and Schopenhauer, who were then hailed by the revolutionary liberal intelligentsia. Grappling with the "agony of having all of his past ideas torn and shaken," Echeverría found purpose in the philosophy of the American pragmatist William James. After immigrating to Chicago, Echeverría started collecting books and formed a library of more than a hundred texts. Speaking about Protestants in Chicago who had tried to court him, Echeverría said: "I have never been especially attracted by the Protestant Church. Its teaching does not agree with what I learned in physiology and natural science. I would like to find some group which was thoroughly modern to which I could belong, some philosophy of life which I could follow, something which would unify my thinking." Drawn to the liberalism of what he called the "liberal American Churches in Hyde Park," Echeverría visited several churches near the University of Chicago and concluded that his background as a Mexican and his work as a laborer set him apart from the Hyde Park congregations, which he identified as consisting of "business and professional people."[10] Worldly working-class Mexican migrants like Echeverría who had received an unorthodox education during the revolution were having trouble finding a place for themselves in Chicago, and Echeverría was no exception. Working- and middle-class migrants who defined themselves as liberals were making their way to Chicago, and they shared Echeverría's sense of estrangement. These migrants wanted to be members of a liberal community that would unite them with their like-minded compatriots. As migrants like Echeverría searched for community, thousands of Mexicans continued to move to Chicagoland.

Remapping Mexican Chicago

Between 1900 and 1930, approximately 1.5 million Mexicans crossed into the United States, and their entry was facilitated by American employers. The Great War and the restrictive immigration acts of 1921 and 1924 deprived American companies of their historic use of European immigrant labor. Between 1905 and 1914, nearly one million Europeans had entered the United States every year. In search of a new mobile, nonunion, and noncitizen workforce that lacked legal protections and would shoulder the layoffs associated with seasonal agricultural work and the vacillating cycles of industrial production, American companies turned to Mexicans, and the federal government accommodated American businessmen by permitting nearly unrestricted Mexican immigration into the United States.[11] Corporate leaders believed they had found ideal laborers in the Mexican people, who could be incorporated into the U.S. workforce when the economy expanded but could be fired and encouraged to return to Mexico when the economy contracted. Southwestern growers hired Mexicans, who crossed a relatively open U.S. border, and midwestern growers and industries hired Mexicans through labor agencies. Some sixteen labor agencies recruited more than eighteen thousand Mexicans to Chicago in one year alone. Labor agencies typically enlisted Mexicans to work in midwestern agriculture, but after arriving in Chicago, many migrants went to work for industrial and manufacturing plants that offered immediate jobs and higher wages. By 1930 Chicago's

Mexican population had climbed to more than twenty thousand persons, and Mexicans came to represent about 40 percent of the maintenance-of-way railroad workforce of the city, 12 percent of steel and metal employees, 5 percent of meatpacking workers, and about 15 percent of all cement, rug-manufacturing, and fruit-packing laborers.[12] Chicago's Mexican population also included a growing number of middle-class proprietors who owned restaurants, groceries, convenience stores, and saloons and white-collar employees who described their occupations as "export managers," "salesmen," "accountants," "physicians," "civil engineers," "teachers," "Spanish-language translators," "photographers," "stenographers," and "clerks."[13]

After securing employment, working- and middle-class Mexicans rented apartments throughout Chicago. Mexicans from various states and regions lived next to each other, among Spanish-speaking immigrants from Spain and Latin America, and near white and black Americans. The maps of Mexican Chicago that the economist Paul Taylor created in the 1920s and that scholars continue to use to this day suggest that Mexican Chicago consisted of three heavily concentrated Mexican neighborhoods on the Near West Side near the railyards, in the Back of the Yards by several meatpacking plants, and in South Chicago adjacent to the steel mills (see figure 1 on the webpage).[14] As early as 1930, at least one scholar questioned this visual depiction of Mexican Chicago, pointing out that more than half of the Mexicans in the city (some fifteen thousand persons) may have lived outside of these three neighborhoods.[15] Mexicans actually resided across Chicagoland: all along Lake Michigan, on the Near North Side, in Lincoln Park, in Lakeview, and in Uptown. They also rented apartments to the west of the city in North Lawndale and Brighton Park and to the south in South Deering and in Blue Island (see figures 2 and 3 on the webpage).

Gabriela Arredondo argues that Mexican immigrants "became Mexican," or developed a Mexican national identity in Chicago as a result of revolutionary nationalism and as they experienced U.S. discrimination and ethnonational diversity.[16] Scholars have described Italian immigrants in a similar fashion. Thomas A. Guglielmo explains that when Italians arrived in Chicago in the nineteenth century, their identities were rooted in their *campanalismo*, "a loyalty to one's region, town, or clan," even though they initially "knew little of the Italian nation and cared about it even less."[17] In support of this interpretation, historians point out that Italians named their fraternal societies after their particular regions of origin, spoke distinct regional dialects of the Italian language, tried to remain regionally endogamous, and chose residencies to reproduce premigration regional communities.[18]

On the one hand, some Mexican immigrants from small towns may have developed a sense of Mexican national identity in Chicago; but on the other hand, the middle-class Mexicans who founded fraternal societies and the working-class Mexicans who started mutual aid organizations (*mutualistas*) typically described themselves as Mexican nationals (i.e., *mexicanos*) as they concurrently recognized their particular regional, state, city, town, and even neighborhood backgrounds. Regional identities, as this book will demonstrate, were important to Mexicans, but the migrants who described themselves as members of distinct regions within Mexico also referred to themselves as mexicanos. Unlike Italians, Mexicans typically named their organizations after the Mexican nation-state or after widely recognized Mexican presidents and national icons (see table 16 in the appendix for a list of Spanish-speaking immigrant societies in Chicagoland). The vast majority of Mexicans spoke in one discernible Spanish language, and it does not appear that Mexican men courted Mexican women based on their premigration region of origin.[19] In regard to their residencies, certain neighborhoods inside and outside of Chicago reflected a regional character, but the migrants who resided in these neighborhoods often identified as Mexican nationals.[20] In fact, in numerous Spanish-speaking neighborhoods, Mexicans from diverse states and regions chose to live near each other (see figure 4 on the webpage). In sum, some Mexicans may have developed a Mexican national identity in Chicagoland, but this book suggests that Mexicans did not so much become Mexican in Chicago as they became more liberal, traditionalist, or radical.[21]

The experiences of Mexican nationals in Chicagoland were made more diverse and complicated, however, by their Spanish-speaking neighbors who were becoming U.S. citizens. The first Mexicans to naturalize in the early 1900s did not leave us with statements explaining their decisions. But as Arredondo, Michael Innis-Jiménez, and other historians have explained, when Mexicans first arrived in Chicago there was no preexisting Mexican or Mexican American community, and these "early immigrants [initially] went without resources of support mechanisms, such as mutual aid societies, contacts for housing and employment, or cultural support."[22] In search of community and a support network, the first Mexican naturalizers sought to assimilate into the United States as U.S. citizens.[23] Naturalization records provide us with rich details about these naturalizers, while the characteristics of those who remained foreign nationals can be gleaned from other sources. The majority of Mexican naturalizers (56 percent) and many Mexican nationals in Chicago emigrated directly from their state, city, or town of birth in Mexico (see table 3 in the appendix). These Mexicans brought their understandings of Mexican politics and culture directly to Chicago and were therefore exposed to Mexico's regional and political diversity (what some scholars call Mexico's "many Mexicos") in the United States.[24] Nearly every Mexican naturalizer (94 percent) and Mexican national entered the United

States through Texas, and more than half of all naturalizers crossed the border at Laredo (see table 2 in the appendix).[25]

The Mexicans who naturalized in Chicago during the first forty years of the twentieth century can be divided into two waves: between 1900 and 1930, approximately 830 Mexicans applied for U.S. citizenship, and another 1,063 applied between 1931 and 1940. In 1920 the U.S. census listed 1,224 Mexicans living in Chicago, and between 1900 and 1920, the first two decades of Mexican settlement in the city, approximately 212 Mexicans applied for naturalization (see table 4 in the appendix).[26] The first naturalizers were primarily from Mexico City, from the border states, and from northwestern Mexico. Every decade after 1920, the number of naturalizers from these regions decreased as the number of naturalizers from the rural Bajío region of Mexico increased. Between 1921 and 1930, the percentage of naturalizers from central Mexico, the border states, and northwestern Mexico dropped to 49 percent; between 1931 and 1940, it dropped to 33 percent. Bajío immigrants, who represented only 19 percent of all naturalizers before 1920, came to represent 37 percent of all naturalizers between 1921 and 1930 and then 50 percent of all naturalizers between 1931 and 1940 (see table 4 in the appendix).[27]

The first wave of naturalizers before 1931 included many *capitalinos* (Mexicans from Mexico City) and a substantial number of urban and middle-class immigrants from the border states in Mexico (see figure 4 on the webpage). Seventeen percent of Mexican naturalizers before 1931 were middle-class migrants who owned small businesses and worked in white-collar sales and office work or in high-end positions as engineers and accountants and in other professions. As the percentage of naturalizers from central Mexico, the border states, and northwestern Mexico decreased, so too did the percentage of middle-class naturalizers. Between 1931 and 1940, the percentage of middle-class naturalizers dropped to 11 percent from a high of 17 percent, and in these years 57 percent of naturalizers were now unskilled blue-collar laborers, and most were from the Bajío (see table 11 in the appendix).[28]

In summation, naturalization records reveal that capitalinos and other urban middle-class Mexicans were the first to seek permanent residence in Chicago as U.S. citizens, but over time, these migrants stopped applying for naturalization in significant numbers and were supplanted by a much larger wave of naturalizers who were less formally educated, worked as blue-collar laborers in Chicago, and hailed from the Bajío. The capitalino pioneers who settled Chicago have left a rich but little-known history. Naturalization records suggest that far more capitalinos migrated to Chicago than to Los Angeles. While capitalinos represented only 8 percent of all naturalizers in Los Angeles before 1940, they would eventually stand for 14 percent of all

naturalizers in Chicago in these same years (see table 1 in the appendix).[29] By
the mid-1920s, however, the majority of capitalinos and urban middle-class
migrants were no longer applying for U.S. citizenship because by this point in
time Mexican liberals were succeeding in creating a nationalist community
in Chicago.

As Mexican liberal nationalists established themselves in Chicago, they
were disturbed to learn that Mexicans who shared their cosmopolitan characteristics were choosing to become American citizens. The liberals believed
that these migrants were applying for U.S. citizenship because they felt iso-
lated and alienated in Chicagoland.[30] Liberals reasoned that they could con-
vince middle-class migrants like themselves to retain their Mexican citizenship by creating a vibrant Mexican community in Chicago, but they thought
that working-class migrants were going to be more difficult to win over. The
liberals concluded that Mexican laborers were most likely to apply for U.S.
naturalization because they lacked a formal Mexican education, which would
have taught them to remain loyal to Mexico.[31] The liberals were in part right.
Between 1900 and 1940, roughly 86 percent of the Mexicans who applied for
naturalization held blue-collar jobs in Chicago. These were not all unskilled
laborers either. A significant 14 percent of them were skilled artisans: machinists, welders, and carpenters, among other tradesmen, but these were
blue-collar folks (see table 11 in the appendix). To discourage working-class
Mexicans (unskilled and skilled alike) from becoming U.S. citizens, the liberals drew on their experiences in creating political communities in Mexico, a
process of community formation that revolved around a press and fraternal
society.

Creating a Mexican Liberal Community in Chicago

On January 12, 1925, a liberal journalist named Julián Xavier Mondragón,
a businessman named F. Patrón Miranda, and five other activists gathered
in a small office at 20 East Jackson Street. On this day, the office was "filled
with great stir and activity" as they all worked feverishly "taking clippings"
from "great stacks of '*El Universal Ilustrado*'" and other imported Mexican
newspapers. Working together, Mondragón and his cohort planned the un-
veiling of *México*, a liberal paper aimed at Mexican immigrants. At this point
in time, Chicago's Spanish-language press fell into three categories: apoliti-
cal papers printed by high school Spanish-language departments, religious
newsprints published by a handful of Protestant churches, and newspapers
written by self-identified "Hispanic Americans" who called for the unifica-
tion of all Spanish-speaking immigrants.[32] Mondragón and Miranda were

active in Hispanic circles, but they were first and foremost Mexican liberal nationalists. In the aftermath of the revolution, Mondragón and his compatriots professed they were a "new type of liberal" who stood for "human rights," "universal suffrage," "public education," and the "emancipat[ion] of the people's religious consciousness."[33] Before he emigrated, Mondragón had written for *El Universal Ilustrado* in Mexico City, and he now worked for the *Tribune* in Chicago. Miranda, meanwhile, had started a tailoring business and was turning toward a career in advertising. Mondragón and Miranda believed Chicago was ready for a Mexican press. Chicago's Mexican population was growing rapidly, and migrants like Mondragón and Miranda were in search of community.[34]

Within weeks, Mondragón, Miranda, and their supporters had inaugurated the liberal paper *México: El Semanario de la Patria*. They were able to start their press by drawing on Mondragón's skills as a journalist, Miranda's finances and contacts as a businessman, and the relationships they had each cultivated among a growing body of community leaders. For over a year, Mondragón managed *México* while Miranda worked as an editor. The paper eventually changed hands between 1926 and 1930, but Mondragón and Miranda remained active in liberal circles. Through *México*, Mondragón and Miranda had set a historical precedent. They had founded a newspaper in Chicago that focused almost exclusively on Mexican migrants. Under Mondragón's leadership, *México* endorsed newly formed liberal societies, encouraged migrants to seek out English- and Spanish-language instruction, offered migrants criminal justice assistance, connected migrants to the Mexican consulate, and discouraged Mexicans from becoming U.S. citizens.[35]

Initially, Mexican liberals started their societies by drawing on the institutional resources of the Chicago settlement houses, which had a long history of assisting European immigrants as they adjusted to life in Chicago. Mexican liberals were nationalists, however, and recognized that the settlements sought to Americanize the immigrants they assisted. The liberals appreciated and respected the settlement houses and the work they did with all immigrants, but Mexican liberals were also cautious about working too closely with the settlement houses because the liberals wanted their societies to be free from the control of white American administrators. It took several years, but by the midtwenties, middle-class Mexicans had managed to pull together enough resources to found two organizations: Lux en Umbra, a Masonic lodge, and the Cruz Azul, a social welfare group led by Mexican women. Initially, middle-class liberals supported the activities of both Lux and the Cruz, but, over time, reform-minded liberals ended up uniting with working-class Mexican activists to guide the entire liberal community away from Lux's elitist activities and toward the Cruz's community-reform agenda, which emphasized the importance of improving the lives of Mexican laborers (see table 16).[36]

In Mexico, influential liberals like Cámilo Arriaga, Enrique Flores Magón, and Francisco Madero all joined the Freemasons. In 1893 there were more than two hundred Masonic lodges in Mexico, and, as James Cockcroft explains, the Masons attracted middle-class Mexicans with liberal, anticlerical, and democratic politics who typically opposed the Díaz dictatorship. Díaz attempted to co-opt the Masons, but many lodges resisted, and some actively contributed to Díaz's downfall.[37]

In South Chicago, middle-class Mexican liberal men founded the Masonic lodge Lux en Umbra and then began organizing private and ritzy nationalist events. The relatively small size of Chicago's Mexican population and its largely working-class composition sparked debates between the liberal elitists who founded Lux and liberal reformers who subscribed to a more inclusive vision of Mexican nationalism. In October 1928 Luis Álvarez Castillo and other liberal migrants contacted the Valley of Mexico Grand Lodge in Mexico City and started Lux en Umbra No. 50 as a division of the Rito Nacional Mexicano. Under the leadership of Venerable Master Castillo, Lux recruited "honorable" Mexicans who were businessmen and professionals. Seeking Mexican state legitimacy, Lux invited the Mexican consul of Chicago, Gen. Carlos Palacios Roji, to join Lux, and Palacios enthusiastically accepted the invitation. Using their own finances, Mexican Masons held posh nationalist celebrations at Mexican-owned restaurants such as La Gardenia in South Chicago and the South American on the Near West Side. During these events, Masons would take turns reading Mexican nationalist poetry, often reciting selections from Amado Nervo, whose lyrics paid tribute to Mexican indigenous leaders, philosophers, and architects and famous Mexican liberals like Benito Juárez. *México* covered all of Lux's festivities as examples of glorious tributes to Mexican patriotism.[38]

As Mexican Masons organized these elite events, working-class migrants who read about Lux in *México* submitted letters to the paper criticizing the liberals for doing nothing for ordinary Mexicans. Mexican liberal women responded to these criticisms by forming the Cruz Azul Mexicana of Chicago, the first Mexican liberal-reform organization in the city. The Cruz was first started in San Antonio, Texas, in 1921 as a social welfare organization that provided migrants with health and childcare assistance. Over time, Cruz brigades, as they were called, emerged in nearly every Mexican community in the Southwest, the Midwest, the East Coast, and even Alaska, where Mexicans were laboring in fishing and canning work. Several scholars have characterized the Cruz as the first nationwide Latina organization in the United States.[39]

In Texas and California, where the Cruz managed more than fifty brigades, Mexican women activists began linking their healthcare work to educational initiatives. Mexican women started Spanish-language libraries at Cruz centers and offered migrants Spanish-language courses. In Chicago, *México* and newly formed liberal papers like *La Noticia Mundial* picked up on the healthcare and educational activities of the Cruz and praised its work. These articles ran in conjunction with letters that criticized Lux. In response, a capitalina named Milla Domínguez, who had worked as a professional singer in Mexico and was now married to the vice consul of Chicago, joined with María Luisa Sánchez, Juana Peña, Eva A. Carreras, and other Mexican women to inaugurate a Cruz brigade on the Near West Side. In her public speeches, Domínguez claimed to privilege a domestic lifestyle over a life of public activism, but in practice, she devoted countless hours to fundraising and networking on behalf of the Cruz. As a singer, Domínguez initially served as the Cruz's director of festivities. By 1931 she had been elected to the presidency of the Cruz's executive board. In this position, Domínguez recruited all her middle-class contacts to back the Cruz, and she secured the support of several Mexican doctors in Chicago, such as S. G. Meixueiro, Eliud García Treviño, and Óscar G. Carrera, who was a known healthcare advocate for Mexican workers. The West Side Cruz eventually created a subbrigade in South Chicago and elected a board of Mexican women to lead its activities.[40]

The Cruz was soon joined by other associations of Mexican women, such as the Sociedad Feminil Mexicana, led by Antonia Aguilar, María Jiménez, and Virginia Chávez. Often working with the Cruz, the Sociedad Feminil engaged in a range of social welfare work well before the New Deal and the creation of the American welfare state. Cruz and Sociedad activists assisted Mexican workers with unemployment, bereavement, and legal assistance. They organized clothing drives for poor Mexican families, bought Christmas presents for orphans, visited the elderly in hospitals, started support networks for widows and disabled workers, and, through their connections to doctors, began organizing educational programs that addressed intimate matters, such as women's "sexual hygiene" practices.[41]

To raise revenue for this social work, Cruz activists turned to the ideology of Mexican nationalism, and Mexican laborers encouraged them in this direction. Beginning in April 1930, *México* received numerous letters signed by laborers who stressed that "true patriots" and "real [Mexican] citizens" would assist the Cruz, Sociedad Feminil, and "our countrymen who are dispossessed." Mexican workers advised the Cruz to redefine its social work as patriotic labor, and they encouraged the Cruz to organize large nationalist fundraisers. At this point in time, Lux had held exclusive nationalist affairs, and these events were typically closed to the general public. Working-class Mexicans recognized the unifying power of nationalism. Many were genuine Mexican patriots, while most could agree that they needed to find ways to raise revenue for the social welfare work of the Cruz and Sociedad Feminil. Mexican laborers consequently pressed the Cruz to organize fundraisers that would honor "the struggles and deeds of our Mexican heroes."[42]

Drawing on these recommendations, the Cruz began blending Mexican nationalism with all of its revenue-raising activities. On May 5, 1930, the Cruz held two Cinco de Mayo fundraisers that "commemorate[d] the anniversary of the glorious Puebla expedition" that defeated French troops. More than four hundred migrants turned out for the Cruz festival at Ashland Auditorium, while another four hundred migrants participated in a parallel event at Community Hall. Adding its support to these nationalist celebrations, the Mexican consulate of Chicago sent delegates to both events. On the Near West Side, Dr. Eliud García Treviño delivered a speech praising liberal "heroes" like Benito Juárez who fought against French imperialism, while *México* bolstered the nationalist overtones of the festivals, noting that migrants had "turned out en masse to do homage to the memory of our heroes, and to show the interest which we still have in the far away land of the Mother country."[43]

Mexican laborers were inspired by the Cruz's dedication to the broader Mexican population, and they started working closely with it. Mexican women's social welfare work began pulling working-class migrants into the emerging liberal-reform community. Throughout the 1920s, Mexican laborers had established their own organizations, which were typically mutualistas.[44] In South Chicago, Mexican steelworkers founded the Sociedad Mutualista Obreros Libres Mexicanos (Sociedad Mutualista). Polish and Italian Americans had their own mutual aid and fraternal groups, but in a few instances, white ethnics like Victor Lapiano were drawn to the enthusiasm of Mexican workers, and they too joined Mexican mutualistas. When Sociedad Mutualista began partnering with the Cruz, it encouraged other mutualistas in Chicago, such as Campamento Emilio Carranza, to do the same. By 1931 Sociedad Mutualista and Campamento Carranza were collaborating with the Cruz, Dr. Treviño, and other Mexican healthcare professionals in a project to curb alcoholism among migrants. José R. Vega, the president of the Sociedad Mutualista, was so moved by the social welfare activism of the Cruz that he wrote a passionate letter to *México* in admiration: "These women have made themselves the idols of men. Each one of the members of this benevolent institution will encounter a supporting hand and heart, eager to help them glorify the dignity of the Mexican woman through their cultural and social work. I wish to stress the fact that the women of this worthy organization have the backing of the Mexican workers."[45]

Julián Mondragón was one of the many liberals in Chicago who supported the Cruz's work, and he began encouraging middle-class migrants to form societies that would continue to engender community while carrying out new social-welfare projects. Following in the footsteps of the working-class Sociedad Mutualista, white-collar workers founded the Sociedad Mutualista Benito Juárez, whose members were "workers, lawyers, doctors, engineers, businessmen, writers, and newspapermen."[46] Then, in the early 1930s, Mondragón, Miranda, and a number of newly arrived liberals, such as Sebastian Rivera (a former lawyer in Mexico), Jesús Maldonado, Fernando Moreno, León Lira, and others, formed La Alianza Fraternal Mexicana (La Alianza), which functioned more as a fraternal society than as a mutualista. At this time, the now-prominent Mexican philosopher and statesmen José Vasconcelos was serving as the rector of the National Autonomous University of Mexico (Universidad Nacional Autónoma de México, UNAM), and he had recently redesigned the university's logo to include the dictum "Por mi raza hablará el espíritu." La Alianza adopted Vasconcelos's words as its own salutation, which it translated and expressed as "Through my race speaks the spirit. Salud!"[47] La Alianza started its own press to attract community support and then began organizing dinner parties to recruit others to the organization.

These networking events were initially held in the homes of liberals, but as new liberal groups emerged, the dinners were reorganized as large banquets at Mexican-owned restaurants. Liberal clubs, like Club Melchor Ocampo (named after the influential lawyer and politician who had served as Mexico's minister of the interior under Benito Juárez), worked with the Sociedad Feminil to recruit all community organizations to the banquets. As these events grew in size, La Alianza requested that Mexican groups send no more than three delegates to every banquet, and many middle-class societies and working-class mutualistas complied. Honored guests included Consul Palacios Roji, Vice Consul Tomás Morlet, Professors Fortunato Ortega Rodríguez and Justino Sánchez, Dr. Eliud García Treviño, and other middle-class Mexicans. "The atmosphere [at the banquets] was purely Mexican," recalled an attendee.[48]

Protestants and Mexican Liberals

Back at the headquarters of La Alianza on the Near West Side, Mondragón discussed providing working-class migrants with secular and nationalist educational courses, and this proposal led La Alianza in search of donors. The liberals were too anticlerical to work with the Catholic Church in Chicago, and they were hesitant to partner too closely with the settlement houses, which they identified as Americanizing institutions, and so they turned to Hispanic Protestants who had access to the resources of wealthy Protestant churches. Hispanic ministers were perceived as men who might challenge Mexicans' commitment to Catholicism but not their loyalty to the Mexican nation-state. As the Mexican population of Chicago grew, Methodists, Presbyterians, and Baptists took notice and started ministering to migrants, and the Protestants who led this work often had experience proselyting in Mexico. Protestants first entered Mexico in significant numbers during the anticlerical and liberal presidency of Benito Juárez (in office 1858–72). In Juárez's effort to curtail the Catholic Church's influence, he invited American Protestants to start schools, missions, and health clinics in Mexico. Through these organizations Protestants established reputations as critics of Catholicism and as liberal social reformers.[49]

Mexican liberals in Mexico and in Chicago could be quite judgmental of the Catholic Church and therefore expressed few qualms about working with Protestants. The majority of liberals, like Mondragón, were Catholics, but they were also anticlerical in their politics, believing that the church wielded too much influence in Mexico. Mexican liberal Catholics saw no contradiction between being a faithful Catholic and an anticlerical patriot. Before working with Hispanic Protestants in Chicago, Mondragón and Miranda decided to reach out to Mexican Protestants in the southwestern United States. In May 1930 *México* published "The Swallows of Becker" by Alberto Rembao, a Mexican Methodist minister and liberal intellectual who had developed a scholarly reputation among ethnic Mexicans in Texas and California. Rembao had recently questioned the liberals' conviction that migrants would eventually return to Mexico. In Mexico, Rembao had worked as a teacher in the extremely Catholic state of Jalisco. After immigrating to Texas, Rembao began working as a journalist in San Antonio for *La Prensa*, the largest Mexican-controlled newspaper in the United States. He later wrote for *La Opinión* in Los Angeles and then in 1930 began publishing *La Nueva Democracia* in New York City. Because Rembao was a migrant who had worked in several U.S. cities as a journalist, an educator, and a Methodist minister, Chicago's Spanish-language press treated him as an intellectual authority figure on contemporary immigration issues. In his editorial for *México*, Rembao began by declaring that he was "speak[ing] as a Mexican of Mexicans, with the pride of my blood, race, and citizenship," and then he went on to elucidate that migrants were once like "swallows" or birds of passage who sought to escape revolutionary turmoil by moving to the United States. While it was "painful" to admit, these migrants were never going to return to Mexico, reasoned Rembao, because they had found decent work in the United States, they had established large families on this side of the border, and their children were losing the Spanish-language "mother tongue" and were internalizing American cultural values. "The American public schools," bemoaned Rembao, "bombard us at night through our own children, who preach to us the doctrines which are taught to them during the day." Mexican parents would never force their children to resettle in Mexico, concluded Rembao; therefore, Mexicans were destined to remain in the United States.[50]

Mondragón and other liberals came to terms with Rembao's argument as they personally witnessed the growth of the population of Mexican children. Throughout the 1920s, Mexicans tended to migrate to Chicago as adults, and they often arrived without any children. As late as 1930, a study of 3,616 Mexican households revealed that 44 percent were childless.[51] Naturalization records support this demographic description of Mexican Chicago as an adult population. Out of a sample of 1,876 Mexicans who settled in Chicago between 1900 and 1940, only 10 percent of these migrants crossed the border as children. The majority, some 70 percent, crossed the border as adults, and most made their way directly to Chicago. By comparison, some 32 percent of the Mexican naturalizers of Los Angeles crossed the border as children, and another 22 percent crossed the border as young adolescents.[52] Mexican Chicago was significantly more adult than Mexican Los Angeles, and adult culture facilitated the growth of Chicago's liberal intellectual community (see table 8 in the appendix).

As the population of Mexican children grew, Mondragón and other liberals began to argue that Mexican children had the power to swing the entire community toward or away from Mexico. Mexican children would either retain the Spanish language and remain intimately connected to Mexico, or they would lose their "mother tongue," adopt American cultural ways, and create permanent lives for themselves in the United States. In his analysis of the children, Mondragón added that they were often the victims of alienating "racial discrimination" in Chicago and were ill prepared to cope with this type of abuse. Mondragón believed that Mexican children often dealt with racism "in private" and in ways destructive to their self-esteem. He argued that anti-Mexican racism needed to be challenged and that Mexican children needed a safe space where they could discuss their racial experiences. He therefore advised liberal societies to help him create the Centro Mexicano (Mexican Center), where the Spanish language and Mexican cultural studies could be taught to both children and adults and where Mexicans could escape the "outrages suffered by many of our people" in "this modern 'Babylon' called Chicago."[53]

Mondragón succeeded in establishing the Centro Mexicano through his Protestant connections and his close personal friendship with a Methodist minister named Guillermo Baquero O'Neill. Of Puerto Rican and Irish ancestry, William B. O'Neill (as he was known by most Americans) came to Mondragón's attention after O'Neill challenged the *Chicago Tribune* for publishing a series of chauvinistic editorials about revolutionary Mexico. "It is saying too much for Mexico to call it medieval," editorialized the *Tribune*. Mexico's "products are . . . waste lands, destroyed resources, illiteracy, poverty, and ignorance. . . . The great masses of primitive peoples are unfit for self-government and the educated classes are equally so."[54] The *Tribune* concluded that the Platt Amendment ought to be extended from Cuba to Mexico. Passed in 1901, the Platt Amendment established, among several stipulations, that Cuba would grant the United States territory for U.S. military bases and would accept that the U.S. government had the right to intervene in Cuban affairs. Outraged by the proposition, O'Neill fired off several passionate letters. "The recent editorial," which recommended "a protectorate for Mexico under the so-called Platt amendment, . . . is rather disgusting. . . . Has Mexico asked for it?" challenged O'Neill. "Mexico, let it be known, does not need a protectorate. The *Chicago Tribune* may rest assured of this fact. We believe she can attend to her own affairs."[55] O'Neill wrote in the first person when defending Mexico, discursively inserting himself into the Mexican community. He had grown fond of Mexicans after ministering to them in several railyard boxcar camps on the outskirts of Chicago, and he now saw all Mexicans as members of his Latino flock.[56]

The Methodist Episcopal Church was eager to support O'Neill's Mexican activities because of developments that had recently transpired in Mexico. After the revolution and several successive anticlerical Mexican presidencies, the Mexican government invited the Methodists to found the Methodist Church of Mexico in Mexico City in July 1930. It was to be independent of the Methodist Episcopal Church of the United States but would be administered by an executive board led by an American named Dr. Ralph E. Diffendorfer. Diffendorfer appointed Juan N. Pascoe to the Episcopate of Mexico's Methodist Church, and by June 1932, Bishop Pascoe was in Chicago, holding meetings with O'Neill about leading the Methodists' missionary work among Mexican migrants in the city.[57] Through Bishop Pascoe's support, O'Neill started a Spanish-language Methodist church in Chicago, the Church of the Good Shepherd.[58] Within a few years, O'Neill had courted a number of migrants to Good Shepherd, the majority of whom worked at International Harvester.[59] Speaking at a religious conference in Chicago in 1931, O'Neill delivered a paper entitled "The Papal Power's Fall."[60] O'Neill's criticisms of the pope and of Rome apparently appealed to Mondragón, and they developed a friendship. O'Neill joined La Alianza, and through the Methodists, Mondragón founded the Centro Mexicano. O'Neill could not finance the construction of an entire community center for Mondragón and the liberals, so he partitioned a large space within an existing Methodist community center, the Marcy Center, and renamed it the Centro Mexicano. In this space, Mondragón and other liberals began teaching Spanish-language classes to Mexican children and adults, started a liberal Spanish-language library, and recruited Mexican and Latin American intellectuals working at the University of Chicago and Northwestern University to deliver lectures at the Centro.[61]

Receiving a Liberal Education in Chicago

As Mondragón worked as a de facto teacher in Chicago, he was assisted by Jesus Mora, who recommended that liberals create educational courses across the city. From Mora's perspective, a poor education placed migrants at an economic disadvantage in Chicago and contributed to their sense of alienation, which might lead migrants to apply for U.S. citizenship. A frequent contributor to *México*, Mora argued that migrants were unaware of "the wonderful traditions of our [Mexican] race." Their poor formal education, Mora contended, led migrants to "feel ashamed of their origin[s] and deny their country either by changing their citizenship or by making up their mind not to come back [to Mexico]." Liberals understood that education and patriotism went hand in hand. One of *México*'s first issues had aggressively lashed out against the Mexican naturalizers of the city, referring to them as those "Who Deny Their Country." The editorial asserted that "the true Mexican . . . proclaim[s] his nationality once and a thousand times . . . saying very proudly to everyone *that he was born in Mexico*, that that is his country, and that he would give everything for his country, including his life."[62] Rather than simply recastigating Mexican naturalizers, Mora theorized that migrants applied for U.S. citizenship because of American national and racial chauvinism. By Mora's reasoning, U.S. racism did not discourage Mexicans from assimilation. On the contrary, racism contributed to migrants' sense of alienation and compelled them to assimilate. "The sons of 'Uncle Sam'" express an "air of superiority . . . toward the Mexicans," explained Mora. "They believe that we are still uncivilized beings," they "reproach us for our illiteracy," and "because their color is white, they classify us as 'colored people.'" Because of their poor education and predominantly nonwhite skin color, contended Mora, Mexicans experienced intense alienating discrimination, which led them to naturalize. Mondragón agreed and added that migrants' low self-esteem was a direct consequence of the Porfiriato, before "[Francisco I.] Madero's Revolution," when Mexicans "were kept in the most profound ignorance, and no opportunities for education were given [to] them." Mora and Mondragón concluded that without education, migrants would remain unable to intellectually defend themselves against U.S. chauvinism.[63]

La Alianza consequently encouraged migrants to take advantage of educational opportunities in Chicago, including both English- and Spanish-language instruction. Well aware of the market advantages to learning the English language, middle- and working-class Mexicans enrolled in English-language courses Chicago officials created to help assimilate the city's large foreign-born population. Between 1926 and 1927, more than 637 Mexicans enrolled in the Chicago Board of Education's night school English-language courses, and another 845 registered between 1927 and 1928. Settlement house workers jubilantly claimed that Mexicans were one of the few immigrant groups whose participation nearly matched their population size within Chicago. In 1920 Mexicans represented about 2 percent of the city's population, and they constituted 1.8 percent of the 47,718 immigrants who enrolled in the board's classes. Settlement house workers and city officials cited these figures as proof that Mexicans wanted to assimilate into the United States as U.S. citizens. Following in the footsteps of the board, Hull House established an English course specifically for Mexicans in 1927 and quickly enrolled over one hundred migrants. Mexican women took advantage of these educational opportunities along with Mexican men. They attended English-language classes at Hull House and represented about a third of the students attending an English class at the Henry Booth House.[64]

While American social workers and educators viewed Mexican migrants' aspiration to learn the English language as an indicator of their desire to become American citizens, the majority of Mexicans never applied for U.S. citizenship, and their decision was supported by Mexican liberal activists. Through *México* and other Spanish-language papers, liberals encouraged Mexicans to learn the English language, but they also urged migrants to safeguard the Spanish language and to decline U.S. citizenship. Beneath the radar of the settlement houses, the Chicago Board of Education, and other Americanizing institutions, the liberals carried out their own Mexican nationalist education project, which included English- and Spanish-language courses and classes in Mexican civics and history. Mondragón taught courses at three locations: the Centro Mexicano, the La Alianza office, and a Young Men's Christian Association branch. In Brighton Park, a Mr. Rodríguez used a vacant storefront as a classroom to assist Mexican adults with their English competency while teaching Mexican children the Spanish language. On the Near North Side, a Mr. Herrera used his residence as a classroom and taught a language course to migrants on a weekly basis. On Ashland Avenue, A. Talamentes, a former teacher in Mexico, taught a language class out of his apartment. Throughout Mexican Chicago, liberals provided migrants with educational courses to reinforce their connections to Mexico and to grow the liberal community by establishing a closer relationship with the Mexicans who valued education.[65]

Criminal Justice Protection

Mora's and Mondragón's understanding of what they called "racial discrimination" was informed by their experience in Chicago and by what they learned from their Mexican students.[66] Mexicans had ambivalent interactions with white ethnic Americans. Chicago was an incredibly diverse and international city in the 1920s. Some European immigrants and ethnic Americans accepted newly arrived Mexicans, and these people tended to be entrepreneurial in outlook. They owned properties and rented rooms and apartments to Mexicans or owned convenience stores and saloons and saw Mexicans as a new pool of customers. Michael Innis-Jimenez found that in South Chicago, German, Austrian, Bulgarian, and Italian Americans who owned homes took in Mexican boarders for extra income.[67] Irish landlords, such as a Mrs. McAvoy, stated they "liked the Mexicans," and McAvoy even defended one of her Mexican tenants from a group of aggressive police officers on one occasion. McAvoy was taken aback and impressed by the Mexicans when she learned that during the "daytime, [Mexicans] go to the public schools to learn English, and at night they come here [to one of her properties] to learn Mexican."[68] While McAvoy sympathized with her Mexican tenants, white ethnic Americans who were not explicitly profiting from Mexican migrants could act aggressively toward Mexicans who moved into their neighborhoods, especially when Mexican men were seen courting white ethnic women. At times, groups of white ethnic men attacked Mexicans, and their behavior was condoned by a segment of the police force.[69] On the Near West Side, two Poles beat a Mexican to death during an altercation. In this same neighborhood, a group of Italians attacked Felipe Ruiz and his wife, mortally wounding both of them. In South Chicago, Luis Mendez, Nicolas González, Luis Vargas, and Pedro Peña were all assaulted by groups of Poles on separate occasions. In yet another incident, thirty Poles chased five Mexicans into an apartment complex, where they pinned them down for several hours by pelting the building with rocks. Part of what distinguished this violence from the fisticuffs and even knife fights that occurred among Mexicans and between Mexicans and African Americans was the support white ethnics received from white police officers. *México* and other liberal papers excoriated "Polish policemen" when they clubbed, shot, and killed Mexicans, arrested them en masse, and allowed white ethnics to destroy Mexican-owned property.[70]

Liberals used their newspapers, *México, La Noticia Mundial,* and *La Lucha,* to document and denounce acts of "racial discrimination" and to warn migrants to avoid certain streets, blocks, and neighborhoods. To protect their "compatriots," the liberals turned to the Mexican consulate of Chicago and demanded that it defend Mexican citizens. Mexican liberals were knowledgeable about the Mexican consulate's legal duties, and at various times, the liberals used the press to shame consular officials when they believed they were not living up to the liberals' nationalist standards.[71] Chicago's liberal community established a working relationship with the consulate, encouraged migrants to fill out their *matrículas* (consular identification and registration records), and advised migrants to contact the consulate if they needed assistance.[72] The Mexican foreign service was started in 1822, but it was fundamentally reorganized after the revolution. In 1923 the Ley Orgánica del Cuerpo Consular Mexicano established that consuls were obligated to defend the "prestige, moral and material progress of the [Mexican] Republic," and they were "to protect the interests and rights of Mexican nationals."[73] Citing Mexican international law, liberals in Chicago published bold headlines, such as "The Consulate Does Not Honor Its Duties!" when liberals felt individual consuls were not abiding by their legal obligation to assist Mexicans.[74] Several consuls served Chicago at different times, but the liberals gained significant assistance from Consul Rafael Avelyra and Vice Consul Luis Lupian.

Consuls were often from Mexico's upper class, but that did not mean that they were elitists unconcerned with the welfare of their countrymen. Gilbert Gonzalez argues that the Mexican consulate has largely been a conservative force in the United States. To be sure, consuls were not radicals: consuls did not try to substantively alter the exploitative relations between Mexican workers and American employers, they were often hostile to Mexican radicals, and they did not always support the unionization efforts of Mexican immigrants.[75] However, Mexican immigrants were often better off with the Mexican consulate than without it. The vast majority of Mexican consuls were nationalists, and they were disturbed by anti-Mexican racism in the United States. At times, individual consuls went out of their way to assist migrants who were in dire straits. In the case of Consul Avelyra, like many liberals, Avelyra was a capitalino and a social reformer. As a student, he had taken courses in administration, music theory, and art. An accomplished cellist and fluent in English, French, and Italian, Avelyra was a humanist who worked as a journalist for *El Monitor Republicano* in Mexico City before joining the consular service.[76] After arriving in Chicago, Avelyra began supporting the liberal community's initiatives.[77]

In the context of several high-profile criminal justice cases, including the arrest and trial of Juanita Guevara, whose story is told in the introduction, Mexican migrants were arrested on criminal charges but then released from custody because of Consul Avelyra's intervention. In November 1924 a group of migrants went into a pool hall, fell into an altercation, and began firing pistols at each other. A white police detective who heard the shots rushed into the pool room and was killed. Enraged by the death of an officer, the police rounded up every Mexican in the vicinity, arresting some fifty migrants. When Mondragón and Miranda learned of the incident, they went straight to Avelyra for assistance. Avelyra became involved and, over time, negotiated the release of forty-eight of those arrested.[78] Even though a white police officer had been shot by a Mexican immigrant and had died during this incident, Consul Avelyra was still able to use his influence to free nearly every Mexican who was arrested.

In other incidents, Mexicans were denied access to Chicago's recreational facilities by white Americans who did not want to share these leisure spaces with them. In South Chicago, Mexicans were prevented from using the field-houses and public showers at Bessemer, Calumet, and Russel Square Parks.[79] Mexican liberals turned to the consulate to put an end to these discriminatory practices, and on one occasion the consulate succeeded. When Mexicans were denied access to the 12th Street Beach in South Chicago, the liberals called on Avelyra. As *México* explained, a group of white Americans had established an extralegal practice of barring nonwhites from the beach. This was "an insult to the people of our race as well as to the Colored and the Filipino people, who were also denied admission," argued Mexican journalists. Avelyra launched an investigation and through what appears to have been a personal contact in city government opened the beach. *México* celebrated: "There is no further discrimination against any race [at the beach]!" Mexican journalists were clearly too optimistic, but they were proud of Avelyra and his commitment to Mexican immigrants.[80] Avelyra gained such a reputation as a social champion that migrants living in Utah and Texas would call on him for support if they were denied assistance by their own consular representatives.[81]

Mexican consuls possessed bona fide legal power, and the liberals understood this and pressed the consulate to use its privilege to assist migrants. As individual consuls helped migrants, they too experienced American chauvinism, which only enraged and motivated them to fight harder on behalf of the Mexican community. Milla Domínguez's husband, Vice Consul Adolfo Domínguez, had taken it upon himself to start sitting in during court proceedings whenever he learned that a Mexican was being tried. While seated in Municipal Court judge Thomas A. Green's courtroom, Domínguez listened closely as Green discussed the case of a migrant who had been arrested on trespassing charges for sleeping in a public alley. Green had a reputation for mistreating Mexicans and would later preside over numerous repatriation cases during the Depression. At one point during the current trial, Green made an offhand remark about Mexico, and Domínguez simply snapped: he rose to his feet and began chastising Green in his own courtroom. Affronted by Domínguez, Green had Domínguez arrested, sentenced him to six months for contempt of court, and fulminated, "I cannot understand why these persons [other judges] use so much wordiness with these [Mexican] consuls. I put them where they belong." As Domínguez was hauled away, however, he yelled out at Green that he had diplomatic immunity and would be back. Within four hours of Domínguez's arrest, the Mexican consulate of Chicago contacted the Mexican ambassador, who spoke with the Foreign Office in Washington, D.C., which called on a federal judge in Illinois, who ordered Domínguez's immediate release. Leaving the jailhouse, Domínguez directed oncoming journalists to his lawyer, who informed the press that Consul Domínguez would be seeking retribution against Judge Green in federal court.[82] In the aftermath of the incident, the State Department and the governor of Illinois intervened and forced Green to retract his contempt of court ruling against Domínguez.[83]

Mexican liberals embraced consulate officials like Avelyra and Domínguez as progressive liberal allies, and community activists were emboldened by the presence of the consulate in Chicago. In the context of these court trials, liberals started sitting in during court proceedings to observe how American judges and district attorneys treated Mexicans, and the defense attorneys of Mexican migrants encouraged this new practice. As one defense lawyer told a migrant, "I believe we should have as many members [of your organization] as possible present at trial" to demonstrate the "prestige of [your] organization" and to convey to judges and district attorneys that they were being watched by the Mexican community.[84] The Mexican consulate and various liberal societies pulled together a network of lawyers, such as Mary Belle Spencer, Bruno Heirich, and Russell Baker, among others, to work with Mexican migrants on various legal issues. Just as the Cruz had organized nationalist fundraisers to pay for its social welfare work, liberal groups followed in this tradition to pay for migrants' legal fees, and Consul Avelyra supported all of these endeavors.[85]

The Rise and Fall of the Mexican Liberal Movement

Through nationalist banquets and fundraisers, social welfare services, Spanish-language education courses, and criminal justice assistance, La Alianza and other liberal groups had created a community and a reform movement in Chicago. The liberal movement was led by middle-class Mexicans, but it attracted working-class migrants who needed social services. As the liberal nationalist community became influential, the percentage of Mexican applicants for U.S. naturalization in Chicago shrank. In 1920, 107 Mexicans applied for U.S. citizenship in Chicago. The U.S. census cites 1,224 foreign-born Mexicans living in Chicago in this year. A conservative calculation might divide the number of Mexican applicants for naturalization in Chicago in a given year by the number of foreign-born Mexicans living in Chicago in the same year to determine a plausible Mexican rate of application for naturalization. Through this cautious method, we can establish that Mexican immigrants in Chicago had a rate of application for naturalization of 9 percent in 1920.[86] The naturalization rate of Mexican nationals across the United States in 1920 was only 3 percent.[87] In 1920, before the rise of the liberal movement, Chicago settlement house officials may have reasonably thought that the majority of their Mexican clients would eventually become U.S. citizens. As the Mexican liberals created a community, however, naturalization records reveal that the proportion of Mexicans seeking U.S. citizenship fell drastically even as the raw number of Mexican applicants for U.S. naturalization increased slightly. Only forty-four Mexicans applied for U.S. citizenship in 1925, fifty-eight in 1927, and seventy in 1929, when the Mexican population of Chicago proper stood as high as twenty thousand persons. The Mexican rate of application for naturalization thus dropped from a high of 9 percent in 1920 to 0.4 percent by 1929.[88] While my research uncovered no examples of Mexicans who completed the naturalization process in Chicago before 1938, a report by the Immigrants' Protective League, a progressive organization that supported immigrant rights, claimed that two Mexicans completed the naturalization process in Chicago in 1926, a mere five in 1927, and a total of fifteen in 1928.[89]

During the Depression, many Mexicans in Chicago lost their jobs, some were targeted for deportation, and others simply left the city. The Mexican population of Chicago, which stood at about 20,000 persons in 1930, was reduced to some 7,200 persons by 1940. The Depression-era deportations dissuaded some Mexicans from approaching courthouses to apply for U.S. citizenship, while Mexicans who had all of their immigration papers in order and felt confident now attempted to apply for naturalization to protect themselves from deportation. Thus, by 1940 the rate of application for naturalization had actually climbed slightly to 2 percent from 0.4 percent in 1929. In short, the Mexican rate of naturalization was at its lowest in Chicago during the peak years of the Mexican liberal nationalist movement between 1925 and 1936.[90]

With relatively limited resources, Mexican liberal nationalists had created a reform movement in Chicago, but international developments ultimately derailed the liberals' future plans. Between 1926 and 1929, conflicts in Mexico between anticlerical liberals and Catholics escalated into the violent Cristero Rebellion, which pushed antiliberal and proclerical Mexican traditionalists out of Mexico and into the United States. Traditionalists, some of whom were Cristero militants, wanted to improve Mexican society, but they were unwilling to abandon the church and the Catholic ethic they argued was a defining characteristic of the Mexican people. In Chicago, traditionalists joined Catholic churches, such as Our Lady of Guadalupe in South Chicago and St. Francis of Assisi on the Near West Side, and then challenged the liberals' right to serve as the figureheads of the Mexican community. In the densely populated Mexican neighborhood of the Near West Side, traditionalist associations such as La Union Nacionalista Mexicana attacked liberal clubs such as Club Plutarco Elias Calles, named after the anticlerical president of Mexico whose policies had engendered the Cristero Rebellion.[91]

While traditionalists marshaled migrants against the liberals, the Depression devastated the liberal community. A third of the Mexican labor force lost their jobs during the Depression, and these were the customers who patronized Mexican-owned restaurants, bakeries, and saloons and who subscribed to the liberal press. Mexican liberal proprietors pleaded with Mexicans "to patronize the stores of our people," but the weight of the recession proved too great, and numerous Mexican businesses went bankrupt, destroying the institutional base of the liberal community. The liberals who lost their businesses often returned to Mexico. Those who remained in Chicago now learned that city welfare administrators were pressuring Mexicans to repatriate. Mondragón and others were disturbed to discover that federal immigration officers, working with local police officers, were detaining, questioning, and sometimes forcing migrants to repatriate.[92] The liberals were ambivalent about repatriation. On the one hand, they condemned deporting Mexicans against their will and coercing them into self-repatriation; on the other hand, liberals did not consider themselves "Americans," and they believed that unemployed and unwanted Mexican citizens might be better off in Mexico. Many liberal leaders repatriated, and some worked with the Mexican consulate to assist migrants who also wanted to return to Mexico. Liberals even criticized the Mexican government for bureaucratically impeding return migration. Within this milieu, Mondragón and other liberals witnessed the decline of their world in Chicago.[93]

As the liberals lost influence, they launched an aggressive campaign against the traditionalists to save what was left of their community. Joining *El Liberal* in 1933, Mondragón personally went on the offensive. When traditionalists leafleted Chicago hailing the Cristero guerrillas who rebelled against the Mexican government, *El Liberal* asked them to "go to school . . . so that they may be able to define the words: Citizenship, Revolution, [and] Right[s] of Man. Because in their utmost inconsistent [news]sheet they exposed their ignorance and clearly show [they are] coward[s and] traitors." For the liberals, the traditionalists' seditious criticisms of the Mexican government, their intense devotion to the Catholic Church, and their support of the Cristero Rebellion were all signs of a traditionalist-led counterrevolution that threatened the future of revolutionary Mexico. Through *El Liberal*, Mondragón and others defended the anticlerical thrust of the revolution and the legacy of liberal leaders such as the "most meritorious statesman of the Americas, Licenciado [lawyer/accredited] don Benito Juárez," the "Great Indian who knew how to manage one by one the administrators of the convents and other similar centers where the most impudent immorality of the epoch was in force." According to Mondragón, President Juárez had improved Mexican society by separating church and state, limiting the influence of clerics in politics, and thereby "teach[ing] us [Mexicans] to respect God as God, and Man as a Man."[94]

In response to the liberal offensive, the Martires Mexicanos, a traditionalist organization operating out of St. Francis of Assisi, began distributing *El Ideal Mexicano* to combat *El Liberal*. Mondragón and other liberals now referred to traditionalist societies as "Associations of Stupid Persons" who wanted to return to the "35 year[s] of [Porfirio] Díaz" when Mexicans were kept "ignoran[t]" and "illiterate" and had "no schools." A few of the Mexicans who wrote for *El Liberal* attempted to explain that they were not anti-Catholic; they simply desired a clear separation between church and state. These liberals emphasized that as patriotic Mexicans, they "kept the picture of Our Lady of Guadalupe together with that of Benito Juárez" over "the head of [their] bed[s]." Yet this synthesis of liberal politics and Catholic beliefs was of little concern to traditionalist activists. From their perspective, the liberals in Mexico and Chicago were anticlerical, and their politics were at odds with a Catholic conceptualization of Mexican national identity. As the Depression continued, liberals lost their businesses, while the traditionalists, organizing out of Catholic churches, kept recruiting migrants, and they organized an influential antiliberal movement. Between 1936 and 1939, the traditionalist mobilization, aided by the effects of the Depression, ruined the liberal community, which would never regain the influence it had achieved in the late 1920s.[95] By the mid-1930s, however, a few liberals would join with Mexican *comunistas* to create a radical movement that would continue to orient many Mexicans toward Mexico.

Conclusion

In Chicago, middle-class Mexican liberal nationalists created a community and a reform movement that dissuaded many migrants from becoming U.S. citizens. Some Mexican liberals were elitists uninterested in interacting with uneducated and poor migrants from rural backgrounds. Many others, however, had a genuine desire to assist their working-class compatriots, to "uplift" them, by providing them with needed welfare, educational, and criminal justice services. Initially, Mexican women like Milla Domínguez led this liberal-reform work, and then men such as Julián Mondragón began encouraging the entire liberal community to engage in reform projects.

Based on the existing literature, it appears that middle-class Mexican liberals were more influential as community leaders in Chicago than they were in the Southwest, in cities such as Los Angeles, Houston, and San Antonio. During the revolution, elite Mexicans and middle- and working-class folks escaped revolutionary violence in Mexico by fleeing across the border and settling in nearby U.S. cities. The elite Mexican exiles who arrived in Los Angeles possessed the wealth, influence, and connections to quickly establish themselves as the figureheads of the Mexican community. Middle-class Mexican professionals and small property owners in Los Angeles largely aligned with the *ricos* (as the elites were called), separating themselves from the larger, poorer, and less educated working-class Mexican population of L.A.

Elite and middle-class Mexicans had migrated into Houston and San Antonio well before the revolution, and, over time, the entrepreneurs within this population established reciprocal commercial relationships with middle-class white Americans. By the 1920s, an influential number of upper- and middle-class Tejanos (or "Texas-Mexicans," as they were named) had come to believe that they had financial investments and futures in the United States. By the 1930s, these Tejanos were well on their way toward asserting themselves as Mexican Americans.[96]

The history of Mexican Chicago is distinct. Very few Mexican ricos migrated all the way to Chicago before or after the revolution. Instead, Chicago was settled by middle- and working-class Mexican migrants. Mexican Chicago's class composition (which lacked a true cohort of elites) engendered a reciprocal relationship between middle-class migrants like those who belonged to the Cruz, Sociedad Feminil, and La Alianza and working-class folks who needed social services and were in search of a Mexican community.[97] To be clear, the formal educations, professions, and tastes of middle-class Mexicans in Chicago distinguished them from the broader working-class population of the city, but Chicago's Mexican middle class collaborated and fraternized with Mexican laborers through social fundraisers, community events, and social reform activities.

Chicago's Mexican liberal community and movement were sustained by the Mexican middle class and by a gainfully employed Mexican working class. During the Depression many Mexicans lost their positions, many repatriated, some were deported, and those who remained in Chicago witnessed the decline of their particular vision of *México de afuera* (outer Mexico).

2 The Counterrevolution Migrates to Chicago and Northwest Indiana

Why is *The Indicator* published? *The Indicator* is a paper destined
to make people think and begins its labor now. [We are] not
moralists. . . . [W]e are liberals lamenting the lack of organization
of the Mexican Colony of Chicago. [Without organization,] the
pride of the race tends to disappear, and the *chaos* draws near.

—*El Indicador*, April 1933

The home is the foundation of every society, the fundamental
motivation for our existence, the indispensable factor of every
institution. . . . Without [a home and a] family, all that would exist
is *chaos*.

—*El Amigo del Hogar*, April 6, 1930, emphasis added

On an early Sunday morning in May 1928, dozens of Mexican families gathered outside of St. Francis of Assisi Church on the Near West Side of Chicago. This church was "quite a large one as churches go," noted an observer, for over the course of several decades, successive waves of Catholic immigrants had added to its size and prosperity. Originally constructed and congregated by Germans, St. Francis was later sustained by Italians and was now transitioning into the hands of Mexicans. On this Sunday, as Mexican men, women, and children filed into church, they seated themselves according to gender. Women sat to the left of the altar, "Mary's side," while men situated themselves to its right, "Joseph's side." This division puzzled an onlooker who had attended numerous Mexican Masses and had never seen such a practice. By 9:30, St. Francis was quite "crowded," forcing many men to stand near the rear entrance, and yet several rows of pews remained available. St. Francis's parishioners had reserved these pews and divided themselves by gender out of respect for their special guests of honor, the men who belonged to one of the most prestigious traditionalist organizations in Chicagoland, El Círculo de Obreros Católicos San José (Círculo).[1]

As the members of the Círculo entered St. Francis they took their place in front of all other parishioners and to the right of all women, as a groom would during a Catholic marriage ceremony. Subscribing to a hierarchical and family-centered worldview, the Círculo's members positioned themselves below God, Christ, and the priest who was about to say Mass but in front of all other attendees as the symbolic heads of Mexican Chicago. These Mexicans were extremely "devoted and their attendance genuine," wrote an observer, as suggested by a Círculo activist who attended Mass despite a debilitating illness that forced him to "be seated during the entire service." Looking at the Círculo's membership, one could see that these were not elites by any monetary standard. These migrants represented a cross section of the male population of Mexican Chicagoland. Some wore "tailor made suits" and "coats," while the majority attended Mass in their working-class "denim pants and overalls." A few of the Círculo's leaders owned small businesses and held white-collar jobs, but most labored in the steel mills that lined the shores of Lake Michigan, extending out from South Chicago into Northwest Indiana. While there were clear distinctions within the Círculo, these Mexicans had united across class and educational lines by their devotion to the Catholic faith.[2] After migrating to Chicagoland, these conservative traditionalists, as I call them, carried out a counterrevolution of sorts that sought to reverse the anticlerical momentum of the Mexican Revolution.

A Migrating Counterrevolution

The Mexican immigrants who founded the Círculo created a political program that stressed the importance of "Christian unity and fraternity" because they were well aware of the numerous contemporary conflicts occurring in Mexico between anticlerical liberals and Catholics. These clashes would eventually escalate into the Cristero Rebellion of 1926, a three-year battle that ended after tens of thousands of deaths. The founders of the Círculo had emigrated from the Bajío state of Jalisco, the citadel of the Cristero movement, and they were deeply disturbed by the influence and effects of anticlerical liberalism in Mexico.[3]

Unlike the liberals who celebrated the revolution, traditionalists denounced it as an anticlerical and bloodletting event. Traditionalists were disgusted by the bellicose anticlericalism, atheism, and radicalism of many revolutionary leaders, which had engendered incredible division, conflict, and "chaos" in Mexico. The revolution had been fought by diverse political factions, but it was led by liberals who wanted to create a less Catholic and more secular, modern, and prosperous Mexico akin to what they believed existed in western

Europe and the United States. Concluding that liberalism and Protestantism were intertwined on some nebulous level, the authoritarian but economically liberal president Plutarco Elías Calles (in office 1924–28) drew together a coalition of influential industrialists, landowners, and intellectuals who believed that secularization and the influence of Protestantism would lead to Mexico's advancement.[4] Catholic prelates and priests, devoted to their faith and fearing a loss of their social position in Mexico, began mobilizing the religious against the Calles presidency. Counseled by the Vatican, Mexican bishops and clergy pulled together faithful landholders and campesinos and urban middle-class Catholics who collectively charged that Mexico's national identity and moral social order were grounded in the Catholic faith.[5]

President Calles initially reacted to his Catholic opponents by attempting to undermine the church's influence through federally funded educational and social service programs that focused on capturing the "conscience of the [Mexican] youth," because, as Calles would say, "the young man and the child belong to the Revolution."[6] Calles increased federal funding for public schools and appointed a Mexican Protestant, Aarón Sáenz Garza, to serve as his secretary of foreign affairs. He then chose José Manuel Puig Casauranc as his secretary of education, who authorized the construction of over two hundred Methodist schools in Mexico.[7] Newly formed Catholic organizations such as the Liga Nacional Defensora de la Libertad Religiosa (Liga) and the Asociación Católica de la Juventud Mexicana (Asociación Católica) felt rightfully threatened by these developments, and they organized protests and economic boycotts against the Calles administration.

As other scholars have made clear, President Calles was an authoritarian who believed the executive branch of government had the right to set the course of national policy in Mexico. Calles thus responded to his intransigent Catholic opponents through repression and threats, declaring he would enforce all of the articles of the Mexican Constitution of 1917, which would in effect expel the church from the public sphere. The constitution embodied the anticlericalism of the liberal politicians and intellectuals who drafted it.[8] If fully enforced, articles 3, 5, 27, and 130 would completely secularize education in Mexico by preventing the church from sponsoring any schools. The articles would further allow the government to expropriate all of the church's property, they would outlaw the clergy from supporting political parties and organizations, and they would censure the clergy from criticizing the government. The Mexican episcopate reacted to Calles's hardline anticlericalism by calling for a moratorium on all religious services. Learning of the episcopate's plans, Calles contemplated, "I believe that we have reached the moment when the lines of battle are definitely drawn; the hour is approaching for the decisive battle; we will see whether the Revolution has triumphed over reaction or whether the victory of the Revolution has been ephemeral."[9]

In August 1926 Calles began enforcing the articles of the constitution, and the Liga and Asociación Católica responded by recruiting Catholic militants from the Bajío states of Jalisco, Michoacán, and Guanajuato into guerrilla units. Battle-crying "Long Live Christ the King!" Catholic rebels (Cristeros) ransacked government offices, destroyed public schools, and then engaged federal troops in all-out warfare.[10]

Calles's troops fought the Cristeros throughout the Bajío. Calles forcefully relocated thousands of Bajío residents from their hometowns and villages and then strafed the Bajío from the sky, leveling entire communities to rubble. The violence that occurred during the rebellion engendered an exodus from the Bajío, and many Bajío migrants made their way into Texas and California and then up into Illinois and Indiana.[11] While the rebellion compelled many Bajío residents to migrate, U.S. labor agents had been recruiting Mexicans from the Bajío to the Midwest since the First World War. Labor recruiters drew Bajío immigrants to numerous cities in the Midwest, including Chicago, East Chicago, and Gary, but Bajío immigrants established their largest and most prominent community in East Chicago.

Mexicans first began arriving in East Chicago, Indiana, during the First World War, when the Inland Steel Company, several railroads, and a meat-packing plant began attracting them to the Calumet region. In 1900 fewer than fifty Mexicans lived in the entire state of Indiana. By 1920 more than four hundred had settled in East Chicago, and another two hundred had migrated to Gary, Indiana. Despite a dip in their population size during the recession of 1920, between 1922 and 1930, the Mexican population of Northwest Indiana soared to nearly ten thousand persons, 70 percent of whom resided in East Chicago. By 1930 Mexicans came to represent between 6 and 10 percent of East Chicago's total population.[12] Proportionally, Mexican East Chicago may have been the largest Mexican community in the Midwest at this time. Approximately three thousand Mexicans worked in steel production, roughly two thousand at Inland Steel, eight hundred at the Gary Works foundry of the Illinois Steel Corporation, and another two hundred at Youngstown Sheet and Tube. Another one thousand Mexicans worked for three railroad companies: the Indiana Harbor; the Western Indiana; and the Chicago, Milwaukee, and Gary Railway. Roughly two hundred or so Mexicans worked at the G. H. Hammond meat company.[13]

Like their counterparts in Chicago, Mexicans in Northwest Indiana lived near white ethnic Americans and African Americans, but unlike Chicago, Mexicans in this locale did not live among many non-Mexican, Spanish-speaking migrants: Mexican East Chicago was a predominantly Bajío community. As Francisco Rosales's early work revealed, after U.S. labor agents began recruiting Bajío migrants to Chicago and Northwest Indiana during the war, these migrants established an effective pattern of chain migration that pulled more Bajío migrants into the region. Bajío migrants secured steel-mill jobs for their relatives living in Jalisco and Michoacán, and this process repeated itself as newly arrived migrants sent remittances back to their families in the Bajío and encouraged others to join them in the United States. Steelwork paid well and was prized above lower-paying meatpacking work and transient railroad jobs. Chicago's larger economy attracted a more diverse range of Mexicans, while East Chicago in Northwest Indiana was founded and settled primarily by Bajío migrants. Throughout the late 1920s, Bajío migrants continued to migrate to East Chicago and to other cities throughout the Midwest.

Creating Traditionalist Communities in Chicago and Northwest Indiana

The Bajío traditionalists who arrived in Chicago, East Chicago, and Gary were assisted by the Catholic Church, but the relationship between the church and traditionalists took time to develop because the Archdiocese of Chicago was undergoing a transition. When Mexicans began appearing in the Midwest, the archbishop of Chicago, George Mundelein, was consolidating Chicago's numerous Catholic parishes, which had been organized around the nationalities of priests and their parishioners. In 1920 Catholics could attend Mass at more than two hundred parishes in Chicago. Within one square mile in the Back of the Yards neighborhood, there were eleven parishes, representing Irish, Polish, Italian, German, Slovakian, Croatian, Lithuanian, and Bohemian Catholics.[14] Mundelein wanted to consolidate parishes, he had little interest in creating new national parishes, and he therefore made few overtures toward newly arriving Mexican migrants whose population numbers were small in comparison to the much larger Irish, Polish, and German Catholic populations of the city. Mexican liberals took advantage of this organizational vacuum and recruited Mexicans into liberal societies. As early as 1925, however, Mundelein began to make concessions to ethnic priests who wanted to preserve their national parishes. Mundelein started granting religious orders the right to carry out work with specific nationalities, and it was then that the Claretians, a Spanish order, began focusing on the needs of Mexican Catholics. Father James Tort, a Claretian Spaniard, was instrumental in this process. Father Tort was a charismatic leader who, in a relatively short amount of time, transformed Our Lady of Guadalupe (Our Lady) in South Chicago into a large Mexican parish, and then he transitioned St. Francis on the Near West Side into a Mexican-serving church. Father Tort succeeded in integrating Mexican Catholics into these two churches by creating an interethnic Catholic community between Mexicans, Irish, and Poles in South Chicago and between Mexicans, Italians, and Germans on the Near West Side.[15]

The anticlerical Calles presidency and then the rebellion shifted the political activities of many Mexican communities in the United States toward Catholic activism and concurrently raised the status of the Claretians within the church. Beginning in the 1880s, Mexican liberals had crossed into the southwestern United States to topple the Porfiriato; Mexican Catholic émigrés now entered the United States seeking to overthrow President Calles. Julia Young's work highlights the degree to which American bishops assisted exiled Mexican clergy and Cristero activists. The archbishop of San Antonio, Arthur Jerome Drossaerts, embraced exiled Mexican archbishops José Mora y Del Rio and Leopoldo Ruiz and the president of the Asociación Católica, René Capistrán Garza, when they escaped Mexico and arrived in Texas. In El Paso, Bishop Anthony J. Schuler offered newly arriving Mexican bishops, priests, and Cristeros the use of all church facilities and provided them with $120,000 in financial assistance. In Los Angeles, Bishop John J. Cantwell welcomed Archbishop Jesús Manríquez y Zarate, one of the most ardent Cristero leaders, whose activities included "working with arms smugglers" to supply Cristeros with weapons, according to Young.[16] These Mexican prelates and Cristero activists, like Capistrán Garza, supported new militant Mexican Catholic societies in the United States, groups like the Vasallos de Cristo Rey; they expanded the circulation of the Spanish-language Catholic press; and they organized massive Cristero demonstrations that could draw together more than ten thousand ethnic Mexicans.[17]

Meanwhile, the Catholic press of the United States educated white American Catholics about the long history of anticlericalism in Mexico, and it began framing Mexican immigrants as religious refugees. Between 1925 and 1929, one of the most influential Catholic newspapers in the Chicago region, the *New World*, published more than six hundred articles about anticlericalism in Mexico. The Claretians in Chicago, who were then attempting to create a Mexican Catholic parish, shaped the conversations white ethnic Catholics were having about Mexicans. Father Tort had served as a priest in Mexico City in 1914 and had personal experience dealing with anticlerical Mexicans, and he urged the *New World* and other Catholic presses to frame contemporary Mexican immigration to the United States as a consequence of the anticlerical Calles presidency.[18] In the context of the rebellion, Calles began deporting Mexican bishops, priests, monks, friars, and nuns, and many of these religious leaders made their way to Chicago, where they were received as heroes by the Chicago archdiocese. When the Cordi-Marian Sisters fled Mexico, they were taken in by the Sisters of St. Francis on the Near West Side. After Calles exiled Father Miguel García from the state of Jalisco, García settled in South Chicago, where he started saying Mass at Our Lady. As the Claretians developed close ties with the exiled clergy, they cut off all contact with the Mexican consulate of Chicago and, by extension, with the Mexican societies the consulate supported. Over the course of the rebellion, some twenty-five hundred Mexican religious entered the United States, and they shaped the political culture of the ethnic Mexican communities of the United States. At St. Francis in Chicago, the Cordi-Marian sisters started parochial education courses for Mexican children, and other Mexican religious refugees began requesting and receiving funding from the church to open new parochial schools in nearly every American city that received Bajío migrants.[19] In further support of the Mexican clergy, American bishops issued the so-called *Pastoral Letter on Mexico*, which condemned the anticlericalism of the Calles administration in the contemporary period and the anticlericalism of former President Benito Juárez in the nineteenth century. The Knights of Columbus, meanwhile, distributed pamphlets entitled *Red Mexico* and *Mexico: Bolshevism the Menace*, which castigated Calles as an anti-Catholic dictator.[20]

Father Tort and the Claretians then oversaw two major religious projects in Chicago that drew Mexican and white ethnic Catholics together and helped create the foundations of a Mexican traditionalist community in Chicagoland. First, Tort modernized Our Lady parish, and then he played a key role in organizing the Twenty-Eighth Eucharistic Congress, a great religious gathering that brought Catholic clergy and laity to Chicago from around the world. Initially, Our Lady parish revolved around a plain wooden chapel in South Chicago that allegedly had been constructed as an army barrack. Claretian priests delivered Masses at Our Lady to Mexicans and local Irish residents who found the location of the chapel convenient. After Mundelein assigned Father Tort to Our Lady, he began building the parish up by recruiting Mexican migrants and middle-class Irish Chicagoans to invest in the construction of a new and massive Our Lady of Guadalupe Church. To draw Mexicans to the church project, Tort created what he called the Mexican Aid Society. Led by Tort, the society did not offer migrants much in mutual aid, but it recruited Mexicans to catechism classes and study groups that centered on the church's teachings, the history of Catholicism in Mexico, and the value in creating a Mexican parish in Chicago. Tort then focused on recruiting influential middle-class Irish Chicagoans to the project, some of whom were members of the Knights of Columbus, which had been carrying out missionary work among Mexicans throughout the Midwest. When delivering sermons to Irish parishioners and when speaking to wealthy Irish donors, Father Tort and other Claretians frequently discussed President Calles's anticlericalism and Cristero martyrdom, a narrative that framed Mexicans as Catholic refugees forced to flee an anti-Catholic state. These arguments must have emotionally moved the devout Irish who had historically defined themselves as Catholic exiles.[21] As prominent Mexican clergy continued to arrive in Chicago, Mundelein, who had been elevated to the cardinalate, announced he would financially support a Mexican parish and the construction of the Our Lady Church. With Mundelein's endorsement, Father Tort received the financial backing of several rich Catholic philanthropists, and in February 1928 Tort started constructing Our Lady.[22]

Tort then organized several grand displays of Catholic interethnic community that spotlighted the up-and-coming Twenty-Eighth Eucharistic Congress, to be held in the United States for the first time. At the groundbreaking of Our Lady, Tort asked local white ethnic politicians to deliver talks in support of Catholic fraternity, and he had exiled Mexican bishop Pascual Díaz deliver the keynote. At the first Mass at Our Lady, Tort secured the attendance of numerous white ethnic Catholic societies and organized them into a parade that stretched three city blocks in length. Impressed observers reported that more than fifteen thousand people attended the procession. During the Our Lady ceremonies, Irish, Polish, Italian, and German Catholic invitees all learned of the intense persecution of Mexican Catholics in Mexico.[23]

Malachy McCarthy convincingly demonstrates that Father Tort clinched the support of the Irish by promising them that he would establish a national shrine at Our Lady, the shrine of Saint Jude Thaddeus, the patron saint of lost causes. According to Catholic folk tradition, few Catholics prayed to Saint Jude because his name was too similar to that of Judas Iscariot, the disciple who had betrayed Jesus, and yet it was precisely because Saint Jude was so rarely called upon that he allegedly was more likely to intervene in one's life, to come to one's rescue, during times of dire need. Father Tort must have foreseen that Saint Jude could attract Irish and Mexican Catholics who had a shared history of coping with religious persecution. Irish Catholics formed a Saint Jude Club at Our Lady in 1929, which replaced the Mexican Aid Society. Its members included Irish Americans and Mexican migrants who later created the Saint Jude League, which developed a national reputation for coordinating the visitations of prominent Saint Jude pilgrims.[24]

Father Tort's role in organizing the Eucharistic Congress further bolstered the prestige of the Claretians and their mission to establish a large and well-supported Mexican Catholic community in Chicago. The first Eucharistic Congress was held in Lille, France, in 1881 and had since developed into a renowned international event that called on Catholics to join together to worship the presence of Jesus in the Eucharist and to hear sermons from clergy on the most pressing Catholic matters of the day. Cardinal Mundelein was given a great honor in hosting the conference, because it had never been held in the United States. Mundelein, in turn, extolled the Claretians when he asked them to chair the Spanish-speaking events at the congress and when he determined that St. Francis would serve as the headquarters of the Spanish-speaking Catholic delegations arriving from Spain, Mexico, and other countries in Latin America. Tort and the Claretians took every opportunity to discuss the persecution of Catholics in Mexico and to emphasize the need to assist Mexican refugees. The congress was a monumental affair. Catholic Masses during the congress held at Soldier Field Stadium and at the St. Mary of the Lake Seminary drew crowds of more than half a million people.[25]

Meanwhile, within the Mexican liberal community of Chicago, Mondragón's *México* devoted few pages to the construction of Our Lady or to the Eucharistic Congress. Instead, *México* defended President Calles's anticlerical policies, arguing that Calles was only enforcing the articles of the Mexican Constitution, which he had the right to do as the president of Mexico. As *México* defended Calles, it ran articles that criticized the church's wealth, highlighting a $1.5 million "gift" that Cardinal Mundelein had recently delivered to Rome.[26]

By 1929 Father Tort and the Claretians had created a Mexican Catholic parish in Chicago, Our Lady of Guadalupe, and were organizing large Catholic events that brought together white ethnic Catholics and Mexican traditionalists from across the city and from Northwest Indiana. Tellingly, the building committee of Our Lady included the names of Tort and ten other white American Catholics, but no ethnic Mexican served on the committee.[27] Likewise, the Mexican Aid Society was founded and led by Tort. When Mexican Catholics first created their own societies at Our Lady, many complained that Tort tried to exercise too much control over them.[28] The creation of Our Lady parish in Chicago was a top-down endeavor, but hundreds of Mexicans were now gathering and attending Mass at Our Lady and at St. Francis, and these migrants were soon joined by passionate Catholic activists who belonged to the Círculo, which had created a Mexican traditionalist community in Northwest Indiana from the ground up.

Traditionalist Mexican immigrants resided throughout Chicagoland, but in East Chicago they arrived in significant numbers before there was a liberal presence, they positioned themselves as community leaders, and they shaped Mexican East Chicago to reflect their values as Mexican Catholic patriots. Their community-building project began in April 1925, when three brothers, Benjamin, Francisco, and Carlos Figueroa, gathered migrants together after a Sunday Mass at St. Demetrius Catholic Church. "The excitement of the group of Mexicans was felt throughout," expressed the Figueroas. "For the first time, [we] were going to discuss unity, love, and patriotism." Mexicans "had been torn from their motherland," believed the Figueroas, but, "as if by divine intervention," their faith had brought them together at St. Demetrius to found the Círculo.[29]

The Círculo's leaders were formally educated migrants, but they set out to create a Catholic organization that would include Mexicans of all educational and occupational backgrounds. Benjamin Figueroa, a known bibliophile, was elected president of the Círculo. Pedro F. Pacheco was chosen as vice president, J. Jesús Cortéz as treasurer, and Ignacio González as secretary. In search of recruits, Círculo organizers canvassed East Chicago and found working-class Catholics eager to join. The majority of these Catholics labored at the Inland Steel Corporation and the Youngstown Sheet and Tube foundry.[30] Holding their first meeting in the basement of St. Demetrius, the Círculo formulated an ambitious plan of action and distributed it through *El Amigo del Hogar* (*El Amigo*), a newspaper started by the Figueroa brothers, who owned a printing business in East Chicago.[31]

The Círculo's program reflected its Mexican Catholic and patriotic politics. Calling out to all Mexicans, the Círculo claimed it would "unify" migrants so that it could "enrich their spirits with the doctrine of Catholicism." The Círculo would raise funds to build a "patriotic and pious" Mexican Catholic church where Mexican citizens could "satisfy [their] spiritual needs with complete freedom." Mexican traditionalists would then introduce "small-town values" to East Chicago through *El Amigo*, the creation of a Catholic Spanish-language library, and the construction of numerous "Catholic schools." The church and schools were most important to the Círculo, which defined them as institutions "where Mexican children can be taught to love and venerate their heroes and traditions" so they would "think of themselves as the legitimate children of their country" through "the study of our obligations as good citizens of Mexico." The Círculo concluded that it would promote a spirit of Catholic cooperation in East Chicago, and it would work with other Mexican societies to provide migrants with spiritual leadership, access to a Catholic education, and social welfare services.[32]

The Círculo in Indiana had an advantage over its traditionalist counterparts in Chicago. The vast majority of Mexicans in East Chicago had emigrated from one region within Mexico: the Bajío. The Círculo recognized that Mexican East Chicago was a Bajío enclave, and its members knew that their "patriotic and religious" church-building project would attract many faithful Jaliscienses, Michoacanos, and Guanajuatenses.[33] While Mexican liberals in Chicago formed partnerships with Hispanic Protestants, the Círculo secured its allies among white ethnic Catholic priests in Northwest Indiana. The Círculo quickly identified an Italian priest named Octavius Zavatta as an ally. Zavatta said Mass at St. Demetrius, a local Romanian Catholic church, and he opened the church to new Mexican migrants as they settled in East Chicago. After meeting with the Círculo's leaders, Zavatta was so moved by their zeal and plans to construct their own church that he decided he would support them wholeheartedly even if it meant irritating some of his Polish and Lithuanian parishioners who were less welcoming toward Mexican migrants. Father Zavatta allowed the Círculo to use St. Demetrius as their headquarters, he delivered numerous Masses in favor of the Círculo's agenda, and he ultimately assisted the Círculo with the actual purchase of the land they used to build their own church.[34]

When Zavatta was called to Rome in October 1927, he was replaced by the Cristero Rebellion expatriate Father Apolinar Santacruz, who hailed the Círculo, affirming that it was "God who wanted me to come here to be a part of . . . the progressive and pleasant Mexican Community of Indiana Harbor."[35] Through the assistance of these priests, the Círculo was able to gather as many as three hundred Mexicans together in support of their church-building project.[36] Drawing on the assistance of the majority of Mexicans in East Chicago, the Círculo organized numerous and large fundraisers, and it succeeded in constructing Santa María de Guadalupe (St. María) in 1928.[37]

In Chicago, Father Tort won over wealthy and middle-class Irish Americans to help finance the costs of the new Our Lady Church. In East Chicago, the Círculo was backed by the entire Bajío community, and the unpaid labor of Mexican women ultimately underwrote the construction of St. María. Traditionalists quickly learned that their fundraisers needed to be festive in order to attract blue-collar steelworkers, who worked long and grueling hours. To attract community participation, traditionalists organized "Grand Festivals" that offered migrants carnival-like nights of music, dancing, games, and home-cooked dishes catered by Mexican women.[38] Slow-cooked tamales, hearty chicken and beef tacos, and refreshing ice-cream desserts were all prepared by teams of women, who were often the wives and daughters of the members of the Círculo.[39] Mexican women also made quilts, serapes (colorful ponchos), and rebozos (shawls), which were raffled throughout the night. Through the unpaid labor of Mexican women, the Círculo raised over $2,000 and was able to establish St. María.[40]

Receiving a Supranational Catholic Education

After building their church, the Círculo began to focus on implementing its pedagogical objectives. The Círculo sought to create a more literate Mexican community in East Chicago, provide migrants with a moral and religious curriculum, and recruit Mexican children to its educational program, because Círculo activists believed that children were most likely to be swayed by the liberals' anticlerical arguments. In Chicago, liberals argued that Mexicans were defined by their birth and upbringing in Mexico and by their Mexican citizenship, and many liberals accepted, albeit with reservations, the anticlerical Calles presidency. In reaction to the revolution and the extreme anticlericalism of President Calles, traditionalists began to claim that real Mexican "patriots" were defined not by their Mexican citizenship but by their Catholicism, their Catholic sense of morality, and their commitments to their families.

Throughout the 1920s, traditionalists would continue to underscore the ways Mexican identity was determined more by the Catholic faith than by Mexican citizenship. Initially, the traditionalists who articulated this theme only sought to distance themselves from the Calles presidency, but, over time, traditionalists began to unintentionally deterritorialize Mexican national identity. That is, they began to decouple *mexicanidad* from the territory governed by the Mexican state. By the late 1930s, some traditionalists would explicitly argue that "real" Mexicans were a supranational Catholic people.[41]

The leaders of the Círculo understood that the vast majority of Mexicans in East Chicago were blue-collar industrial workers who possessed limited formal educations but might not want to spend their free time attending Catholic study groups. So traditionalists emphasized that education in general and Catholic literacy in particular could offer migrants opportunities for economic upward mobility while freeing their "soul" from the day-to-day drudgery of factory work. The Círculo's Ignacio González, who worked in a steel mill, frequently implored Mexican laborers: "*We need to study!* We believe that after 8 to 10 hours of working in the factories, we have nothing more to do. Well, no, sir," urged González, "we should dedicate a couple of hours, at least, to our own personal education by which we will better ourselves socially and economically."[42] Through the Círculo's finances, González established a Spanish-language library at St. María that would serve as both an intellectual salon and a job resource center.[43] At the library, Mexicans could learn about job training and work opportunities in the Chicago region, and they would be offered pamphlets and books on the history of Catholicism and on contemporary Catholic issues. Carlos Figueroa, an avid reader and one of the Círculo's founders, stocked the library with Spanish-language books on Catholic theology, literature, poetry, and art and Catholic monographs on sociology and science so, as Figueroa would say, the library would "embody the sophistication of a race of people who are striving for their own intellectual elevation."[44] To reinforce the Catholic orientation of the library, the Círculo purchased a sixteen-volume history of Mexico from a bookstore in Jalisco, "the heartland of militant Catholicism."[45] The Círculo's educational initiatives had a significant impact on the broader Mexican population of East Chicago. At times, the Círculo would organize book swaps, and batches of novels would pour into the Círculo's office, revealing the degree to which migrants were reading.[46]

Throughout the 1920s, the traditionalist press published numerous articles that stressed that Mexico had become an immoral nation because it had been led by postrevolutionary anticlerical presidencies.[47] Traditionalists therefore set out to provide migrants with a religious education that would allow them "to shape, little by little, their moral personae."[48] In developing their moral curriculum, traditionalists understood they would have to tackle the liberals' philosophical and scientific challenges to faith-based instruction. "Education is not about filling our brains with texts and theories. . . . True education lies in . . . practicing our moral virtues," explained *El Amigo*.[49] Addressing the relationship between science and religion, traditionalist writers claimed, "There is no antagonism between science and faith. What is science?" asked *El Amigo*, "It is in great part the fruit of the investigations of humanity: it is faith[, and] faith is the experience and discoveries of other men." Science that sought to "destroy religion," however, was "false science." The liberal's overemphasis on materialism and "science," argued the traditionalist press, ignored the spiritual ties that bound humanity together.[50] Mexican migrants were often drawn to the Círculo's "moral" arguments that stressed human connectivity, given that most migrants were living far apart from their extended families, who resided in Mexico.

Círculo members often claimed that the "home" was the "foundation of every society," which led traditionalists to conclude that their educational work needed to include both home-school lessons and the creation of "Catholic schools."[51] Given that most of the Círculo's male membership worked irregular hours in factories, traditionalists argued that Mexican wives were in the unique position to morally educate children and combat the corrosive influence of liberalism. While Mexican adults could defend their faith-based beliefs, "children and adolescents" were in a precarious position because the liberal "secularization of every sphere of life" threatened to "tear out the seeds of Faith [in children] before they had a chance to germinate and develop."[52] Mexican women already "managed homes," argued the Círculo; they now needed to safeguard children from anticlerical liberalism.[53] "[Public] Schooling," explained traditionalists, was the "terrible weapon that the enemies of the church wielded." Traditionalists were not against schools, progress, or science, as some liberals charged, but they were opposed to "secular" education, which they stressed ignored the "moral" lessons that underscored human connectivity and empathy.[54] Settlement houses in Chicago, Detroit, and Los Angeles that attempted to assimilate immigrants often focused their energies on winning over migrant women, believing they would then teach their children "American values." The Círculo agreed with this rationale, and so it recruited Mexican women to educate children on the importance of internalizing a Catholic sense of morality.[55]

Mexican women were inspired to participate in the Círculo's educational program by articles that appeared in *El Amigo* that showcased the Cristero activism of women in Mexico.[56] As *El Amigo* published articles on Cristero women activists, a woman named María Rodríguez and a tireless Catholic community activist named Rosaura Herrera started teaching children's classes at St. María. These courses included lessons in the Spanish language and in Mexican Catholic history.[57] The Círculo "admire[d] and respect[ed]" Rodríguez and Herrera for their "grand work" with the children.[58] When explaining her reasons for serving the Círculo as a teacher, Herrera expressed her own patriotic and Catholic sentiments, saying that "it is criminal . . . to not cultivate in our children's hearts a love of their country along with our most saintly affections."[59]

The diasporic lives of Mexican immigrants prompted intellectuals within the traditionalist community to underscore the ways Catholicism united Mexicans across international borders. As the Círculo's Ignacio González explained, "Christianity is found across the entire world": "Like a state whose leader is God . . . she makes us see that all men are brothers, that they all have the same needs and the same rights to benefits."[60] In this piece and in others, González argued that Mexicans on both sides of the border were bound neither by their Mexican citizenship nor by their allegiance to the Mexican state but by their Catholicism, which was a transnational ideology. The traditionalists who argued that "all men are brothers [and] all have the same needs and the same rights to benefits" expressed that these rights were inalienable and transcended place of birth, residence, and citizenship status. This was an incredibly attractive and moving argument to Mexican Catholics who had been exiled by Calles and were now living and laboring in the United States.

Catholic Cooperation and the Legacy of the Cristero Rebellion

Mexican migrants in East Chicago who subscribed to their own visions of Mexican community formed organizations apart from the Círculo.[61] The leaders of these groups learned of the Círculo's call for unity, their Catholic educational courses, and their plans to offer migrants social services. Back in Chicago, conflicts developed between Mexican liberals and Catholics after Calles's election and during the rebellion; in Indiana, a spirit of cooperation developed between most Mexican organizations throughout these years. By the late 1920s, Mexican men in East Chicago and Gary, Indiana, had formed eight societies, while Mexican women had started a local chapter of the Cruz Azul.[62] These groups were often led by middle-class Mexicans, but working-class migrants also joined this organizational network, and Mexican laborers at Inland Steel formed their own *mutualista*, the Sociedad Mutualista Benito Juárez (Sociedad Mutualista). Although these Mexican laborers chose to name their mutualista after an anticlerical liberal, the leaders of the Sociedad Mutualista understood that by working with the Círculo, they could offer their members more substantive welfare services. Consequently, the Sociedad Mutualista formed a tight-knit partnership with the Círculo, avoided addressing Juárez's anticlericalism, and elected sincere devout Catholics to positions of leadership.[63] The Círculo reciprocated by supporting fundraisers organized by the Sociedad Mutualista.[64] These practices of Catholic fraternity and cooperation allowed the Círculo to carry out activities well beyond East Chicago. Over time, the Círculo formed Círculo branches throughout Chicagoland and in the state of Michigan.[65]

Working together, the Círculo, the Sociedad Mutualista, and the local Cruz Azul provided Mexican workers with numerous social welfare services. Cruz Azul women activists such as Elvira Peña and Rosaura Herrera (who served the Círculo as a teacher) offered steelworkers hospital care subsidies, disability assistance, and bereavement funds.[66] They purchased food, medicine, clothes, shoes, and Christmas presents for working-class Mexican families, and through these activities, they encouraged all Mexican laborers to join one of the existing Mexican societies in East Chicago. To pay for these endeavors, these women organized fundraisers such as dances, art fairs, and plays, which were well attended.[67]

Círculo members worked in difficult, dangerous, and nonunionized steel mills, and, at times, these migrants experienced discrimination in Northwest Indiana. Yet Círculo leaders maintained that hardship and racial discrimination did not define the Mexican people's lives. Liberal societies in Chicago, like La Alianza Fraternal Mexicana, frequently criticized racial discrimination in the United States and tacitly endorsed the unionization of Mexican laborers. The Círculo did not oppose unionization, but the Círculo recognized that unions attracted militant labor activists who often subscribed to atheistic radical political beliefs. For the Círculo, unionization opened the door to discussions about class inequities and alternatives to capitalism, which could then raise questions about the relationship between Christianity, private property, and the market economy. The Círculo's leaders accepted that migrants might need to join unions to improve their lives, but Círculo members did not actively promote unionization. In this same vein, when addressing anti-Mexican racial discrimination and altercations between white ethnics and Mexicans, the Círculo asked Mexicans to consider whether they had "behaved shamefully" or "honorably" during the incidents in question. The Círculo advised Mexicans to look inward and to take personal responsibility for their actions. The Círculo acknowledged that Mexicans experienced discrimination, but they recommended that migrants focus on improving their spiritual and material lives.[68]

The Mexican migrants who led the Círculo were devout Catholics who believed they would return to Mexico at some point in the future. Overall, their writings did not focus on issues of labor and race; instead, they wrote about spirituality, their church activities, and the horrors of the Cristero Rebellion. For migrants in East Chicago, El Amigo served as a line of communication between Mexico and the United States, and it depicted Mexico as a country that was about to collapse as a result of anticlerical liberal and Catholic division. Traditionalists read that President Calles deported Mexican clergy and laity and that Catholic organizations organized massive protests against his administration, as when an estimated two hundred thousand Catholics demonstrated in front of the Basilica of Our Lady of Guadalupe in Mexico City, demanding that the government repeal its "restrictive laws against Catholics."[69] When traditionalists learned that Calles had turned his back on the liberal principle of freedom of the press by closing down the offices of El Excélsior, which had become critical of Calles, they asked their readership, "If this constitutional principle can be violated, in the very shade of the buildings that represent our three branches of government and in front of the department of foreign diplomatic affairs, what might be occurring in other parts of the country?"[70] Traditionalists did not have to imagine what was occurring throughout Mexico. *El Amigo* brought the gory rebellion to their doorsteps.[71]

Nothing tested traditionalists' devotion to Mexico more than the extreme violence that occurred during the rebellion. These "acts of barbarism," as *El Amigo* reported, bolstered the Círculo's Catholicism, compelled it to take a partisan stand in favor of the Cristeros, and led it to continue to question the essence of Mexican identity. "A people without God," grieved *El Amigo*, "cannot abide by any logic other than that of their passions, their propensity for violence, brutality, and ferocious savageness."[72] For the Círculo, the secular society the liberals wanted to create would lead to violence, "chaos," and the disintegration of the very Mexican nation-state the liberals claimed to cherish. In "Poor Mexico" and other articles, traditionalists read about bloody battles raging across the Bajío.[73] When the rebellion began, the Círculo advocated "impartiality" and "temperance and moderation [because some Mexicans] see an affront in every act of our Government." As the violence escalated and as members of the Círculo learned that hundreds of Catholic youth were dying, the Círculo declared that "as Mexicans and Catholics [we] must raise our voices."[74] Denouncing the federal troops who did not hesitate to execute Cristeros, *El Amigo* cried out, "These martyrs . . . died in the name of the Faith with the same enthusiasm and valor as the first Christians. . . . Their only crime was to defend the Church." "Christ the King [was] being crucified in [Mexico]," avowed traditionalists, but as all Christians knew, "crucified Christ always rises: history proves this."[75]

The carnage during the rebellion compelled the Círculo to take a partisan stand in favor of the Cristeros, but it refrained from fanatically endorsing their military exploits. The rebellion broke the hearts of traditionalists who were initially genuine patriots disgusted by the grotesque reality that Mexicans were slaughtering each other by the thousands. *El Amigo* estimated that the "latest revolution [the rebellion]" had already cost Mexico eleven thousand lives, hundreds of miles of destroyed train tracks, and a crippled national economy. Moreover, Mexico had lost face, for it "had provided the world with a macabre spectacle."[76]

Traditionalists in Indiana blamed the rebellion on Calles, anticlerical Mexican liberalism, and the Mexican Revolution and praised the United States for offering U.S. citizens and immigrant residents religious freedom. Mexican liberal newspapers in Chicago, such as *El Liberal*, excoriated the Cristeros and accused traditionalists of seeking to regress Mexican society back into the era of Porfirio Díaz. For liberals, Diaz was a dictator, and the revolution was a liberal, democratic, and egalitarian revolt.[77] Traditionalists saw it quite differently, contending that "the regime of Diaz is the only one in the 400 years of Mexican history during which Mexico prospered and the government was stable." From "the savage [Mexican] Revolution, to the recent vulgar tragedy [the rebellion], to the killings with no end [that] have soaked our land with blood," anticlerical liberal revolutions fostered a "horrific immorality," bemoaned traditionalists.[78] Traditionalists now began to praise the political stability and religious freedom they were experiencing in the United States. The Círculo cited numerous examples of public and massive Catholic Masses in the United States, such as those organized by Father Tort in Chicago, as proof that American citizens experienced "true liberty!"[79]

If the United States represented "true liberty," traditionalists were not abandoning Mexico just yet. After completing his presidential term, Plutarco Calles continued to shape Mexican politics as the *jefe máximo* (supreme leader) through his control of the military and his hand-picked presidential successors. During this period in Mexican history, known as the Maximato (1928–34), Calles, under the advice of U.S. ambassador Dwight Morrow, agreed to cooperate with the Vatican to put an end to the rebellion. In the early months of 1929, Calles attended a series of meetings with Vatican officials, clergy from Mexico and the United States, and Morrow. While still in office Calles had founded the National Revolutionary Party (Partido Nacional Revolucionario, PNR), and under Calles's direction, the PNR nominated Pascual Ortiz Rubio as their presidential candidate. Ortiz Rubio did not have a reputation as an anticlerical politician, and he publicly stated he would seek peace with the church. The Vatican, Cristero groups, and many traditionalists in Mexico and in the United States were therefore optimistic when Ortiz Rubio was elected president of Mexico in 1930, defeating José Vasconcelos.[80]

Vasconcelos was hardly anticlerical in his politics, but the limited support he received from traditionalists in Chicagoland reveals the complexity of Mexican politics in this era and the degree to which liberals and traditionalists were polarized. Like other Mexican liberals, Vasconcelos was a sharp critic of U.S. imperialism and U.S. racial beliefs that privileged whiteness, but, unlike the liberal *puros* (the liberal "pure ones," who rejected compromises with the church), Vasconcelos maintained that the Catholic Church had a place in Mexican society. For Vasconcelos, the church was a cultural and spiritual bulwark against U.S. culture and thus U.S. imperialism. Liberal puros in Mexico and Chicagoland believed Vasconcelos was too Catholic and too soft on the question of the church. For pro-Cristero traditionalists, Vasconcelos was too closely associated with the anticlerical liberalism of the revolution. Ortiz Rubio was Calles's chosen successor, but he was promising reconciliation. Thus, when Vasconcelos and Ortiz Rubio visited Chicago during their presidential campaigns, it appears that moderate liberals formed ad hoc societies, such as Cómite Pro-Vasconcelos, and organized fundraisers on his behalf, while moderate traditionalists in Chicago and in Indiana welcomed Ortiz Rubio to the United States.[81] Liberal puros and hardline Cristero traditionalists were dissatisfied with both candidates. After Ortiz Rubio won the election, he followed through on his promise and cooperated with the church to end the rebellion. In this regard, he permitted exiled bishops and clergy to return to Mexico.[82] By June 1929 peace agreements had been signed, and the rebellion was declared over.

Deporting a Catholic Community

With the end of the rebellion, Mexican politics seemed to be improving in the eyes of many traditionalists. But just as the last of the Cristeros laid down their weapons, the U.S. economy slipped into the Depression. As unemployment rose, a nativist movement developed across the United States that engendered a deportation drive. In East Chicago, the cry to deport Mexicans was not initiated by the elites of the city but by ordinary Americans, a number of whom were members of the American Legion. Some Mexicans in East Chicago could sense that something was amiss in the way they were being treated by white East Chicagoans, but traditionalist leaders initially tried to dispel their fears. In June 1929 *El Amigo* communicated, "There is no need to be alarmed. An exaggerated rumor has spread among our compatriots out of a fear that there will be a mass deportation campaign. . . . Nothing has justified this sense of unease."[83] As the Depression continued, Círculo leaders would learn that they had underestimated the nativist sentiments of their white American neighbors.[84]

The severity of the Depression prompted a local branch of the American Legion to call on its members to investigate the citizenship status of those in Northwest Indiana who were drawing on local charities for economic relief. Russell F. Robinson, the post commander of the legion in East Chicago and president of the local Emergency Relief Association, requested formal reports from legionnaires who worked for social welfare agencies in the region.[85] After assessing their findings, Robinson determined that the legion could "relieve . . . welfare agencies . . . so they could do all possible for the native American population" by "remov[ing] the nationalists, especially the Mexicans," from Northwest Indiana.[86] To remove the "nationalists," the legion first attempted to obtain the assistance of the U.S. Immigration Bureau, which declined to assist the legion, explaining that a repatriation campaign would strain diplomatic relations with Mexico. The legion then appealed to the Department of Labor, which conducted a study in East Chicago and found that many if not the majority of the Mexicans in the city could not be deported without violating the existing immigration laws of the United States. Most Mexicans in East Chicago appear to have entered the country legally, many had documented paperwork that proved their legal status, and the vast majority were law-abiding community members with no criminal records—most Mexican immigrants had simply lost their jobs during the Depression.[87] Determined to free up welfare resources for American citizens, legionnaire Paul E. Kelly contacted railroad and industry officials, including representatives of Inland Steel, and convinced them to finance a repatriation campaign if Kelly could ensure that they would be reimbursed by the city of East Chicago through tax credits.[88] The legion now approached Mexican consul Rafael Avelyra for his assistance, and Avelyra acquiesced to the legion's proposal. Consul Avelyra had a reputation of assisting Mexicans in need, but he was not in a position to offer jobs to unemployed and unwanted Mexican immigrants. Avelyra, like many Mexican community leaders, believed that impoverished migrants might be better off in Mexico given their present circumstances and the increasingly dangerous climate of nativism in the United States.

Between 1930 and 1937, the legion cooperated with East Chicago's trustee's office, the Emergency Relief Association, the East Chicago Manufacturers Association, and many ordinary local citizens, who collectively encouraged, nudged, and, at times, coerced some three thousand Mexicans to repatriate to Mexico. Over in Gary, Indiana, the Gary Commercial Club and the local Chamber of Commerce also aggressively prodded Mexicans to repatriate.[89] Under this nativist pressure, several Círculo leaders repatriated and left for Mexico, while the majority of working-class Círculo members remained in Indiana.[90] Throughout East Chicago, Mexicans witnessed acts of intimation during the repatriation campaign and learned of migrants who were deceived into returning to Mexico.[91] As the repatriations continued, traditionalists watched as the Catholic community they had worked hard to create was reduced to less than half of its size. The Círculo and Sociedad Mutualista members who remained in East Chicago, such as Mexican immigrant Basil Pacheco, a future union organizer for the United Steelworkers of America, concluded that their Catholic community's stability, the freedom of worship, and the "true liberty" they had come to cherish in the United States required U.S. citizenship.

Conclusion

In the 1920s, liberal activists in Mexico had the upper hand because they had the tacit and sometimes explicit support of the Mexican government; in the

United States, traditionalists had the advantage because they were directly assisted by the secure, well-organized, and influential Catholic Church. The Mexican liberals in Chicago were too anticlerical to work with the church and too nationalist to work closely with the Americanizing settlement houses of Chicago, while Mexican traditionalists were able to draw on the resources and the institutional backing of the church from the Southwest to the Midwest.

In Chicago, the Claretians created a Mexican Catholic parish, Our Lady of Guadalupe, that brought traditionalists together from across the region, while in Northwest Indiana traditionalists established a Catholic community through their own grassroots initiatives. The Claretians were able to successfully establish the new Our Lady Church in Chicago in part by creating an interethnic community between Mexicans and white ethnic Catholics. Through their community-building initiatives, Father Tort and other Claretians framed Mexicans as religious exiles fleeing an anti-Catholic Mexican state. This narrative appears to have drawn the sympathy of Irish Catholics who defined themselves as Catholic exiles. Wealthy and middle-class Irish Americans helped finance the creation of the first large Mexican parish in Chicagoland. By comparison, traditionalists in Northwest Indiana built their church, St. María, and their Catholic community from the ground up, and they were able to do so because traditionalists in Northwest Indiana did not have to compete with liberals for the hearts and minds of the Mexican people of East Chicago. Mexican East Chicago was a Bajío enclave where traditionalists from Jalisco had founded a Catholic society, a press, and an educational program, and these Mexicans served as the community's leaders.

Over the course of the Calles presidency and during the Cristero Rebellion, traditionalist neighborhoods throughout Chicagoland received an influx of Mexican clergy and Bajío émigrés who encouraged Mexican Catholics to become politically active. The grotesque violence that occurred during the rebellion disheartened traditionalists, who began to question their commitment to the anticlerical Mexican nation-state and the value of their Mexican citizenship. The revolution, the Calles presidency, and the rebellion deeply alienated traditionalists from the Mexican state.

The Depression-era deportations only further spurred traditionalists to relinquish their Mexican citizenship. The Depression ushered in a nativist movement that devastated Mexican Northwest Indiana. While Mexicans were deported from Chicago proper, the threat of expulsion was even greater in East Chicago. In Chicago, it appears that the reputations of the liberal settlement houses and other Americanizing institutions and the overall foreign-born culture of the city created a more tolerant climate for Mexican migrants. While the evidence remains limited, it also appears that the interethnic Catholic community the Claretians helped create in Chicago mitigated anti-Mexican nativism. Traditionalists in Indiana were farther removed from the Chicago settlement houses and Chicago archdiocese, and they were consequently more aggressively expelled from Northwest Indiana.[92] The traditionalists who saw their numbers cut in half and felt that painful loss concluded that their Mexican citizenship could cost them the Catholic communities they had worked hard to create in the United States.

3 Mexican Immigrant Understandings of Empire, Race, and Gender

> While the pride of the present masters of the world asserts through the mouth of their scientists the ethnic and mental superiority of the Whites from the north, any teacher can corroborate that the children and youths descendant from Scandinavian, Dutch and English found in North American universities, are much slower, and almost dull, compared with the mestizo children and youths from the south.
>
> —José Vasconcelos, *The Cosmic Race: A Bilingual Edition*

> The ambitious North Americans are not content with monopolizing our industries and our petroleum, they have taken the first steps to monopolize our ideas and our spirits.
>
> —*El Amigo del Hogar*, September 4, 1927

This chapter compares Mexican liberal and traditionalist understandings of empire, race, and gender to explain why the liberals often rebuffed U.S. citizenship and why traditionalists became amenable to U.S. naturalization. In Chicago, Mexican liberals created "Hispanic" coalitions with liberal Puerto Ricans, Nicaraguans, and other Latin Americans. Mexican liberals adopted the term "Hispanic" because they believed that the Spanish language facilitated unity and coalition building between Latin Americans in a way that no other characteristic could. As Mexicans befriended Puerto Ricans and Nicaraguans, they began to aggressively denounce U.S. interventions in Latin America as examples of "the imperialism of the United States."[1] In Mexico, liberals had embraced a kind of Mexican nationalism that was critical of European and U.S. imperialism and celebratory of the indigenous and *mestizaje* heritage of Mexicans. The Mexican liberals in Chicago who commemorated their mestizaje identities concurrently criticized U.S. notions of race, segregation, and whiteness. Mexican liberals ultimately refused to become U.S.

citizens because they were put off by U.S. imperialism and a U.S. society they argued was too racially exclusive and, as we shall see, too gender egalitarian.

By contrast, traditionalists rarely entertained discussions about U.S. imperialism or racial discrimination, and they disregarded the writings of Mexican intellectuals who promoted mestizaje because these writers were often liberals. A few traditionalists acknowledged that the United States practiced imperialism in Latin America, but the majority embraced the political culture of the United States for granting citizens and immigrant residents alike with religious freedom, and they further praised the U.S. government for offering exiled Mexican clergy and laity a refuge from the postrevolutionary, anticlerical Mexican government. As traditionalists challenged the liberals' anticlerical and mestizaje politics, they accentuated all that was Catholic and thus Spanish in Mexico. In so doing, they exalted Catholic Spain and inadvertently created an intellectual culture that was more congruous with the Eurocentric ideas of race, whiteness, and citizenship that were dominant in the United States. While the liberals continued to criticize U.S. imperialism, white supremacy, and U.S. naturalization, traditionalists concluded that they could create lives for themselves in the United States as Americans.

Mexican Liberal Understandings of American Imperialism

During the nineteenth century, American businessmen migrated into Latin America and created powerful enclaves that shaped Latin American perceptions of the United States. In the 1880s American financiers and the representatives of the Atchison, Topeka and Santa Fe Railroad entered Mexico to construct a binational railway that would facilitate the extraction of natural resources from Latin America and the export of U.S.-manufactured goods into new southern markets. As the Santa Fe and other railroads coupled Mexico to the United States, the Guggenheim Exploration Company began acquiring mines in the states of Durango, Chihuahua, Coahuila, and Zacatecas. In Chihuahua, the Hearsts, starting with U.S. senator George Hearst and continuing with his son, William Randolph Hearst, secured more than 1.6 million acres of land, which they used to launch a massive and profitable cattle-ranching operation. In Sonora, William Greene developed the mining town of Cananea through his acquisition of the largest deposit of copper ore in Mexico. Along the Gulf of Mexico, in Tampico and Tuxpan, Tamaulipas, the fortune hunter Edward Doheny first struck oil and then took hold of more than 600,000 acres of land, only to prompt Standard Oil to expand its operations in Mexico. By 1910 more than seventy-five thousand Americans were living in Mexico, and in cities like Tampico, Americans opened hotels, restaurants, bars, candy shops, and a Presbyterian church.[2]

Assessing these American migrants and their ventures, Mexican liberals developed a critical analysis of the United States. The leftists within the Partido Liberal Mexicano began castigating the United States for what they called "American imperialism in Mexico."[3] Isidro Fabela Alfaro, a more moderate liberal professor and government official, published a treatise on U.S. foreign affairs that became, in the words of John A. Britton, "a standard in the repertoire of anti-US rhetoric" in Latin America.[4] In *Los Estados Unidos contra la libertad* (The United States against liberty), Fabela argued that the United States practiced imperialism, but he emphasized that U.S. imperial policies emanated from Washington and not from ordinary Americans, who did not directly determine their country's foreign policies. Fabela explained that U.S. statesmen were discursively democratic but imperialist in practice, and he supported this claim by citing multiple examples of U.S. filibustering and interventions in Nicaragua, Cuba, Panama, the Philippines, and the Dominican Republic while making references to U.S. military actions in Hawaii, Samoa, Haiti, and Puerto Rico. Both ardent and moderate liberals in Mexico agreed: the United States practiced imperialism.[5]

Throughout Latin America, liberal nationalists were making similar arguments. Both the Nicaraguan Augusto César Sandino and the Cuban José Martí described the United States as an empire. Between 1850 and 1913, the U.S. Marines carried out six interventions in Nicaragua alone. When the liberal presidential administration of José Santos Zelaya declared it would impose higher taxes on U.S. companies operating in Nicaragua, the United States pressured Zelaya to resign. Nicaraguan liberals turned away from Zelaya's successor, U.S.-supported president Adolfo Díaz and instigated a civil war against him. The Díaz forces triumphed in 1917, and Díaz then ratified the Chamorro-Bryan Treaty, which granted the United States a military base in the Gulf of Fonseca. Costa Rica and El Salvador protested, arguing that the U.S. base infringed on their sovereignty, but the United States dismissed their claims. Summarizing this history in the 1920s, Sandino wrote, "The entire civilized world knows . . . there has been a situation of unalterable struggle to maintain our territorial integrity against the menace of U.S. imperialism."[6]

As Sandino condemned "U.S. imperialism," Mexican liberals migrated to Chicagoland and developed friendships with Puerto Ricans, Nicaraguans, and other Spanish speakers.[7] Mexicans like Julián Xavier Mondragón, the editor of the liberal paper *México: El Semanario de la Patria*, befriended Puerto Ricans such as Julio I. Puente, who worked as a lawyer in Chicago and published *El Heraldo de las Américas*. These Hispanics joined with Nicaraguans like Celio H. Barreto, who worked at a financial firm in Chicago, and Miguel Ibarra, a journalist from Managua. Barreto and Ibarra had recently started a liberal press, *La Noticia Mundial*, and had formed a fraternal society, the Unión Centroamericano. Central American and Caribbean migrants, who were few in number in Chicago in the 1920s, joined with Mexican liberals who could organize large events of upward of eight hundred Spanish-speaking migrants. Mexican liberals, on their part, worked with these other Hispanics to offer Mexicans a broader fundraising network, more social services, and additional opportunities.[8]

Little is known about the non-Mexican Hispanic population of Chicago before the Second World War. The U.S. census offers us an amorphous description of these Hispanics by grouping Central Americans with South Americans and by combining Spanish-speaking Cubans and Dominicans with all immigrants from the "West Indies." Tentative calculations suggest the non-Mexican Hispanic population was increasing in size before the Depression and then went into a period of decline. The census listed 617 Central and South American immigrants in Chicago in 1920, 1,281 in 1930, and 1,062 in 1940.[9] These figures imply that the Depression resulted in a 17 percent reduction in the size of the Central and South American population of the city. The immigrants of the West Indies, which included Cubans and Dominicans, numbered 773 in 1920 but only 373 in 1940. They appear to have suffered a population loss of 52 percent over the course of the Depression. It is quite plausible that during the Depression some of these Hispanics were deported alongside Mexicans or simply lost their jobs and left Chicago. The U.S. government conferred citizenship on Puerto Ricans in 1917, which largely shielded them from deportation. Although Puerto Ricans possessed U.S. citizenship, which eased their travel to and from the United States, relatively few appear to have migrated to Chicago before the Second World War.[10]

Naturalization records clarify our portrait of Hispanic Chicago and provide us with the opportunity to compare the characteristics of the non-Mexican Hispanic liberal nationalists (or the nationalists) to those of the non-Mexican Hispanics who applied for U.S. naturalization (or the naturalizers). Between 1900 and 1940, 795 South American, Central American, and Caribbean immigrants applied for U.S. citizenship in Chicago. The majority of these naturalizers (478 applicants) were from South America, 159 were from the Caribbean (which included 149 Cubans and 10 Dominicans), and 158 were from Central America, the majority of whom were from Nicaragua (51 applicants). Between 1900 and 1940, 422 immigrants from Spain also applied for U.S. naturalization in Chicago. Spaniards participated in Mexican community activities in the 1920s, but they established a closer relationship with Mexicans during the

Spanish Civil War in the 1930s, a development discussed in chapter 4. This chapter references Spanish naturalizers only for comparative purposes.[11]

Non-Mexican Hispanic nationalists and naturalizers had much in common, and because they were few in number in Chicago, they rarely engaged in serious disputes and instead formed a fluid Spanish-speaking community. Central American and Caribbean nationalists and naturalizers shared a similar middle-class (white-collar) and skilled blue-collar occupational status in Chicago. Central American and Puerto Rican nationalists like Barreto, Ibarra, and Puente, mentioned above, worked as professionals in Chicago, and a slight majority (37 percent) of all Central American naturalizers were professionals, while another 35 percent of Central American naturalizers were skilled artisans and semiskilled factory operatives. Similarly, 35 percent of all Caribbean naturalizers were white-collar workers, while another 41 percent were skilled and semiskilled laborers. In total, Central American and Caribbean naturalizers were proportionally more middle class than other Hispanics, while a significant share of Caribbean (41 percent), South American (41 percent), and Spanish (40 percent) immigrants worked in skilled and semiskilled blue-collar occupations. In comparison to the Mexican population of Chicago, the non-Mexican Hispanic population was significantly more educated and more skilled (see table 12 in the appendix).

Central American and Caribbean nationalists and naturalizers also tended to emigrate from similar urban centers. The Nicaraguan nationalists who appear in the Spanish-language press were often from Managua, the largest city in Nicaragua, and more than a quarter of Nicaraguan naturalizers were from León, the second-largest city in Nicaragua. Less is known about the Cuban nationalists in Chicago, but Cuban naturalizers tended to be from Havana. South American naturalizers, which included a cohort of Argentines, were typically from Buenos Aires (see table 7 in the appendix). In sum, naturalization records reveal that the non-Mexican Hispanic community of Chicago was quite urban, educated, and skilled, and these Hispanics shared the middle-class tastes and sensibilities of the Mexican liberal nationalists of Chicago, which explains why all of these Hispanics were coming together.[12]

Mexican liberal nationalists tended to be more cosmopolitan—urban, formally educated, and civically engaged—than the majority of Mexicans in Chicago, but they commiserated with their working-class compatriots, for they all experienced degrees of racial discrimination. The liberals' affinity with the broader Mexican population on issues of race developed, in part, because in the United States the majority of Mexican and non-Mexican Hispanic liberals were considered to have a "dark" complexion, a racial marker they shared with the majority of Mexican migrants. While scholars often describe middle-class Hispanics as light-skinned people, middle-class Mexicans in Chicago, like Julián X. Mondragón, were perceived as brown-skinned Mexicans by white Americans. Immigration administrators described Mondragón in the same way they characterized the majority of Mexicans, as members of the "Mexican" race and as having a dark complexion.[13]

Scholars of race in the United States often reiterate that Mexicans were assigned "whiteness," or a status as white persons, by the Treaty of Guadalupe Hidalgo (1848), which ended the Mexican-American War and granted the Mexicans living in the newly acquired southwestern territory U.S. federal citizenship at a time when federal citizenship was only available to "free white persons." In further support of this claim, historians emphasize that the U.S. decennial census typically enumerated Mexicans as "whites" except during the Depression, when Mexicans were targeted for deportation. During the Depression-era deportations, Mexicans were reclassified by U.S. census takers as members of the nonwhite "Mexican" race.[14] While Mexicans were usually counted as racially white people by census officials in the years prior to and after the Depression, it is important to note that in these same years (1900–1940), U.S. immigration and naturalization administrators typically classified Mexicans as members of the so-called "Mexican race" and as "dark"-skinned people under a "color" category they created to evaluate all immigrants.

In many ways, immigration and naturalization records are more useful in determining how Mexicans were perceived by white American officials because these documents include data on the skin color of Mexicans, while the census does not include such data. Naturalization records reveal that immigration and naturalization officers perceived the majority of Mexicans as dark-skinned. In Chicago, between 1900 and 1930, 69 percent of Mexican naturalizers were defined as dark-skinned, 22 percent as fair-skinned, and 9 percent as medium in skin tone. Many middle-class liberals, like Mondragón, were dark-skinned, and naturalization papers reveal that 61 percent of all white-collar Mexican naturalizers were perceived as having dark skin.[15] The Mexican middle class was far "darker" than what other monographs suggest. Working-class Mexican naturalizers were, as one might expect, even more likely to be seen as dark-skinned. In fact, as the proportion of working-class Mexican naturalizers increased between 1931 and 1940, the proportion of dark-skinned Mexican naturalizers rose. In total, between 1900 and 1940, 77 percent of Mexican naturalizers were perceived as dark-skinned by the white Americans who processed their naturalization papers (see table 9 in the appendix).

Comparing Mexican Chicago to Mexican Los Angeles reveals that slightly more fair-skinned Mexicans naturalized in Chicago than in Los Angeles, but the vast majority of Mexican naturalizers in Chicago (77–79 percent) and in Los Angeles (83 percent) were still seen as dark-skinned people.[16] In Chicago, Mexican naturalizers were actually perceived as the darkest Hispanic naturalizers. They were preceded in proportional size by Central Americans (75 percent of whom were seen as dark-skinned), Caribbean migrants (67 percent), South Americans (55 percent), and lastly Spaniards (50 percent; see table 10 in the appendix).

Chicago's Hispanic community, which included migrants from various countries in Latin America, was largely middle class, but these Hispanics were perceived as people with very dark features—darker than those of the average European American. The dark phenotypes of Hispanics and the discussions they had with each other about imperialism and racism help explain why Hispanics were critical of U.S. military interventions in the Third World, U.S. opinions of race and whiteness, and U.S. naturalization.

The Hispanic community was able to successfully use Spanish-language newspapers to criticize imperialism and racism because of the high degree of literacy and "preliteracy" of Mexicans.[17] In the 1920s American social scientists and settlement house workers often emphasized Mexican illiteracy when trying to rationalize Mexican immigrants' low rate of U.S. naturalization.[18] These sympathetic but paternalistic Americans assumed Mexicans did not understand the naturalization process because they were uneducated. A close examination of Chicagoland reveals a counternarrative. In every major Mexican neighborhood in Chicago and Northwest Indiana, Mexicans established libraries and bookstores. Nearly every Mexican-owned pool hall and grocery store sold Spanish-language newspapers, books, and magazines. When *El Heraldo*, one of a dozen Spanish-language papers in Chicago, held a raffle, more than four thousand people purchased tickets for it, an indication of the readership that sustained this weekly. The holdings of Mexican libraries in Chicagoland reveal that Mexican and Hispanic immigrants read popular novels and the works of Homer, Euripides, Shakespeare, Rubén Darío, José Vasconcelos, Immanuel Kant, Arthur Schopenhauer, and William James.[19]

This Hispanic literary community published newspapers in Chicago that defined U.S. interventions as examples of imperialism, and it continued in the tradition (theorized by Isidro Fabela Alfaro) of reproaching U.S. policy makers more than ordinary American citizens. This was a critical decision on the part of the liberals, because this top-down critique of U.S. imperialism was acceptable to Mexicans who could have positive experiences in the United

States. Drawing on Vasconcelos, Mexican liberals in Chicago explained that Mexico had yet to realize its potential as a nation-state because it had been "a colony, first, of the Spanish conquistadors [and] at present [was] a colony of the wealthy local and foreign exploiters." "The citizens of the United States," according to the liberal press, had an interest in opposing "Yankee conquests," for "imperialism . . . always becomes oppressive at home before oppressing abroad."[20] Through Vasconcelos, liberals claimed that there was an inherent contradiction between American ideals of democratic governance and American practices of conquest. Mexican liberals believed that ordinary Americans would oppose U.S. imperialism and ally with anti-imperialist Hispanics if they only knew what their government and their corporations did "beneath the United States."[21]

Mexican liberals became more anti-imperialist as they closely befriended Puerto Ricans and Nicaraguans. Puerto Ricans like Puente and Guillermo Baquero O'Neill (introduced in chapter 1) were appalled by the way so many Americans could unabashedly accept that the United States had the right to invade other people's territories and intervene in their affairs. Puente's and O'Neill's perspectives were informed by the history of U.S.–Puerto Rico relations. The United States occupied Puerto Rico along with Cuba, the Philippines, and Guam after the Spanish-American War (1898), and then, in the Treaty of Paris, simply proclaimed the right to determine the "political conditions of the natural inhabitants of the [occupied] territories."[22] Petitioning Congress, Puerto Rican leaders asked, "Are we [now U.S.] citizens, or are we subjects? Are we brothers and our property territory, or are we the bondmen of a war and our island a colony?"[23] Through the Foraker Act (1900) and the Insular Cases (1901–5), the United States answered these critical questions: Puerto Rico would not become a member state of the United States, the Puerto Rican people would be denied the right to self-rule, Puerto Ricans would not be granted U.S. citizenship, and the U.S. Constitution would not be fully extended to them. In all but terminology, Puerto Rico was now a colony of the United States.

Puerto Rico was simply too valuable to the United States to allow Puerto Ricans the autonomy to establish policies that could challenge American ambitions in the region. Puerto Rico straddled the Anegada and Mona Passages, and it, along with Cuba, the Philippines, and Guam, were all identified as strategic locales for U.S. military bases where American battleships could reload, refuel, and repair and extend the U.S. military's reach across the Caribbean and into the Pacific.

After the war, American agricultural interests began assessing the island's potential. Some investors promoted Puerto Rico as a new and lucrative "garden," while others held reservations. As one American expressed it, "The opportunities for investment are good if the laws and methods of taxation were such as to make an investment safe."[24] In response to the specific appeals of U.S. sugar producers, Congress ruled that sugar could be imported into the United States from Puerto Rico tariff free. U.S. sugar companies now began to seize arable land. By the 1920s, the amount of Puerto Rican land devoted to sugar production had increased to 230,000 acres from 61,000, and this development had a deleterious effect on domestic food production. The majority of foodstuffs in Puerto Rico had once been produced locally by small farmers; now that the island was under U.S. control, more than 75 percent of all of the food consumed in Puerto Rico was imported, and the majority of these imports were shipped in from the United States to the benefit of American farmers. Given the decline in local food cultivation, many Puerto Rican families were now spending 90 percent of their weekly wages on food, and Puerto Rican laborers could not even depend on year-long employment because the island's economy had been so skewed toward seasonal sugar production.[25] As a Puerto Rican political leader scoffed, Puerto Rico was now "Uncle Sam's second largest sweatshop," with a "company store [located] in the United States."[26] With the start of the First World War, intellectuals and policy makers engaged in an international dialogue about sovereignty, democracy, and the future of interstate relations, and in this context, the United States attempted to rebut criticisms of U.S. imperialism in Latin America by assuaging the growing Puerto Rican movement for independence. Congress therefore extended U.S. federal citizenship to Puerto Ricans in 1917, granting Puerto Ricans more legislative rights while continuing to deny them statehood and a voting representative in the U.S. Congress. Disappointed Puerto Rican nationalists, like María Mas Pozo, openly expressed their disapproval: "*We do not want a North American citizenship that humiliates us, depriving us of our dignity, after having been stripped, in the name of humanity, of our blessed land.*"[27]

Nicaraguan immigrants in the United States further personalized and intensified the anti-imperialism of Mexican liberals through their denunciation of the U.S. occupation of Nicaragua in 1926. Nicaraguans gave the entire Hispanic community pause when celebrating the United States and contemplating U.S. naturalization. "More Nicaraguans Killed by U.S. Marines," ran a typical headline in the Central American–owned *La Noticia Mundial*. Under the pretext of suppressing banditry, argued *La Noticia*, "the U.S. air force ha[d] assassinated" Nicaraguan patriots and "rained terror" on Nicaragua. *La Noticia* was owned and managed by Central American migrants and therefore had the freedom to offer Hispanics a critical analysis of the U.S. occupation. *La Noticia*'s Central American and Mexican reporters compiled and published Nicaraguan casualty statistics to challenge the U.S. government's figures; they translated reports from the League of Nations, which condemned the occupation; and they quoted Russian analysts who claimed the United States was establishing a sphere of influence in Central America through its military bases and a strategy of proxy warfare.[28]

In the 1960s Chicanos and their Latino allies would adopt the Argentine Ernesto "Che" Guevara as an anti-imperialist icon. In the 1920s Nicaraguan and Mexican migrants in Chicago celebrated the Nicaraguan Augusto Cesar Sandino as the personification of anti-U.S. hegemony. Between 1927 and 1934, Sandino led a guerrilla movement against the U.S. marines. The *New York Times* reported that Sandino lacked broad support among the Nicaraguan people and was "the only disturbing element in Nicaragua."[29] Nicaraguans in Chicago disagreed. They alleged that Sandino was backed by well-educated Nicaraguan liberals who understood that he was no guerrilla but a "civilized and formally educated" patriot who was forced to resort to arms because of "Mr. Coolidge" and the "foreigners [who] were treading all over his [Sandino's] country."[30] Nicaraguans took the lead in censuring the occupation and convinced many Mexicans to support their cause. Over time, the Mexican liberal press likened Sandino to Pancho Villa, who was also recast as an anti-imperialist.[31] Mondragón's *México* printed reproachful headlines, such as "U.S. Marines Killed Innocents in Nicaragua," and accompanied them with heroicized photos of Sandino.[32]

While Mexican liberals became more critical of the United States, the traditionalist press ignored the occupation of Nicaragua and ran numerous articles on the Cristero Rebellion in Mexico, the conflict between the Catholic Church and the anticlerical administration of President Plutarco Calles. When the rebellion began, a few traditionalist reporters initially blamed it on U.S. "imperialist intentions." "Alert!" advised a traditionalist journalist in Chicago "The ambitious North Americans are not content with monopolizing our industries and our petroleum, they have taken the first steps to monopolize our ideas [and] our spirits." President Calles had encouraged Protestant ministries in Mexico, and Protestantism was "one of the most powerful weapons that the Colossal Yankee [could] wield against Mexico," argued this journalist. "The North American enemy knows that the Catholic Church is the strongest obstacle against the de-Mexicanization of our people," and U.S. imperialists sought the "de-Mexicanization" of Mexico via the "cold religion" of the "Nordic people" of the United States. "We Protest against Protestantism!" seethed this traditionalist.[33]

Chicago's traditionalist community understood that Protestant leaders were largely supportive of the Calles administration. In December 1926 more than a hundred Protestant delegates gathered together in El Paso, Texas, to participate in the Interdenominational Conference on Work among the Spanish Speaking People of the United States. Assessing the conference, Malachy McCarthy found that Calles officials were invited to participate and were received warmly by numerous Protestant ministers who praised Calles's open attitude toward Protestantism. American Catholic leaders, meanwhile, were shocked and offended to learn that American Protestants were describing the incredibly anticlerical Calles as "tolerant" and his policies against the Catholic Church as "negligible."[34]

Catholic traditionalists in Chicagoland recognized the deep Protestant heritage of the United States, but they also believed that the U.S. Constitution and the political culture of the country granted U.S. citizens the right to practice their own individual religious beliefs. Traditionalists did not delve into the constitutional complexities, limits, and legalities of religious freedom; instead, they simply noted that in the United States ordinary American people were allowed and even encouraged to experience religion in their everyday lives. Traditionalists were impressed by what they saw in the United States and speculated that U.S. religious tolerance was connected to an American sense of democracy. The traditionalist press noted that presidential elections in the United States were conducted in "a very democratic manner and the loser was the first to congratulate the winner." By contrast, in Mexico, this was simply not the case. Pointing to a gubernatorial election that had taken place in the state of Puebla, Mexico, traditionalists lamented that it resulted in a riot "without even knowing who is now going to serve as the governor." In yet another example, journalists pointed out that in San Antonio, Texas, more than forty thousand Americans had gathered with the American Legion, U.S. military officials, and delegates of the American Federation of Labor for a public Catholic Mass. "How beautiful is the practice of true liberty!" proclaimed traditionalists, for Americans were not "ashamed of their [religious] beliefs, they practice[d] them publicly. . . . When will the army and the government of our homeland imitate this noble example?" Sadly, reasoned traditionalists, "it seems that it is characteristic of *la raza* [our race / our people] to obtain our objectives by whatever means necessary without considering either the consequences or the results."[35]

U.S. political stability, congressional practices, and religious freedom all appealed to traditionalists as they created Mexican Catholic communities in the United States free of the oversight of the Mexican government. The traditionalists who continued to praise U.S. stability while lamenting Mexican discord soon began to philosophize about the root causes of the divergent political cultures of the United States and Mexico, and they initiated a dialogue about the historic role of racial mixture in Mexico. Mexican liberals were also having these types of discussions about Mexican civic culture and racial identity, but liberals and traditionalists arrived at fundamentally different conclusions about these contentious topics.

Liberal and Traditionalist Understandings of Race

Mexican liberals in Chicago subscribed to a mixed-race understanding of Mexican civic identity, a mestizaje nationalism. These Mexican immigrants rejected white supremacist ideologies and often declined U.S. citizenship because they were offended that first-class U.S. citizenship was conferred only on persons deemed white by the U.S. government. The liberals' sense of mestizaje was formulated in Mexico and was debated by numerous writers and artists who shared an anti–white supremacist desire to redeem Mexico's mixed-race heritage.[36]

Scholars of American race relations are currently assessing the idea of mestizaje, and some dismiss it as resting on "white-supremacist assumption[s]."[37] Yet the idea of mestizaje was quite anti–white supremacist in the 1920s when it was popularized. In this decade, the majority of prominent American and European intellectuals accepted an intellectual canon that divided humanity into a hierarchy of fixed races. Influential scholars such as Charles Davenport of Harvard University and Michael F. Guyer of the University of Wisconsin as well as powerful philanthropists like Madison Grant were advocates of eugenics, and they argued that racial mixture led to biological degeneration, or "mongrelization," as they put it.[38] Seeking to redeem the mixed-race Mexican polity, José Vasconcelos attacked the theory of mixed-race degeneration by turning it on its head. In the heyday of eugenics, Vasconcelos published *La raza cósmica* (*The Cosmic Race*), which argued that multiracial Mexicans were not an inferior people, as the eugenicists claimed, but a superior people because of their multiraciality. Like his contemporaries, Vasconcelos accepted an essentialist understanding of race that at times validated "the whites," but as a Mexican patriot he could not accept that multiracial Mexican citizens were degenerates. Vasconcelos philosophized that if there were "four racial trunks: the Black, the Indian, the Mongol, and the White," and each possessed static traits, then mixed-race Mexicans, who were the progeny of all "four racial trunks," possessed the best fixed traits of humanity. Moreover, in an increasingly interconnected world, multiracial Mexicans were not some debased race of the past but the race of the future, which Vasconcelos poetically called "the cosmic race."[39] While Vasconcelos acknowledged the African heritage of Mexico, many advocates of mestizaje did not. Over time, mestizaje came to mean the mixture or "forging" of Indians and Spaniards, which erased the African people in Mexico from the country's national narrative. Scholars debate how the concept of mestizaje came to exclude Afro-Mexicans, but most point to the history of antiblack racism in Spain and then New Spain (colonial Mexico) and the way antiblack racism was carried over into Mexico's independence movement, continued into the years of the revolution, and exists in various forms in Mexico to this day. But when Mexicans in Chicagoland were adopting the ideology of mestizaje, Mexican intellectuals were promoting this construct to rebut white supremacist arguments about Mexicans, condemn Spanish and European imperialism, and, most importantly, recognize and revere the racially exploited Amerindians who were autochthonous to Mexico and vastly outnumbered all other peoples in Mexico.[40]

As problematic as the idea of mestizaje was and continued to be, Mexican migrants embraced the concept to defend themselves against white supremacy. Mexican migrants were therefore not just another "in-between people" but a mixed-race people who arrived in Chicago with the intellectual means to challenge white supremacy.[41] Through historiography, iconography, poetry, plays, and other cultural productions, liberals asserted their brownness and criticized U.S. citizenship, a citizenship that privileged whiteness. Liberals celebrated the "glory [of] bronze men," including Amerindians such as Netzahualcoyotl, the poet king of Texcoco; the "Bronze Cuauhtémoc," the last ruler of the Mexica; and Benito Juárez, Mexico's Zapotec president, or "our man of bronze color," as the Mexican liberals of Chicago called him.[42] Although liberals commemorated the multiracial Vicente Guerrero, Juárez was their hero.[43] Juárez, "the most meritorious statesmen of the Americas," the "Great Indian," was "bronze-skinned," like the majority of Mexicans, and yet Juárez rose in prominence through a liberal education, obtained the presidency, defended Mexico's sovereignty, and then directed Mexico down a liberal path of secularization.[44] Liberals in Chicago, like liberals in Mexico, rejected the racially essentialist denigration of the Mexican indigene and chose to underscore the adaptability and universality of liberal ideology. At a time when first-class American citizenship was conferred only on persons deemed white by U.S. judges and statesmen, Mexican liberals explicitly stated that "true Mexican[s]" had "dark skin" and would proudly declare their Mexican nationality "a thousand times." Liberals understood that some Mexicans might consider applying for U.S. citizenship and that some of these migrants could pass as white. Liberal writers denounced these Mexicans as "renegades" and added that this kind of Mexican would attempt to deny his Mexican heritage "no matter how dark-skinned he [was]" and would even try "passing [himself] off as Spanish" as opposed to Mexican.[45]

Mexican liberals were not just expressing ideological pride in their brown-ness. It appears that the most fair-skinned Mexican liberals chose to live in the most heavily concentrated neighborhoods of dark-skinned Mexican migrants. In fact, my analysis of 1,321 Mexican residencies in Chicago reveals that the majority of fair-skinned Mexicans lived among dark-skinned Mexi-cans. More provocatively still, dark-skinned Mexicans appear to have been more residentially dispersed in Chicago than fair-skinned Mexicans. Mexican immigrants did not self-segregate by skin color. To be sure, fair-skinned Mexican liberals held racial prejudices, but fair-skinned liberals were not so prejudiced against their dark-skinned compatriots as to live apart from them (see figure 7 and figure 4 on the webpage).

While Mexican liberal nationalists internalized and promoted mestizaje, these Mexicans were not racial egalitarians. In several instances, mestizaje nationalists described Chinese businessmen in Mexico in sinophobic ways, and in at least one incident, mestizaje nationalists used the diminutive when referring to *los negros* (the blacks) of Chicago. In this instance, a few Mexicans were robbed by a few African Americans, and the mestizaje nationalist jour-nalist who covered the matter described the African Americans as *negritos* to demean them.[46] Liberal mestizaje nationalists may not have been racial egalitarians, but they also did not define themselves as white persons. These Mexicans characterized themselves as mestizos and believed in prioritizing and privileging their own Mexican people.

Throughout the 1920s, liberal and Catholic conflicts in Mexico intensi-fied, and traditionalists in Chicagoland started undercutting the liberals' mestizaje message by emphasizing the Catholic and thus European heritage of Mexico, which unwittingly created a broad intellectual opening for the American ideology of whiteness. Through their own cultural productions, traditionalists produced a Catholic and European interpretation of the Con-quest (1521), Mexican Independence (1810–21), and Cinco de Mayo (1862). Traditionalists defended the Spanish colonization of the Americas, which they argued brought "a civilization, a religion, [and] a faith" to a "virgin land." Assessing the exploits of Christopher Columbus, Hernán Cortés, and Fran-cisco Pizarro, traditionalists ignored their violent plunder and emphasized their Christianity, which traditionalists claimed "saved the indigenous race" by abolishing their "bloody forms of worship."[47]

Whereas liberals placed "pagan" Amerindians on pedestals, ignoring their human sacrifices, traditionalists heroicized the "Good Priest," Father Miguel Hidalgo y Costilla, the Spanish criollo who initiated Mexican independence.[48] Aware that liberals were recounting the so-called glory of Mexican indigenes, traditionalists reminded Mexican migrants that they "should be proud . . .

to have in [their] veins the blood of the Indian blended with the blood of the Spaniards . . . the same blood that ran through the veins of Hidalgo, the Priest of Dolores."[49] When celebrating Cinco de Mayo, liberals exalted Juárez, who oversaw the French army's defeat at the Battle of Puebla. Traditionalists circumvented the anticlerical Juárez by honoring his criollo general, Ignacio Zaragoza Seguín, pointing out that Zaragoza Seguín had actually bested the French battalion.[50] President Juárez was the architect of La Reforma (1855–60) and represented the ascension of anticlerical liberalism in Mexico; he was consequently lauded by liberals and minimized by traditionalists.

Speaking directly to the liberals, traditionalists lectured that intra-Mexican violence during La Reforma, the Mexican Revolution, and now the Cristero Rebellion all proved that liberalism could not amalgamate Mexico's "racial hybridity." The recent and gory rebellion proved that "it simply was true that [we] Mexicans don't know how to love ourselves." Focusing on select examples of intra-Mexican violence, traditionalists argued that politically and racially divided Mexicans could only find unity through their Catholic faith, for "Catholicism was the only bond of unity that has remained among our deplorable discord, [and] once broken, our nationality will perish."[51]

The liberals responded to these challenges by passionately defending the ideology of mestizaje and by recruiting Mexicans to their cause, but they did not seek much support outside the Mexican community. Given that Mexican liberals in Chicago rejected whiteness, created community between dark- and fair-skinned Mexicans, and experienced racial discrimination, it would seem that some mestizaje nationalists and African Americans would have found solidarity with each other. But in Chicagoland, Mexicans and African Americans were "neither enemies nor friends."[52] Mexicans did not have much power or authority over the lives of African Americans. Mexicans did not deny African Americans jobs, housing, educational opportunities, or social services, and there is little evidence of Mexican-led pogroms against African Americans.

As Mexicans sought housing in Chicago, some chose to live among African Americans. In the "Black Belt" of South Chicago, African Americans rented low-cost basements and backyard sheds to Mexicans seeking affordable and temporary housing. When Victor García encountered hostile white ethnics in South Chicago, he simply moved away from them and decided to board with an African American family. Seeking to add to their household incomes, African Americans boarded Mexican and Slavic migrants who had not yet internalized an American understanding of racial segregation.[53] Concomitantly, African American businessmen who owned groceries, saloons, and billiard halls catered to Mexican customers, and Mexican businessmen responded in kind, soliciting African American patrons. In the 1920s, contemporary white Americans perceived that there were, at times, violent conflicts between white ethnics and Mexicans but "very little trouble" between Mexicans and African Americans.[54]

Living near black and white Americans, Mexican men developed intimate relations with women in both of these communities. Mexican men visited black and white sex workers and dated and married black and white American women. A white University of Chicago student expressed "surprise" when he met a Mexican who chose to live in an African American neighborhood, married a black woman, and claimed he "fe[lt] no prejudice against the negroes."[55] Commenting on these relationships, a pastor in Chicago simply remarked, "I have seen happy marriages of negroes and Mexicans."[56] Today, scholars tend to say that marriages between Mexicans and African Americans were rare, but in Chicago, the existing evidence suggests that these marriages were not much rarer than marriages between Mexicans and white Americans.[57] Out of a sample of 863 married Mexican male immigrants in Chicago, 77 percent chose to marry a Mexican-born spouse (see table 13 in the appendix).[58] Overall, Mexican men preferred to date and marry Mexican women and therefore did not seek wives in black *or* white communities.[59]

Mexican and African American intimate relations stood out to white Americans who had adopted a separatist white civic identity. White Americans who "liked the Mexicans" encouraged them to move away from "negro streets," while white city officials who held more power tried to coerce Mexicans into accepting segregation.[60] When Mexican immigrant Philip Martínez decided to open a pool hall, he applied for a permit with the Chicago Billiard Commission, which was governed by twelve of Chicago's aldermen. Eyeing the proposed location for the hall, Chairman Joseph B. McDonough rejected Martínez's application on the ostensible grounds that he "was not a citizen of the United States." Given that no law barred noncitizens from opening billiard halls, Martínez appealed to the Mexican consulate, which reprimanded the commission for practicing "discrimination between citizens, and noncitizens." The commission then contacted Chicago federal judge William E. Dever for support, citing a police report that cryptically explained that the "kind" (read "integrated") of hall that Martínez wanted to open did not currently exist in the neighborhood that Martínez had selected. The commission went on to explain that "people of this kind [Mexicans like Martínez] are not desirable characters" and then disclosed, "We know of places where Mexicans are now playing pool mixed with the white people just a few blocks away from this particular location. While this is not the law, the Commission have tried to prevent Mexicans with the white people and up to the present time, we have been successful."[61]

In a segregated America, Martínez was seeking to create a commercial space open to all paying customers: black, white, and Mexican. This was simply an un-American proposal for Chicago's aldermen. Becoming aware of the problem, Martínez chose a new site. The commission now rewarded Martínez for reselecting a "location among his own people" and "recommend[ed] that the license be issued immediately."[62] In yet another example, a Mexican-owned pool hall open to both "Mexican and Negro clientele" was closed due to vaguely characterized "opposition[al] neighbors."[63] Mexicans were learning from these experiences: white Americans did not want them to blur the color line.

Mexican and African American conflicts rarely occurred as a result of neighborhood boundaries or sexual relations. Instead, conflicts between African Americans and Mexicans revolved around job competition. Competition for work led to intense rivalries between African Americans and Mexicans, but because African Americans and Mexicans did not have the partisan support of the police, their quarrels rarely escalated to a level of group-on-group violence. Other historians frequently emphasize the racism of the Mexican people to explain "the failure of Black-Brown solidarity."[64] While racism within the Mexican community is certainly an obstacle to solidarity, these scholars rarely tell us what African Americans thought of Mexicans and the periodic deportation campaigns that occurred over the course of the long U.S. civil rights movement.

Evaluating African American understandings of Mexicans and their deportation, Arnold Shankman, Lawrence H. Fuchs, and Jeff Diamond explain that African American journalists and political leaders perceived Mexicans as labor competitors, a viewpoint that engendered antagonism, not solidarity. Since the end of the Civil War, white employers had given preference to white Americans and European immigrants over African Americans for better jobs, while predominantly white unions admitted European immigrants before accepting African Americans, further limiting African American opportunities. Labor historians have found that in various industries, managers sought to maintain an ethnically and racially stratified workforce that would not conceive of itself as a community with shared interests. As the number of European immigrant industrial workers declined in the years after World War I, companies hired more Mexicans and African Americans to maintain a diverse and divided labor force. In addition, at times, managers chose to hire Mexicans over African Americans so that a company would not have to build separate cafeterias and showers to accommodate the legal segregation practices of white Americans.[65] As a result of this oppressive history of racial discrimination aimed at African Americans, black journalists could resort to harsh criticisms when assessing Mexican job seekers. Shankman quotes African American journalists referring to Mexicans as "densely ignorant son[s] of Aztecs," as "grossly illiterate and greasy," and as "unnaturalized labor" that "care[d] nothing about our [American] civilization" and "t[ook] bread from the mouths of colored people" by taking American jobs.[66] Fuchs adds that African Americans juxtaposed their status as Americans against the foreignness of Mexicans to argue why employers ought to hire African Americans.[67]

African Americans and Mexicans competed with each other for their livelihoods and for the security of their families and therefore rarely sought solidarity with each other. Black-brown solidarity required a radical leadership that would seek occupational equity between African Americans and Mexicans, but job competition consistently defeated black-brown unity. African American intellectuals, such as Charles Johnson of Fisk University, challenged anti-Mexican sentiments by arguing that Mexicans were not the African American community's main obstacle to better jobs. Yet forced to compete with Mexicans for work, frustrated African American laborers from the Southwest to the Midwest could express positions in favor of restricting immigration from Mexico. "I think they should not let the Mexicans come in here," explained a black worker in Texas. "It makes it hard for the American people to get work. The Mexicans will work cheaper and keep the prices down. They can live on next to nothing. . . . More Negroes would come down here [to Texas] if there were not so many Mexicans and they could get better wages."[68] In an attempt to secure work during the recession of 1920–21, African American and white American workers in Fort Worth, Texas, marched together on city hall to protest against hiring Mexicans to work on city construction projects.[69]

During the Great Depression, white Americans frequently expressed anti-Mexican restrictionism, and economist Paul Taylor noted that in Chicago, African American congressman Oscar De Priest "actively favored application of quota law to immigration from Mexico."[70] When Mexicans were deported during the Depression, Shankman and Fuchs claim that most African American politicians and journalists did not voice opposition. As one African American journalist reasoned, "With the repatriation of the Mexicans the labor market for colored workers will be considerably improved."[71] European Americans and African Americans were not alone in expressing restrictionism. As Mexicans became Americans, they too could be unsympathetic toward Mexican migrants. During the late 1940s and early 1950s, the Mexican American leaders of the League of United Latin American Citizens and the GI Forum expressed restrictionism and, in some instances, advocated deporting Mexican nationals. In the end, the restrictionism that Mexican migrants experienced in the United States reinforced their identities as Mexican nationals—politically divided Mexican nationals, but Mexican nationals nevertheless.

The Depression turned many Americans toward restrictionist politics, and it concurrently destroyed the liberal mestizaje movement, which depended on Mexican-owned small businesses and employed Mexican workers for its existence. Throughout the Midwest, Mexican people—middle class, working class, liberal, and traditionalist—were fired and then targeted for deportation. While some Mexicans simply lost their jobs and decided to return to Mexico, Mexicans were made painfully aware of the restrictionist attitudes of many Americans.[72] As thirty Mexican families bemoaned in one collectively signed letter, "In this month [during the Depression], we Mexicans were fired, simply because we are Mexicans, in order to provide jobs for Americans and Europeans."[73] The Mexican Midwest was transformed during the Depression by both the impersonal market economy and the personal decisions of Americans to target Mexicans for deportation. In this hostile context, a small segment of the Mexican community began advocating U.S. civic and racial assimilation. In Northwest Indiana, some traditionalist leaders, already receptive to establishing permanent lives in the United States, surrendered their Mexican citizenship and advised other migrants to do the same.[74] In Chicago, a more disturbing process unfolded. In the largest Mexican neighborhood in the city, the Near West Side, Mexicans were known to patronize an African American–owned funeral home, and a Mexican newspaper now argued against this practice:

> We are not antagonistic, nor have we any prejudice against the Negro. The white resident, native or foreign, has a very low opinion of the Negro. He despises his standards and his mercantile and social activities. Concomitantly are despised those who associate with the Negro in any way. . . . [T]hey are despised more than the Negro. . . . The economy of the price paid to a Negro undertaker for a modest funeral is not sufficient to pay for the bad name we acquire . . . from the point of view of those who consider that the Negro race should be forced to live entirely isolated. . . . Placing [Mexican] corpses in the hands of undertakers who are not well accepted in the social system of the country we live in is to make them unworthy of a better funeral. . . . [L]et us place our dead in the hands of our own people, the *white race*.[75]

My research unearthed this one example of Mexican immigrants referring to themselves as members of the "white race." Note that the Mexican journalist who penned this statement began by speaking of "white resident[s]" (native and foreign) as a group separate from Mexicans but then discursively inserted Mexicans into the white race. This type of racial and civic argument was uncommon among Mexican immigrants during the 1920s and 1930s in Chicagoland, but a small minority of Mexicans began articulating this position during the decline of the mestizaje nationalist movement and during the Depression-era deportations, when Mexicans found few friends in the European American and African American communities of the United States. If Mexicans were going to be disciplined for blurring the color line, if they would not find solidarity with European Americans or African Americans, and, most importantly, if they were going to be targeted for deportation during recessions, then some Mexican migrants concluded that it was in their best interest to insert themselves into "the white race" while they lived in the United States.

Liberal and Traditionalist Understandings of Gender

In the aftermath of the revolution, Mexican liberals attempted to balance their belief in individual rights with their patriarchal understanding of gender.[76] Indicative of this trend, Hispanic liberals in Chicago endorsed women's suffrage and women's right to divorce.[77] Through the writings of the Honduran feminist Lucila Gamero de Medina, liberals advocated women's liberation via their entry into the professional workforce and thus applauded the anticlerical Mexican president Calles when he appointed Soledad González to serve as his personal secretary and advisor, a position traditionally held by a man.[78]

Hispanic liberals also endorsed women's voting and marriage rights, but liberal women raised the bar, sharpening the contradictions within the liberal community by castigating Mexican men for their role in women's oppression. Liberal women distributed the work of local artists who denounced sexism, and they published articles by Mexican women, such as María Luisa de la Torre de Otero, who condemned "the selfishness of men." In a near call to arms, Torre de Otero charged, "Within her [the Mexican woman] beats a rebellious spirit that can destroy all of the injustice of men, the injustice that she has carried on her shoulders as a heavy burden throughout the centuries."[79]

Mexican liberal men advocated women's rights but derided women who deviated too much from patriarchal gender roles. Their criticisms were often directed at the 1920s New Woman, represented by the flapper.[80] In the Mexican communities of Los Angeles and Detroit, Mexican men also chided these women.[81] The Mexican liberal Mondragón wrote multiple articles belittling flappers as frivolous and licentious women.[82] The liberals described the flapper as a "bad woman" because she drank, smoked, ignored curfews and chaperones, and, in short, behaved like many Mexican men.[83] The flapper threatened men because she rejected the prescribed gender roles that in part upheld Mexican patriarchy.

The liberals' disapproval of the flapper soon dovetailed with their criticisms of whiteness, and they took aim at the "[seemingly] cute blonde American woman." Mondragón and other liberals worried that some Mexican men would be "demexicaniz[ed] in lieu of [their] choice to have a North American girlfriend." Mondragón forewarned these Mexican men and caricatured white American women as superficial and callous. American women purportedly loved "big Mexican part[ies]" but were bored until fights broke out, which confirmed that the women were in the company of "very Mexican and very manly" men. Mondragón admonished white women for allegedly fetishizing Mexican masculinity, for taking pleasure from Mexican-on-Mexican violence, and for treating Mexico as a fantasy "land of romance, of great emotions and thrilling adventures!"[84]

As some Mexican liberals ridiculed white women, others criticized gendered whiteness through a gendered mestizaje construct that extolled the phenotypic and cultural "beauty of the Mexican [w]oman." According to these male voices, Mexican women, "the beautiful women of the land of [Benito] Juárez," possessed an "Indian grace," "large dark eyes," "dark features," and an overall "beauty uncommon among northern [i.e., white] women." As the "physical perfection" of the "European races" and "Indo-American race," Mexican women were "admired by the entire world." Note that this gendered mestizaje ignored the African heritage of Mexicans—and the Jewish, Arab, East Asian, and South Asian lineages of Mexicans that Vasconcelos acknowledged in *The Cosmic Race*—but it beatified mixed-race people and Amerindian phenotypes as a challenge to whiteness. This idealized notion of gendered mestizaje also meshed with a negative trope regarding white women's alleged promiscuity. The "blue mixture" of white women's eyes "reveal[ed] indecision and lack of character," according to the liberal press, while Mexican women were "a thousand times more virtuous."[85]

Liberal criticisms of white women were part of a broader disapproval of an America that privileged whiteness and supposedly produced egalitarian gender roles. And yet in the context of several criminal justice cases, some liberals identified a culture of benevolent patriarchy within the United States that made America palatable. When Santiago Rivera learned that his mother had been sexually assaulted, "he became enraged, because the bandit who had trampled *his* [Rivera's] honor was proud of his deed." As a patriarchal Mexican, Rivera felt that the assault on "his" mother diminished "his" honor. Rivera hunted down the "sex offender" and killed him. Arrested for murder, Rivera was tried by Judge B. David. "It was an impressive act," proclaimed Mexican liberals when Judge David declared, "I would have done the same as this young man ha[s] done in those circumstances; therefore, in the Law's name I declare you [Rivera] innocent." This white American judge, the liberals affirmed, was an "honest man [and] was just."[86] Most liberals suggested that the United States was too gender egalitarian, but over time some liberals came to believe that U.S. and Latin American gender relations differed in degree and not in kind.

In Indiana, traditionalist men, already critical of liberalism, did not try to strike a balance between individual rights and women's rights. Instead, they proudly advocated a patriarchal ideology that elevated men above women and elevated God, Christ, and the Catholic clergy above the laity. Traditionalist men promoted a dualist theory of gender, assigning reason to men and "heart" or morality to women.[87]

Traditionalist men were not interested in promoting women's rights, but women appropriated the traditionalist community's gendered logic to advance their interests. Writing to the traditionalist press, Julieta González Tapía argued, "[If a] moral education was the solid base upon which communities built their churches," as traditionalists often claimed, then the "cultural advancement" of the community required the "moral and intellectual perfection of women."[88] In East Chicago, Indiana, the male membership of the traditionalist organization the Círculo responded to this type of argument by hiring a learned woman named Manuela Pimentel to address educational "matters of morals" in the pages of their newspaper, *El Amigo del Hogar*.[89]

In her new role as a public intellectual, Pimentel contested extreme patriarchy and advocated a brand of Catholic feminism. Pimentel's writings did not promote women's suffrage or the right to divorce, and they often upheld the ideology of separate spheres, but she expanded the traditionalists' definition of women's education beyond lessons in "cooking and hygiene" to include what she called an "intellectual education."[90] Pimentel drew male criticism and appropriated Catholic morality to defend her position. "Many men detest the learned woman," charged Pimentel. "I classify these men into three categories: ignorant, unconscionable, and evil." By conjoining Catholic morality with education, Pimentel could then damn a Catholic man if he chose to stand in the way of the education of his wife or daughter. Addressing the character of Mexican men, Pimentel advised women, "Don't allow yourself to be seduced by promises or idle words," for "[Mexican] men rarely honor what they claim to offer." Yet always aware of her male employers and readership, Pimentel would typically soften her criticisms of men with the suggestive remark: "I have much, too much to say about the education of women, but I do not want to tire my readers."[91]

Within the United States, traditionalist and liberal women pushed at the boundaries of patriarchy, struggling for their advancement against Mexican men. Through print culture, art, and women's associational life, Mexican women in Illinois and Indiana assertively entered the public sphere. These women won the support of many blue-collar male workers through their reform work, which provided Mexican laborers with social services.[92] Middle-class liberal men tolerated their wives' public activism and advocated women's rights, but they derided what they perceived to be American egalitarian gender roles. Inflexible liberal men rejected egalitarian notions of gender and snubbed U.S. naturalization. A few moderate liberals encountered patriarchal American men who showed them that the United States was patriarchal enough, but these Mexican liberals still continued to criticize U.S. imperialism and racism. Mexican traditionalists, by comparison, largely circumvented debates about American imperialism and racism and continued to contemplate and, at times, advocate U.S. naturalization. Traditionalists embraced and celebrated the pluralistic culture of religious freedom they experienced in the United States, which allowed traditionalist men to create Catholic and patriarchal communities.

Conclusion

At present, there are scholars who claim that "prior to the Chicana/o movement, no segment of the Mexican community had self-consciously embraced and affirmatively proclaimed a brown identity."[93] The history of Mexican liberals in Chicago revises this claim and begins to bridge the academic divide between the Mexican immigrant and Mexican American experience. In Chicago, Mexican liberals created a counterhegemonic "racial project" that "sought to turn non-white status into a badge of pride."[94] Mexican liberals did not systematically confront the U.S. white racial state, but in an Antonio Gramscian sense of a "war of position," the liberals intellectually positioned the Mexican community so that it could defend itself against U.S. racial and national chauvinism.[95]

While Mexican liberals were insightful in their understandings of U.S. imperial practices and race relations, the liberals' record on gender was far less sophisticated and egalitarian. Mexican liberals could see the equality of the human "races" in the diverse faces of their male compatriots, but they largely failed to see the equality of the sexes. Some Mexican men advocated women's rights, but many ridiculed women who deviated too much from the men's patriarchal view of gender. In both Mexico and the United States, Mexican women had to struggle for their advancement against the "selfishness of men."

By comparison, Mexican traditionalists subscribed to a distinct political culture. The traditionalists were just as intellectual and political as the liberals, but in their battles with the liberals, they emphasized the Catholic heritage of Mexico, which underscored the European and white facets of Mexican identity. As traditionalists exalted their Catholicism as a counterweight to the liberals' anticlericalism, the gruesome intra-Mexican violence of the rebellion continued to test the traditionalists' allegiance to the Mexican state. Traditionalists soon began comparing the political stability they experienced in the United States with the "chaos" occurring in Mexico. The traditionalists ultimately concluded that Catholicism was the only ideology that could unify the politically divided and mixed-race Mexican people. Traditionalists did not deny the existence of U.S. imperialism or racism. They simply remained silent on U.S. interventions and discrimination and expressed admiration for the United States, which granted traditionalists the freedom to practice their Catholic beliefs in relative peace.

4 The Rise of the Postrevolution Mexican Left in Chicago

Mexicans, let us never forget or cease to show interest in our
country and in the land in which we first saw the light of day. For, if
we are here working hard and suffering, it will not always be so. We
are but the Children of Israel who are passing through our Egypt
here in the United States doing the onerous labors, swallowing our
pride, bracing up under the indignities heaped upon us here. If we
expect to return and escape all this, as all good Mexicans ought to,
then we should show interest in the affairs of our country from this
Egypt of ours.

—José Vasconcelos, speaking in Chicago during his candidacy for
the Mexican presidency in 1928

In the early 1930s, Mexican radicals in the Distrito Federal, Tampico, and
Torreón and in agricultural regions in Michoacán and the Comarca Lagunera
covertly organized against the Maximato (1928–34), the final and most authoritarian years of Plutarco Elías Calles's rule in Mexico. The leaders of these
protests were often members of the Partido Comunista Mexicano (Mexican
Communist Party, PCM), and an influential number of these Mexican Marx-
ists were "organic intellectuals" who worked as schoolteachers, educational
administrators, journalists, artists, and musicians.[1] While the PCM struggled
to win over rank-and-file workers in the critical industries of oil and steel
production, it was very successful at recruiting young teachers who had a
historic reputation in Mexico as agents of progressive social change. The
PCM would eventually acquire influence within Mexico's Ministry of Education (Secretaria de Educación Pública, SEP), as teachers would come to
represent roughly 30 percent of the PCM's membership.[2] Radical teachers
were passionate advocates of civic engagement and devoted themselves to
mobilizing the masses through organized protests and the publication of
pamphlets and newspapers that analyzed the rise and growth of Fascism in
Europe, U.S. imperialism in Latin America, and the capitalist causes of the

global Great Depression. By the mid-1930s, PCM activists felt emboldened and called to action by the international Communist movement's shift toward a broad anti-Fascist popular front strategy and by the presidency of Lázaro Cárdenas (in office 1934–40), which in June 1935 broke with the Maximato, purged Calles supporters from political office, and then shifted Mexico's political policies to the left. The growth of the popular front and *cardenismo* in Mexico inspired a few Mexican liberal immigrants and many working-class migrants in Chicago to band together and form the Frente Popular Mexicano (Frente), a transnational organization that was first started by the PCM in Mexico City.[3]

After organizing a chapter of the Frente in Chicago, Frentistas (members of the Frente) set out to radicalize the broader Mexican population. Frentistas were too impoverished during the Depression to offer migrants substantive social services or large-scale cultural festivals, so they focused on winning migrants to their politics by assigning value to the Mexican working class and by recruiting Mexican laborers to serve as leaders within the Chicago Frente. Through various educational initiatives, the Frente advocated anti-imperialist Mexican nationalism, international labor rights, and the importance of participating in the Chicago labor movement. The Frente connected working-class migrants with progressive Mexican intellectuals at the University of Chicago, radical officials working at the Mexican consulate, and journalists and student activists who were members of popular front organizations in Mexico and in other Latin American countries. As Frentistas created a community in Chicago, they established relationships with Spanish Republicans active in the Spanish Civil War, Cuban union organizers who were fundraising in Chicago, and white and black American labor activists, many of whom were seeking to unionize the meatpacking and steel industries of Chicago through the recently formed Congress of Industrial Organizations (CIO). In the southwestern United States, in cities like Los Angeles, Mexican migrants were drawn to the CIO as they developed identities as ethnic Americans. In Chicagoland, radical Mexican nationalists—both Communists and *cardenistas*—joined the CIO because they believed that only a united international labor movement could stop the march of Fascism, protect Mexico's sovereignty from U.S. and European imperialism, and forge a better world for the diasporic Mexican working class.

The Formation of the Frente

The PCM formed the Frente in Mexico City in response to the Cárdenas presidency and the international Communist movement's shift toward popular front politics. The Depression compelled the Cárdenas administration to carry out a number of broad-scale social reforms. Cárdenas distributed millions of acres of land to campesinos, passed labor legislation that invigorated a national unionization movement, and encouraged existing unions and labor associations to consolidate within labor federations such as the National Peasant Confederation (Confederación Nacional Campesina); the Confederation of Mexican Workers (Confederación de Trabajadores de México, CTM), led by the Marxist Vicente Lombardo Toledano; and the Federation of Mexican Teachers (Confederación Mexicana de Maestros, CMM), whose membership included hundreds of Marxian militants.[4] These labor federations offered workers government resources and state legitimacy, but they also incorporated the Mexican working class into the folds of the national political party, the Party of the Mexican Revolution (precursor to the Partido Revolucionario Institucional, PRI).[5]

Through this process of state incorporation or corporatism, the Cárdenas administration sought to create national unity out of a politically divided society. Like the liberal leaders who preceded him, Cárdenas attempted to use educational initiatives to unite and mold the Mexican citizenry. He expanded the power and scope of the SEP, which was charged with developing and implementing national educational policy. To win Marxian unionists within the CTM and CMM to his educational agenda, Cárdenas endorsed teaching "socialist education." The concept of socialist education varied, but exponents typically blended the liberal citizenship-rights ideas enshrined in the Mexican Constitution of 1917 with the discourse of Marxism, encouraging Mexicans to participate in civic and collective but nonviolent activities. As cardenista politicians endorsed, defined, and grappled with the application of socialist education, international conditions led the PCM to shift toward a popular front orientation.[6]

In 1935 the Soviet Comintern's Seventh Congress directed all Communist Parties to form popular front coalitions against Fascism. Responding to the directive, the PCM founded the organizing committee of the Frente Popular Antiimperialista (FPA) in Mexico City, which began recruiting activists who were already involved in labor, agricultural, student, and women's groups. For the FPA, fascism and imperialism were intertwined products of capitalism. The "imperialist" nations were coping with the Depression, argued the FPA, by turning to Fascist forms of governance so they could more "intensely exploit" the countries they had imperialized during the era of European colonization. Analyzing Italy's invasion of Ethiopia, the rise of Nazism in Germany, and Japanese aggression against China, FPA analysts claimed that Mexican citizens needed to safeguard Mexico's "independence" by forming a broad umbrella coalition against foreign Fascists and the Mexican elites aligned with the "imperialist capitalism" of the United States.[7]

The FPA affirmed that the United States practiced imperialism but drew a line between ordinary U.S. citizens and U.S. corporate and political leaders, the actual exporters of "imperialist capitalism," a kind of capitalism that derived from the directives of U.S. bankers and financiers who used the U.S. government and its military to protect their international investments. In the case of Mexico, U.S. imperialism was particularly complicated because it was made possible by a "counterrevolutionary" class of elite Mexican businessmen, landowners, and politicians, men like former president Plutarco Calles who had betrayed the revolution and had aligned themselves with reactionary foreign capitalists. The FPA lamented that after struggling for "liberty" through the Wars of Independence and the Mexican Revolution, "Mexico remained a backward state, semifeudal and semicolonial, without its own industries, dependent on foreign capital, and obligated to operate like a fountain of raw materials and cheap labor and a market for foreign industrial products." To combat imperialism and Fascism, the FPA needed to work with all genuinely patriotic Mexican institutions, which included the Cárdenas administration, which the FPA identified as an ally because of its land and labor policies and its advocacy of socialist education. The FPA defined socialist education "as a progressive system of education" that would be "totally and effectively free education" and would advance the "anti-imperialist consciousness of the [Mexican] youth."[8]

Between the 1880s and the 1920s the Mexican liberal revolution and the conservative counterrevolution immigrated into the United States; in the 1930s the radical wing of the revolution was making its way north. In January 1936 Mexicans in Cleveland, Ohio, established a chapter of the FPA, which they renamed the Frente Popular Mexicano (Frente), under the authority of an FPA delegation from Mexico City. A few weeks later, Nicholas M. Hernández formed Section One of the Chicago Frente at the University of Chicago settlement house in the Back of the Yards. Soon after, Fidencio Moreno started Section Three at Hull House on the Near West Side. In South Chicago, A. Escamilla formed a section at the Byrd Memorial Community Center. Impoverished during the Depression, radical Mexican immigrants did not possess the finances of the Mexican liberals and were therefore unable to start autonomous Frente sections. Radical Mexicans were forced to launch the Frente through the Chicago settlement houses. When Hernández first approached settlement house officials to charter Section One, he was translating and conserving Spanish-language newspapers through a Works Progress Administration program. Taking advantage of this work, Hernández was one of several Mexican immigrants who preserved the history of the liberal movement in Chicago. His decision to found the Chicago Frente attracted the support of Henrique Venegas and Jesús Flores, two well-educated middle-class Mexican immigrants. Venegas owned a pool hall and a cigar shop in South Chicago and a restaurant on the Near West Side. Flores, an immigrant from Mexico City, obtained a high-level education in Mexico, but his politics were rooted in the radical Mexican working class. Within a year, Hernandez and his comrades had organized five sections of the Frente, dispersed throughout Chicago.[9]

Unlike the Mexican liberals who preceded them, Hernández, Venegas, and Flores wanted to build a radical organization that would create community leaders out of blue-collar Mexican workers. To attract working-class Mexicans to the Frente, Hernández organized a recruitment event in Bowen Hall at Hull House where Mexican laborers would be offered the opportunity to discuss their needs and wants. In the neighborhood of South Chicago, Frente activist A. Escamilla had won over Juan Uribe, who edited *La Lucha*, a Spanish-language paper that had survived the Depression. Through announcements in *La Lucha*, the Frente filled Bowen Hall to capacity, forcing some fifty migrants to remain standing during the gathering. While the majority of the attendees were male, Mexican women were also present. Both "professionals" and "laborers" attended the gathering, but "the latter [laborers] outnumbered the former [professionals] by a ratio of at least twenty to one."[10]

During the meeting, Mexican laborers bemoaned the Depression and what they described as a cultural crisis. Mexican workers took turns lamenting that they had left their "cultural advantages" in Mexico and had been unable to "transplant" their way of life to the United States. The liberals of the 1920s had founded middle-class Mexican organizations in Chicago that had improved the lives of some Mexican laborers through their social reform work, but the liberals organized events that revolved around the interests and tastes of the Mexican middle class. Frente organizers, some of whom were also of middle-class backgrounds, had been influenced by cardenismo and popular front politics, and they wanted to create a community and a movement that would emphasize their conviction that the Mexican working class was the authentic backbone of Mexican society. Frentistas listened carefully to the grievances of Mexican migrants and decided to address the attendees' disaffection with their lives in the United States through a plan that overlapped with the Mexico City–based FPA's commitment to a "socialist education" that would advance "the anti-imperialist consciousness of the youth." Cheered by the attendees, Frente activists proclaimed that they would call upon the Cárdenas administration to finance the construction of Spanish-language libraries and schools in Chicago for both adults and children, and they would start a scholarship program for "talented young students who may return to Mexico" to be trained in the "arts and professions" so they could become "leaders of their own people both here and in Mexico." Frentistas, reminiscent of the liberals and traditionalists, understood that the future of Mexican Chicago rested with the youth. They consequently sought to provide young Mexicans, both those born in Mexico and those born in the United States, with a Spanish-language education that would keep them intellectually and emotionally connected to Mexico.[11]

Receiving a Radical Education in Chicago

In the context of the politically polarized 1930s, Frentistas had come to believe that Mexican workers needed to join the international struggle against Fascism and imperialism, which, if left unchecked, could threaten Mexico's sovereignty. Lacking the financial resources of a middle-class organization, the Frente decided that a Mexican-government-financed and volunteer-run educational project could most feasibly transmit their radical politics to the Mexican migrants living in Chicago. Unlike the liberals, Frentistas rarely promoted education for the purpose of upward mobility. Instead, the Frente framed education as a means to transform Mexicans into radicals.

Committed to cultivating working-class leaders, the Frente applied a developmental pedagogy to their membership. When Frentistas convened to elect their leadership team, they primarily chose formally educated individuals: Venegas was elected to the position of general secretary; Hernández, the secretary of propaganda; Flores, the secretary of education; and a migrant named José Pedraza was asked to serve as the secretary of the interior. Although Venegas, Hernández, and Flores possessed advanced Spanish- and English-language skills, Pedraza did not, but the Frente refused to use formal education as a litmus test for leadership. As Pedraza began carrying out his duties, he realized that he was in over his head, and he decided it was best to resign because of his lack of formal education. Speaking in broken Spanish during a meeting, Pedraza explained, "When I see you one at a time, when I see you all together I lose my tongue. Now if it was a matter of ploughing a field, that would suit me better. You can't get bananas from an orange . . . from apple trees . . . neither can you get fine words from a man who has not gone to school." Emotionally moved by Pedraza's sincerity, Frente officers applauded him and rejected his resignation. After asking the members to vote on the issue, the Frente appointed a formally educated migrant to serve as Pedraza's personal assistant so that Pedraza could continue at his post.[12] The Frente understood that many working-class Mexicans lacked education, but the organization was committed to providing Mexicans with the assistance they needed to become community leaders.

Frente activists were relatively poor during the Depression but were able to start their educational project through the support of the Cárdenas administration's Secretaria de Educación Pública (SEP). The Frente's secretary of education, Jesús Flores, wanted to provide Mexican migrants with a "history of their own people," or what one might call a people's history of Mexico. To this end, Flores reached out to the SEP, which enthusiastically responded to the Chicago Frente by sending it a collection of Spanish-language textbooks and mimeographed educational materials. Through the SEP, the Frente started a radical Spanish-language library in Chicago that was open to the public and included texts on politics, economics, and the labor movement in Mexico. To advertise the library and to incentivize Frentistas to use it, Flores created a public debate team that traveled throughout the Chicago area, delivered lectures, and debated liberal and conservative Mexican societies about contemporary politics. The SEP boosted the morale of radical Mexican migrants by showing them that they mattered to the Cárdenas administration.[13]

The Frente recognized that Mexican children in Chicago were often "bombard[ed]" by American cultural productions that denigrated Mexico. Popular films in Chicago, such as *A Trip through Barbarous Mexico* and *Soldiers of Fortune*, depicted Mexicans as uneducated bandits and buffoons.[14] The Frente confronted these stereotypes by providing Mexican children with an alternative representation, a radical and nationalist understanding of Mexico's people and place in world history. Flores led this work, and he began by organizing a series of Spanish-language courses for children. Flores could not afford to hire teachers, and so he drew on the educational skills of the radical Mexican women who joined the Frente. To offer the classes free of charge to the students and to make the classes accessible, Flores used the settlement houses' free facilities, and he created a family-friendly class schedule. While Frente organizers met for their weekly meetings in the living room of the University of Chicago settlement, between eight and ten Mexican children gathered in the game room to be taught by a Mrs. García and another Mexican woman, both of whom were members of the Frente. As more children enrolled in the course, the Frente's educational program expanded to include courses on revolutionary art and music. All five sections of the Frente eventually organized children's classes, and their popularity led the Frente to launch a citywide fundraising campaign to create a summer school program.[15]

Throughout the 1930s, the Cárdenas administration was also busy at work recruiting Mexican women to transform the children of the Mexican working class. The SEP hired thousands of Mexican women during the Cárdenas presidency. Some worked in educational administration, while the majority

became federal schoolteachers in rural communities. As educational administrators and teachers, Mexican women shaped the cardenista curriculum,
teaching lessons on women's historic participation in the revolution, women's
rights, and personal matters regarding marriage and sex. Employing progressive theories of "action pedagogy," many of these women went beyond formal
curriculums to teach Mexican families how to form labor unions, start worker
cooperatives, and write government grants and grievances. As Jocelyn Olcott
has shown, Mexican teachers taught "revolutionary [Mexican] citizenship,"
and cardenista politicians supported them and "officially incorporat[ed]
activism into teachers' duties."[16] Frente women in Chicago, like Mrs. Garcia,
were teaching a similar revolutionary curriculum, but they were doing so
outside the borders of the Mexican nation-state and without the full support
of the SEP. On the one hand, this meant that they had limited access to the
SEP's resources; on the other hand, they were also free from governmental
oversight and therefore had the power to define Mexican "revolutionary citizenship" in ways that addressed the particular educational needs of Mexican
migrants.

While the Frente could draw on its membership to teach children Spanish-
language skills and social studies, they wanted to recruit an expert with an
advanced education to teach adult learners. Initially turning to the Mexican consulate for assistance, the Frente encountered immediate opposition
from Consul Eugenio Pesqueira. Mexican consuls had a significant degree of
freedom in the United States and chose to assist, hinder, or ignore Mexican
migrants based on their personal politics and preferences. Former consul
Rafael Avelyra, for example, had supported Chicago's liberal community,
but his replacement, Pesqueira, detested the radical Frente and repeatedly
sidestepped its invitations to its events and cooperative proposals. He even
publicly repudiated the Frente's self-proclaimed ties to the SEP, stating that
the Frente "had nothing to do with the Mexican government" and was by
and large a "selfish group." Two years into the Cárdenas presidency, Pesqueira
was recalled to Mexico and was replaced by Consul Antonio Schmidt and
Vice Consul Manuel Aguilar, both of whom enthusiastically supported the
Frente. With the changing of the guard, the Frente gained the help of a highly
educated consular administrator named Dr. Ramón Alcazar, who joined the
Frente and started teaching advanced courses in Mexican literature, history,
and civics.[17]

Through the support of the SEP and the Mexican consulate, the Frente
was slowly creating a radical Mexican nationalist educational program in
Chicago, and it now linked its educational initiatives more closely to its
radical agenda, organizing a lecture series featuring members of the PCM.
The series was inaugurated by Angélica Arenal, who delivered several talks

at the University of Chicago settlement. At the time, Arenal worked as a journalist for *El Nacional* in Mexico City but was living in New York City with her husband, David Alfaro Siqueiros, the renowned muralist and PCM activist.[18]

Unlike liberal and traditionalist women, radical Mexican women lived relatively independent lives as *comunistas*. For example, like Arenal, PCM organizer and SEP employee Concha Michel also moved to New York City in the 1930s. Immersing herself in New York's radical and international culture, Michel was inspired to move to the Soviet Union, where she lived and studied the lives of women under socialism. Returning to Mexico, Michel continued to work for the SEP and devoted herself to teaching women how to obtain their own means of production through access to ejido (Mexican communal farm) land grants. Ofelia Domínguez Navarro, a Cuban journalist, was exiled from Cuba for her activism against the dictatorship of Gerardo Machado. Moving to Mexico City, Domínguez Navarro joined the Frente-affiliated United Front for Women's Rights (Único Pro-Derechos de la Mujer) and then worked to incorporate the Distrito Federal's numerous women's societies into the Frente.[19]

Radical Mexican women were living the transnational Mexican Revolution through a network that linked activists from Mexico City, New York City, and Chicago. After moving to New York, Angélica Arenal attended numerous radical events and conferences, including the politically left-of-center International Conference for Writers. Progressive Latin American and American journalists at this gathering encouraged Arenal to travel to Spain to cover the political conflicts developing there between conservatives and progressives. Arenal would eventually make her way to Spain, but she first stopped in Chicago because she had already accepted an invitation by the Chicago Frente to deliver several talks on contemporary Mexican politics. Speaking at the University of Chicago settlement house, Arenal gave a "zealous" speech about the "plans being unfolded by El Frente Popular in Mexico in favor of the Mexican workers." She provided Mexican migrants with a firsthand account of "the progress made in education in Mexico" and concluded by offering migrants a "fraternal salutation" from the "workers of Mexico." In solidarity, the Chicago Frente pulled together a monetary collection, which they entrusted to Arenal to deliver to the Mexico City FPA. As a radical journalist and PCM fellow traveler, Arenal embodied the leftist Mexican culture the Frente was attempting to transplant in Chicago, and Arenal's presence in the United States energized radical Mexican migrants who remained invested in Mexico's future. Arenal now headed off to Spain, where she would write a series of articles on what would become the Spanish Civil War.[20]

Radical Mexicans and Spaniards United against Fascism

In July 1936 a group of Spanish military generals launched a coup against the Republican government of Spain, initiating the Spanish Civil War, which lasted for three years and concluded with more than half a million casualties. The military coup was supported by the "Nationalists," which included various conservative groups such as the Spanish Confederation of the Autonomous Right and the Fascist Falange. The Nationalists united under Gen. Francisco Franco, and they received support from Nazi Germany and Fascist Italy. The Republican government was defended by a number of liberal organizations, social democrats, and Communist-led popular front groups, which secured the assistance of the Soviet Union, Mexico, and numerous International Brigades that included more than forty thousand foreigners. The Spanish Civil War captured the attention of political activists around the world who believed the outcome would have far-reaching consequences for their respective organizations and for international relations.[21]

After the start of the war, the Chicago Frente began holding meetings to discuss the "liberation of the Spanish-speaking peoples" and the effects of the war on the "working classes in Spain." These Frente gatherings drew large crowds according to observers, which was a testament to the Mexican organizers who were pulling in Mexicans from throughout Chicagoland. Frente officer Nicolas Hernández informed attendees that he feared the civil war would have grave consequences for the Mexican working class. In a speech entitled "Significance of the Frente Popular throughout the Whole World!" Hernández argued that the "monied classes have been constantly oppressing the laboring class and for that reason the latter has been uniting throughout the world." Hernandez believed that the reactionaries had gone on the offensive in Spain as a result of the growth of the Left, which had gained influence during the Depression. If the Republicans lost the war, Hernandez reasoned, their defeat would embolden the Mexican "capitalist class" in its conflicts with the laboring class. Frentistas now determined that they needed to encourage Mexican migrants to assist the Spanish Republicans. The Frente reached out to a newly formed popular front organization in Chicago named the Spanish Popular Front and worked with it to facilitate the arrival of a group of Republican delegates, which included the journalist, writer, and Spanish minister to Sweden Isabel de Palencia, the noted pro-Republican theologian Reverend Luis Sarasola, and the Republican Left Party's Marcelino Domingo. These Spaniards came to the United States to fundraise for the Republican cause. The Mexican Frente leafleted Chicago on behalf of the Spaniards, helped secure accommodations for the delegates, and encouraged all Spanish-speaking immigrants to attend their events.[22]

Little is known of the Spanish immigrant community of metropolitan Chicago during the interwar years (Spanish immigrants are often referred to as the "invisible immigrants" and the "forgotten immigrants" by scholars), and yet, through the Spanish-language press and naturalization records, we can reconstruct the characteristics of this population, which explain why Spanish immigrants in Chicago overwhelmingly supported the Republicans during the war.[23] The U.S. census lists 640 Spaniards in Chicago in 1930 and another 619 in the state of Indiana.[24] Before the Depression, Spanish immigrants formed mutual aid societies, such as the Unión Benéfica Española and La Sociedad Española, which established joint chapters in Chicago and Gary, Indiana.[25] During the 1920s these societies organized numerous cultural events that celebrated the birth of the Second Spanish Republic. By the mid-1930s the leaders of these groups had begun applying for U.S. citizenship, but with the start of the civil war, they reimmersed themselves in Spanish political activities in favor of Republican Spain.[26]

The Spaniards who engaged in community actions included Maximilian Olay, who was born in the town of Collado Mediano in the province of Madrid. Olay immigrated to the United States in 1908 after a brief stop in Cuba. By the mid-1920s, Olay was living in Chicago's Logan Square alongside other Spanish-speaking migrants (see figure 2 on the webpage). After the Fascist coup, Olay founded the pro-Republican Committee for the Defense of Spanish Liberties and recruited other Spaniards to his organization, some of whom had been politically active within the Mexican Frente and others who had just joined the recently formed Spanish Popular Front.[27]

The membership rolls of Olay's group have not been preserved, but between 1900 and 1940, approximately 422 Spaniards, Olay among them, applied for U.S. citizenship in Chicago. The majority of these Spaniards worked as skilled and semiskilled blue-collar laborers in Chicago and had emigrated from the province of Asturias, a Republican stronghold during the war (see tables 7 and 12 in the appendix).[28] In 1934 working-class miners in Asturias had organized a strike after the general election of 1933 granted the Spanish Confederation of the Autonomous Right more leverage within the government of Spain. Spanish anarchists and socialists agitated against the growing influence of the Right by calling for a larger general strike. While a number of unions struck, most soon returned to work nearly everywhere but in Asturias, where miners occupied several towns and established what one scholar has called "the first revolutionary commune in western Europe since

Paris in 1871."[29] In reaction to the Asturias uprising, the Spanish government called on Franco to regain control of the region. Franco viciously crushed the strike, killing an estimated three thousand miners. Their deaths and the climate of fear created by Franco in the aftermath of the strike enraged working-class Asturians who passionately opposed the military coup in 1936 and remained strong supporters of the Republican government throughout the war. My review of the Spanish-language press in Chicago suggests that very few Spaniards supported Franco and the Nationalists during the war. The Spanish Civil War served to unite radical and moderate Spaniards with radical Mexicans, who came together in opposition to Franco and Fascism.

Radical Mexicans Support the International and Local Labor Movement

The Frentistas who collaborated with Spanish Republicans soon began reaching out to Latin American labor organizers in the Chicago area. Mexican migrants had already established a history of forming coalitions with other Spanish-speaking immigrants. In the 1920s Mexican liberals worked with Central Americans and Puerto Ricans on various initiatives. With the start of the Depression, the Mexican liberal movement collapsed, and so did these early Hispanic alliances. Frente organizers drew lessons from this history and joined with Spaniards to re-create a Hispanic community, but one devoted to radical ends. Frentistas now approached Cuban unionists who were passing through Chicago on their way to labor events in Mexico City.

The Cubans who collaborated with the Frente only reinforced the anti-imperialist politics of radical Mexican immigrants. A Cuban unionist referred to as "Martín" began participating in the Frente's intellectual activities. Martín delivered several talks in Chicago, and the fragments of his speeches that have survived in the records suggest that he addressed the Cuban labor movement's contemporary experience, which had taught radical Cuban unionists that ordinary working-class people were willing to engage in militant strikes under the right conditions. Between the 1920s and the 1930s, roughly two-thirds of the Cuban population worked in sugar production, and in 1933 U.S. and other foreign corporations and banks controlled approximately 100 out of the 135 sugar mills in Cuba. As in Mexico, U.S. companies in Cuba often placed English-speaking American managers in charge of unskilled Latin American workers. In this era, it was not uncommon for U.S. managers to refer to their Latin American employees as "our peons" or "greasers."[30] The conflicts that eventually developed between American managers and Latin American laborers engendered intense feelings of antiforeign nationalism in both Cuba and Mexico. Martín discussed these dynamics, addressing the ways American companies "exploit[ed]" Cuban workers, but he qualified his remarks, explaining that "labor interests in Cuba [were] not anti-American but against American capitalism."[31] Martín, like many Mexican workers, drew a distinction between U.S. corporations in Latin America, defined as agents of imperialism, and ordinary American citizens, who could embody a range of political positions.[32]

In Cuba, sugar workers lived especially precarious lives because their jobs were dependent on the international sugar market, which dipped at various points during the 1920s and then plummeted during the Depression. Cuba's president, Gen. Gerardo Machado (in office 1925–33), like Porfirio Díaz in Mexico during the nineteenth century, encouraged foreign corporations to invest in Cuba, and during a visit to New York City, Machado boasted to U.S. businessmen that he would never allow a strike to last longer than a day in Cuba. Under Machado's rule, Cuban union organizers were fired, blacklisted, arrested, exiled, and sometimes assassinated. Cuba's largest labor federation, the Cuban National Labor Confederation (Confederación Nacional Obrera de Cuba, CNOC), influenced by Cuban anarchists and Communists, was forced underground. As the economy worsened during the Depression, more than a million Cubans lost their jobs, while the wages of employed sugar workers plummeted.[33]

Meanwhile, in Havana, teachers, students, and journalists began organizing massive protests against the Machado regime. In opposition to Machado, in July 1933 bus drivers and then teachers went on strike, and the CNOC supported them by calling for a mass general strike. Longshoremen heeded the call, as did typographers, telegraph operators, and railway workers. Violence ensued as police officers suppressed these strikes. It appeared to all that Machado was losing control of the country, and his support within the Cuban military began to wane. In August 1933 Machado resigned and fled to the Bahamas. His exile created a power struggle within the military that resulted in a rebellion and then paralysis. As the military was embroiled in its own internal conflict, some two hundred thousand sugar cane and mill workers seized the opportunity and took over more than one hundred sugar mills. This was a rank-and-file spontaneous act that caught the CNOC and Cuban Left by surprise. The working-class occupiers demanded higher wages, improved working conditions, better treatment from company managers, and the legal recognition of unions in Cuba. While workers were in control of the mills, they began carrying out radical experiments: labor committees parceled out unused corporate-owned land to rural folk, provided unemployed workers with food from company cafeterias, and confiscated the artillery of company security forces to create worker militias. Believing that the United States would intervene to protect the private property of the U.S. mill owners, Cuban workers grew alarmed when a U.S. destroyer entered Havana's harbor and began communicating with the American managers of a local sugar mill. Cuban Communists circulated handbills that warned, "The Imperialists and their national lackeys, the Wall Street bankers, threaten with an imperialistic military intervention [to] come to our country chiefly and principally to intimidate the laboring class, the peasants, the soldiers, and the students and to drown the movement in blood."[34]

The Cuban Left called on all Latin Americans to oppose a U.S. intervention. Several months earlier, U.S. president Franklin Delano Roosevelt had delivered his "good neighbor" speech, expressing that in the field of international relations the United States would respect the sovereignty of its southern neighbors. Given the impact of the Depression on the U.S. economy and Roosevelt's "good neighbor" position, the U.S. military did not intervene in Cuba. But in the interim, Sgt. Fulgencio Batista had taken control of the Cuban military, and he announced he would take whatever steps were necessary to settle the sugar crisis. Seeking to avoid a bloodbath and the martyrdom of Cuban workers in the aftermath of what workers were now calling the "revolution of 1933," Batista and the managers of several sugar mills met with Cuban labor leaders and conceded to many of their demands. Batista and the owners of the mills granted sugar workers an increase in pay, allowed strike leaders and known union organizers to return to their jobs, and accepted the creation of worker-appointed labor stewards, who would mitigate labor grievances within the sugar mills. In short, sugar workers gained more control over production than they had ever had. Over the course of Batista's rule, the Cuban labor movement would lose ground, but sugar workers had tasted victory in 1933 by seizing the majority of mills, and they had done so without the leadership of the CNOC or Cuban Communists and anarchists.[35] The Mexican Frente in Chicago "enthusiastically received" Martín's lectures on the Cuban labor movement, which must have communicated that ordinary workers were willing and ready to take militant action if they believed they could win.[36] Frente leaders now made plans to speak to union officials from the Confederación de Trabajadores de México (CTM).

Frentistas had family members in Mexico who had joined the CTM and were participating in massive strikes. The Chicago Frente received correspondence from their relatives on strike, and through these letters the Frente discussed the correlation between labor militancy and labor gains under the Cárdenas presidency. In 1936 the brother of Jesus Flores (the Frente's secretary of education) went on strike in Mexico City; it appears he may have been involved in a railway strike that involved more than forty-eight thousand workers.[37] In February 1936 Cárdenas decreed that workers deserved one paid day off per workweek and that his administration would "intervene in the class struggle on the side of labor" in order to ensure that workers received this "paid free day."[38] Emboldened by Cárdenas, the CTM-affiliated Union of Railroad Workers (Sindicato de Trabajadores Ferrocarrileros de la República Mexicana), which had been seeking a pay raise, decided to test Cárdenas's commitment to labor by calling a strike against the National Railways of Mexico, a company directed by the Mexican government but owned in part by U.S. investors who had developed the railways during the Porfiriato. As railroad workers called their strike, red-and-black flags were hung outside railway offices in Mexico City to the cheers of crowds of Mexican citizens. A year prior, Cárdenas had prevented a railway strike, and his involvement had resulted in a labor contract that most workers accepted. The Cárdenas administration responded to the new conflict by assessing the railways' financial records. After determining that the company could not afford to pay its workers more, much less provide them with one paid day off per week, the government's Federal Board of Conciliation asked railway workers to return to their jobs. In a demonstration of trust and loyalty to Cárdenas, the railroad laborers went back to work. Within a year, railway workers were again seeking to strike, and this time around the Cárdenas administration acted more decisively in their favor. Cárdenas nationalized the railways in June 1937 and then placed them in the administrative control of a workers' committee.[39]

Both railway strikes were celebrated by workers throughout Mexico, and in their aftermath, Chicago Frente leaders contacted the CTM and requested it to send delegates to Chicago to discuss these events and their implications. Frentistas were no longer interested in hearing and reading about labor issues in Latin America; instead, they wanted to establish some type of formal relationship with the CTM. Scholars of Mexican Chicago have argued that Mexican immigrants were practically cut off from Mexico during the Depression, but radical Mexican immigrants actually grew closer to Mexico in these years, when Mexico was under the Cárdenas presidency and when the CTM was led by Vicente Lombardo Toledano.

Lombardo Toledano was a radical intellectual who steered the CTM to the left. Educated at the prestigious Universidad Nacional Autónoma de México, Lombardo earned a law degree and a doctorate and then began teaching at his alma mater and at La Universidad Popular Mexicana. He first emerged as a workers' rights leader within a union of white-collar professionals, La Liga de Profesores in the Distrito Federal, and then gained a national reputation when he was nominated to serve as secretary of the Federación National de Maestros. In February 1936 Lombardo helped form the CTM by uniting three unions that had large constituencies in Mexico City. His goal was to create a labor federation *depurada* (purified) of corruption and devoted to the genuine interests of workers through class struggle, defined as short-term labor strikes. Toledano had been heavily influenced by Marxism, and he created the CTM as a federation committed to socialism and the abolition of capitalist exploitation. But in order to create a socialist Mexico, Lombardo believed Mexico needed to be freed from the yoke of imperialism, especially that of the United States. When President Cárdenas broke with the Maximato in 1935, Lombardo threw his support to the president, and Cárdenas reciprocated by siding with Lombardo-affiliated unions during strikes. Lombardo's standing grew, as did the size of the CTM. By 1940 approximately 878,000 workers belonged to a union in Mexico.[40]

As a Marxist educator and passionate anti-imperialist, Lombardo directed the CTM to engage in educational projects that would build support for the Cárdenas administration's expropriation of foreign-owned corporations. Within three months of the formation of the CTM, it had already responded to the Chicago Frente's request, and it sent CTM delegates Dr. Manuel Villaseñor, Dr. Rafael Carrillo, and Eduardo Inez to Chicago. The Frente housed these CTM officials and organized a lecture series by them at Union Hall on the Near West Side.[41] Within a year, the CTM sent a larger delegation to the United States, and these CTM representatives recruited radical American activists to attend seminars at the newly created Workers' University (Universidad Obrera de México) in Mexico City, an educational institution funded by the CTM and directed by Lombardo. While traveling throughout the United States, CTM officials frequently focused on garnering support for the Cárdenas administration's radical expropriation of foreign-owned private property. After nationalizing the railways, Cárdenas backed striking electrical workers against the British-owned Mexican Light and Power Company and rubber workers against the Atlas factory in San Luis Potosí. The Atlas strike came to an end when Cárdenas expropriated the factory and turned it into a worker-run cooperative. British and U.S. oil companies, including Royal Dutch Shell (British controlled) and Standard Oil, were arguably the most powerful corporate entities in Mexico in the 1930s, and they were symbols of foreign power on Mexican soil. Cárdenas wanted to demonstrate the Mexican government's authority, and he began pressuring the oil companies to pay higher taxes, raise wages, and improve conditions for Mexican laborers. When oil workers struck in 1937, Cárdenas first publicly sided with labor, and then in an aggressive and unprecedented move he nationalized seventeen foreign-owned oil companies in March 1938.[42] The international business community and many European governments denounced Cárdenas, but throughout Mexico, ordinary Mexican citizens applauded him and sent his administration thousands of letters of support, some of which included small donations to help pay for the expropriations. Mexican citizens celebrated Cárdenas's bold measures as acts of defiance against the United States and Great Britain. Historians tend to emphasize that throughout this period, Cárdenas actually sought to co-opt Mexico's labor movement in order to guide it away from radical alternatives to capitalist forms of production.[43] Perhaps, but Cárdenas instilled incredible national pride in the Mexican working class, and the CTM officials who went to Chicago and then traveled throughout the United States convinced many Mexican migrants that Cárdenas was a genuine patriot who would stand with Mexican labor against foreign capital.

After meeting with Cuban and CTM unionists who advocated militant class struggle and the far more radical concept of private-property expropriation, Frentistas understood that many liberal Americans and liberal Mexicans would disapprove of their increasingly radical orientation. The Frente frequently argued that there was an inherent irreconcilable contradiction between capital and labor, and Frentistas were starting to question the sanctity of private property. Frente leaders now began holding clandestine meetings outside of the purview of the settlement houses. During one of these assemblies, held in secret on the rooftop of the University of Chicago settlement house, Frente officers discussed the "effects of the capitalist system in Mexico and the U.S.," and more than one officer began to blame the "system" for the impoverishment of the Mexican working class in both countries.[44]

The stakes were high for the Mexican working class, and so Frente leaders agreed that they needed to forge ahead with their radical mission. Over a short period of time, the Frente formed relationships with several progressive and radical American labor groups, including the International Workers League, the Illinois Workers Alliance, and the CIO's Packinghouse Workers Organizing Committee (PWOC) and Steel Workers Organizing Committee (SWOC). Through these partnerships, the Frente created a more multiethnic and multiracial world for Mexican immigrant radicals. These new ties also provided Mexican radicals with new theories and a new discourse through which to express their place in American society. The Workers League first sent Joseph Roth to the Frente, and he delivered a talk that argued that the U.S. government was using deportation as a strike-breaking weapon against

Mexican immigrants. Apparently, Roth provided examples of Mexican labor activists in the Southwest who had been deported because of their participation in the labor movement. Roth's talk made intuitive sense to many
Mexicans. They were concerned about deportation and were well aware that
as noncitizens they could be deported by immigration agents if they were
deemed too radical, too subversive. While Frente activists were impressed
by Roth's analysis, a settlement house administrator who overheard Roth
reported that "his ideas [were] destructive rather than constructive." By contrast, Frentistas were so impressed by Roth that a number of them joined Alliance Locals 32 and 36, which were then lobbying the Illinois state legislature
on behalf of Works Progress Administration employees. Returning from an
Alliance convention at Grant Park, Frente delegates informed the broader
membership that several "W.P.A. groups" had spent their time discussing "the
oppression on the working class from the part of the capitalistic group."[45]

In the late 1930s, the CIO launched unionization campaigns in meatpacking and steel production. When the CIO's PWOC began recruiting Mexicans
to join the union, Frente activists had already laid the groundwork for the
committee's unionization initiative among Mexicans. The Frente had Cuban
and CTM unionists speak to Mexican migrants about the value of a strong
labor movement, the need for militant action, and even the legitimacy of
expropriating the private property of businessmen. In the Back of the Yards
neighborhood, Frentistas began holding pro-CIO meetings and encouraged
Mexicans not simply to join PWOC and SWOC but to become CIO leaders.
At the start of the CIO campaign, PWOC worried that Mexican migrants
would resist unionization, given that several Catholic churches in Mexican
neighborhoods had taken a critical position against the CIO. PWOC unionists remembered Frentistas telling them, "Don't worry about the Mexicans,
we'll get you the signed [union] cards." Shortly after, PWOC received batches
of union cards signed and initialed "FPM," or Frente Popular Mexicano.[46]

While Frentistas encouraged Mexican immigrants to join the CIO, they
remained Mexican nationalist in their politics and had no intention of becoming U.S. citizens. Frente activists had intellectually reconciled the contradiction between Mexican nationalism, that is, their loyalty to the Mexican
nation-state, and Mexican immigration into the United States, which, in
effect, involved leaving or "abandoning" Mexico to work in another nation-
state. In several ways, Mexican liberals had provided the radicals with their
intellectual reasoning. In the 1920s liberal Mexican nationalists had defined
the United States as a country that practiced imperialism in Latin America,
and the liberals often implied that American imperialism and the presence of
so many American corporations in Latin America justified the right of Latin

Americans to migrate and work in the United States. The liberals, however, were incredibly nationalist in their politics, and so they framed Mexicans as citizens of Mexico and always stopped short of describing Mexicans in internationalist terms, as global citizens or as working-class "workers of the world." The liberals wanted Mexico to be so prosperous that Mexican citizens would not have to emigrate. Radical Mexican immigrants drew on this older liberal analysis but inserted it into a Marxian schema that exalted both the subaltern class position and the cultural mexicanidad of Mexican migrants. Radical Mexicans seethed with indignation and were offended that, in their words, "Americans in Mexico were treated with the greatest cariño (love and affection)" and were granted access to so much of Mexico's wealth, while Mexican laborers "in this country [the United States] were exploited by the great corporations, especially by the railroads and steel mills." Frentistas were aware that Mexicans were recruited into the United States when their labor was needed, but then, during recessions, they were laid off, shamelessly denied relief, and even deported after they had generated incredible wealth for the U.S. companies that had hired them.[47] The Frentistas who made these types of arguments were typically from the Distrito Federal, Tampico, and other cities where the Partido Comunista Mexicano had a significant following. Throughout the 1930s, radical Mexican immigrants from these Mexican cities had a much lower rate of U.S. naturalization than migrants from other locales in Mexico (see table 5 in the appendix).

As members of the Frente theorized about their subordinate place within the United States, they began joining the CIO, and they engaged white American unionists in discussions about nationalism. Some American CIO unionists debated and pressured Frentistas to become U.S. citizens. Time and again, Frentistas refused. In fact, at one point, Frente officers proposed excluding U.S.-born Mexicans and Mexican naturalizers from joining the Frente. When this proposal was discussed, the vast majority of Frentistas accepted the motion with "wild applause," but a few young Mexican Americans in attendance voiced their opposition. One attendee in particular, a young Mexican American named Frank Paz, who would go on to become an influential community activist in Chicago in the 1940s, rose to his feet and delivered a passionate counterpoint to the proposal. Paz argued that the plan would exclude him and other Mexican American children from being a part of the political community of their parents and relatives. With some reluctance, Frente leaders conceded Paz's point: the Frente would allow young Mexican Americans to participate in its activities, but it would continue to dissuade Mexican nationals from becoming U.S. citizens. Frente activists chastised Mexicans who even considered naturalization, calling them "gringo renegades," the term Mexican liberals had used to insult Mexican naturalizers. Through their influence in Chicago, the Frente reaffirmed Mexican immigrants' commitment to Mexico under the leadership of Lázaro Cárdenas, who was now facing opposition from numerous corners.[48]

In the border states and in the Bajío, conservative groups mobilized Mexicans against comunistas and cardenistas. In Chihuahua, a reactionary organization called the Dorados attacked Mexican Communists, blamed unemployment and the poor state of the Mexican economy on Jewish Mexicans and Arab and Chinese immigrants in Mexico, and attempted to invalidate arguments about U.S. and European imperialism in Latin America. In the Bajío, the Unión Nacional Sinarquista emerged as a branch of the conservative Catholic organization El Base. The very word *sinarquismo* was meant to represent the inversion of anarchism. Sinarquistas stressed the primacy of authority, order, the Mexican family, and private property. They drew recruits from the militant Catholic communities in the Bajío that had supplied the Cristero Rebellion with soldiers. Sinarquistas established cells across the Bajío and, in particular, in Cárdenas's home state of Michoacán, where Catholic groups were distraught by his increasingly radical rhetoric and policies. The historian Jean Meyer estimates that as many as eighty-five thousand Mexicans participated in sinarquista activities in Michoacán, another seventy-five thousand in Guanajuato, and perhaps twenty thousand in Jalisco.[49] By contrast, in the more radical milieu of the Distrito Federal, Mexican Communists and cardenistas closed ranks and built the Frente into a formidable organization that contained the Dorados and Sinarquistas by intellectually and physically sparring with them, as when Frentistas pummeled a group of Dorados in the Zócalo in Mexico City.[50]

Back in Chicago, as the Frente gained a reputation as a cardenista and comunista organization, Mexicans who subscribed to a more conservative vision of Mexican identity and politics went on the offensive. I could find no evidence of a Dorado or a Sinarquista presence in Chicago, but Mexican Catholic traditionalists aggressively attacked the Frente. At St. Francis on the Near West Side, the conservative Martires Mexicanos, which had opposed the liberal movement in the 1920s, now turned their attention to the Frente. Through *El Ideal Mexicano*, the Martires warned Mexicans about the dangerous ideas presented in radical literature. While radical Mexicans and Spanish immigrants in Chicago supported the Republicans during the Spanish Civil War, the Martires sided with the Nationalists, claiming they would "liberate" Spaniards from "Bolshevik degradation." Concomitantly, the Martires argued that "Communism was crucifying [Christ in] Mexico" under President Cárdenas or the "Chicharronero (the one who fries pork)," as they derogatorily called him. At the University of Chicago settlement house, a Mexican employee named José Rosales began positioning settlement house administrators against the Frente, and at Hull House, a Mexican woman named Hortensia de la Mora moved against the Frente. From de la Mora's paternalistic perspective, Mexican migrants were "simple" and "uneducated," and an "intellectual" radical group like the Frente was simply too "dangerous because of this!"[51]

José Rosales had participated in the 1920s liberal movement, but after joining the University of Chicago settlement house as a social worker in the 1930s, he became critical of the Frente's radicalism and began secretly monitoring the group and undermining its activities.[52] Rosales was more liberal than the Mexicans who joined the conservative Martires, but as a liberal, he believed in parliamentarian democracy, private property, and the power of education and entrepreneurship as a means to improve society. Liberals like Rosales simply did not share the Frente's radical values. Historians often point to the Nazi-Soviet Nonaggression Pact as a watershed moment for liberal and radical alliances in that it led to the decline of many popular front groups in the United States, but Frentistas were deserted and denounced by American and Mexican liberals well before the pact. In 1939 Nazi Germany and the Soviet Union signed a treaty that established they would not engage each other in warfare nor aid each other's enemies. Many liberals and Communists were confused and disillusioned by the nonaggression treaty, because they had joined together within popular front organizations in order to combat Fascism. In the aftermath of the treaty, some Communists continued agitating against the Nazis, believing that the treaty was simply a Soviet ploy to forestall Nazi aggression. The Soviet Comintern, on the other hand, actually pressured Communist organizations to scale down their anti-Nazi activism. Many Communists took the Comintern's directives seriously, curtailed their criticisms of the Nazis, and then intensified their objections to FDR and the New Deal. American Communists started calling the American Popular Front movement the Democratic Front to emphasize its bourgeois and parliamentarian essence. In their efforts to explain their new political position, Communists underscored the difference between the popular front, defined as a coalition of Communists, radicals of various political persuasions, and anti-Fascist progressive liberals, and a bona fide Communist organization like the Communist Party of the United States (CPUSA), which was committed to the abolition of capitalism. Communist criticisms of the popular front, FDR, and the New Deal stressed the legitimate political differences between radicals and liberals, and many popular front organizations did indeed collapse after 1939 as American Communists and liberals withdrew from each other.[53]

Well before the Nazi-Soviet treaty, liberal Mexican immigrants and liberal Americans began criticizing the Frente. So long as the Frente focused on implementing educational projects, it did not make many liberal enemies in Chicago. Most liberals (Mexicans and Americans alike) seemed to think that the Frente's educational work erred in its assumptions but was relatively harmless. It was only when the Frente began collaborating with radical labor activists and union organizers that anti-Communist liberals and conservatives started actively opposing all of the Frente's activities. Frentistas understood this might happen, and they became more secretive in their endeavors and organization style, but they concurrently continued to push at the boundaries of their relationships with the liberal settlement houses.

Frentistas wanted to create a radical Mexican community and movement in Chicago, and so they pressed ahead with their charge and invited a Mexican national named Natalio Vázquez Pallares to consult them in their activities. Vázquez was then the general secretary of the student branch of the Frente Popular Antiimperialista in Mexico City, and after arriving in Chicago, he delivered several leftist public lectures, including one entitled "Socialist Education in Mexico." During his talks, Vázquez argued that the U.S. educational system was "controlled by capitalism" and was training American students to serve as technocrats who would be taught to accept capitalist social inequality so that the "Rockefellers and the Morgans could better exploit [their] high technical knowledge." Under Cárdenas, however, the SEP educated students to consider the welfare of all Mexicans. Vázquez affirmed that Mexico's educational system was in fact "socialist" because it stressed that "since the laboring masses are the real producers [of Mexican society], they should receive a larger share of the wealth produced within the country."[54]

The Frente was proud of the young Vázquez and was thrilled with the talks he gave at the settlement houses. Emboldened by Vázquez, the Frente now moved to strengthen its ties to the Chicago groups that claimed to represent the interests of "the laboring masses . . . the real producers." Frentistas in the Back of the Yards led the way, contacting and then receiving an invitation to join the American League Against War and Fascism, a CPUSA affiliate. Upon learning that the Frente was going to join the League, José Rosales and several unnamed settlement house administrators confronted the Frente and expelled it from the University of Chicago settlement house. Soon after, the Frente was cast out of Hull House and then was driven out of the remaining settlement houses in Chicago.[55] The majority of Frentistas were unemployed working-class Mexican migrants, and they could not afford to rent or purchase new institutional spaces in Chicago. The expulsions did not lead to the Frente's immediate collapse, but it encouraged anti-Communist Mexican traditionalists to attack the Frente with confidence and zeal. The Frente had introduced Mexican migrants in Chicago to radical labor activists from Cuba and Mexico and to local union organizers, including representatives of two of the early organizing committees of the CIO. After the Frente was evicted from the settlements, the organization shrank in size, but its working-class members continued to join the CIO, and these Mexican migrants would go on to participate in the largest unionization movement in U.S. history.

Conclusion

Cardenismo, *comunismo*, and popular front anti-Fascist politics inspired a handful of middle-class liberals and numerous working-class migrants to form the Chicago Frente as a transnational extension of the Mexico City Frente Popular Antiimperialista, founded by the Partido Comunista Mexicano. Chicago Frentistas possessed few resources during the Depression. They did not have the means to secure their own private institutional spaces in Chicago and were therefore forced to partner with the Chicago settlement houses. Despite this limitation, through its determination and the assistance of the Secretaria de Educación Pública and the Mexican consulate, Frentistas managed to launch a "socialist education" project in Chicago that recruited, trained, and encouraged working-class migrants to become community activists connected to leftist social movements in Spain, Cuba, and Mexico.

Over time, Frentistas developed relationships with Americans who were members of the CIO, the CPUSA, and other labor and radical groups. The Frentistas who joined the CIO in the 1930s were not U.S. citizens. These were proud Mexican nationals motivated to join the American labor movement by the radical turn in Mexican politics represented by the rise of President Lázaro Cárdenas.

Through a number of cross-cultural activities with white Americans, Frentistas gained experience explaining and defending their radical nationalist politics. Some Americans urged Mexican radicals to become U.S. citizens, but these Mexicans held their ground and steadfastly refused because they had developed an ideological position on U.S. naturalization that reconciled their right to live and work in the United States as Mexican citizens. Since the 1920s, liberal Mexican immigrants had criticized the United States for practicing imperialism in Latin America. The liberals acknowledged the exploitation of Mexican migrants in the United States and tacitly encouraged migrants to join labor unions. Frentistas drew on these liberal positions but gave them a hardened Marxian edge. In short, radical Mexican immigrants argued that they should be treated with the same respect, rights, and freedom of choice accorded to the American businessmen and corporations operating and profiting in Mexico.

As the Frente created a community and a movement and established alliances with radical American organizations, including those affiliated with the CPUSA, they came under scrutiny and attack by anti-Communist Mexican liberals and traditionalists who were fundamentally opposed to the radicalization of the Mexican immigrant population of the city. Eventually, settlement house administrators also came to oppose the Frente's ultraradicalism, and they expelled the Frente from their institutions and support networks. As Mexican radicals lost the support of the liberals, those who had joined the CIO continued to organize Mexican immigrants but now did so within large and ethnically and racially diverse American unions.

5 Mexican Radicals and Traditionalists Unionize Workers in the United States

So when are we going to start the revolution?
—A radical Mexican immigrant and UPWA organizer, Vicky Starr, interview, November 2003

You cannot dig a hole unless you put something in it.
—A traditionalist Mexican immigrant and USWA organizer in Northwest Indiana, Basil Pacheco, Mexican American folder 1, East Chicago Room, East Chicago Public Library

This chapter follows the revolutionary generation into the Congress of Industrial Organizations (CIO). In both Chicago and Northwest Indiana, Mexican radicals and traditionalists entered the ranks of the CIO-affiliated United Packinghouse Workers of America (UPWA) and the United Steelworkers of America (USWA) and contributed to the largest union-organizing movement in the history of the United States.

Mexican immigrants remain largely absent from the CIO's history, and, when referenced, they are often characterized as strikebreakers or as workers who were difficult to unionize.[1] While many Mexican immigrants and American citizens were grateful for the jobs they held during the Depression, skeptical of the value of unions, and hesitant to join unions because they feared employer retaliation, a dedicated and influential number of Mexican immigrant radicals and traditionalists became CIO organizers and laid the groundwork for the future participation of Latinos in the American labor movement.[2] Mexican radicals and traditionalists were receptive to the CIO because they had already been organized by Mexican immigrant societies and because they had already accepted the value of community mobilization and collective action.[3]

Mexican radicals and traditionalists found a common cause in their support for unionization, but they never reconciled their political differences.

The biographies of immigrant CIO leaders suggest that after joining the labor movement, radicals remained left of center in their politics and proud of their identities as Mexican nationals, a sense of pride bolstered by the radical presidency of Lázaro Cárdenas (in office 1934–40). Immigrant traditionalists, by comparison, also entered the CIO and continued to define themselves as faithful Catholics opposed to radical politics. The traditionalists, who had denounced the anticlerical and socialist policies of the Mexican government under President Calles in the 1920s and President Cárdenas in the 1930s, continued to question the value of their Mexican citizenship and their commitment to the Mexican state. By the late 1940s, working-class traditionalists were advancing a deterritorialized brand of Mexican nationalism divorced from any civic allegiance to Mexico. As CIO traditionalists became American citizens in significant numbers, they encouraged other Mexican immigrants to naturalize so they could support the New Deal.

From Immigrant Societies to the CIO

During the revolution, Porfirio Díaz exiled the liberal Magonistas, Ricardo and Enrique Flores Magón and their followers, into the United States, where they became radicals who encouraged Mexican immigrants to join unions and engage in class struggle. In Texas, Arizona, California, and Missouri, the Flores Magón brothers, Librado Rivera, Juan Sarabia, Práxedis Guerrero, and others experienced racial discrimination and repression at the hands of American detective agencies working for the Díaz government, U.S. federal agents, and local police officers, who all tried to suppress the Magonistas' anti-Díaz revolutionary activities. Fleeing their pursuers by moving from state to state, the Magonistas witnessed the superexploitation of Mexican migrants across the Southwest. The Magonistas entered the United States as liberals, but they became disillusioned with liberalism as a result of their U.S. experience. They redefined themselves as anarchists and began struggling for the liberation of the international Mexican working class. The Magonistas' press, *Regeneración,* changed its motto from "Periódico Independiente de Combate" to "¡Tierra y Libertad!" and began regularly publishing the writings of the anarchist Peter Kropotkin.[4]

Revolutionary immigrant activists like Práxedis Guerrero were highly influential in spurring the Magonistas to form coalitions with working-class Mexican migrants. In Mexico, Guerrero had been born into an elite and extremely wealthy land-owning family. Influenced by Marx and Kropotkin, Guerrero was soon reading Mikhail Bakunin, Errico Malatesta, and Carlos Malato. Forsaking his family's wealth, Guerrero embraced revolutionary anarchism early on and challenged other Magonistas to do the same. As the Magonistas became anarchists as a cohort, Guerrero reached out to and befriended anarchists living in the United States such as Emma Goldman, Alexander Berkman, Florencio Bozora, and the leaders of the anarchosyndicalist Industrial Workers of the World (Wobblies). Mexican immigrants like Primo Tapia joined the Magonistas and then the Wobblies and then went off to unionize ethnic Mexican miners in Colorado and agricultural workers in the Midwest. Guerrero, meanwhile, joined with Manuel Sarabia (Juan Sarabia's cousin) to unionize Mexican miners throughout the state of Arizona in Douglas, Morenci, Metcalf, Miami, and Globe. By the 1920s, Ricardo Flores Magón and his comrades had become renowned radicals in the United States. Magonistas were arrested frequently, and Ricardo was eventually convicted of sedition and sentenced to prison in Leavenworth, Kansas, where he died in 1922. Ricardo Flores Magón was now a martyr to Mexican radicals, who continued to agitate for unionization in his name. In the mid-1920s, in La Placita in Los Angeles, Magonistas could be found delivering long and passionate speeches against the clergy and capitalism and in favor of anarchism and unionization.[5]

Well before the New Deal and the formation of the CIO, working-class Mexican immigrant societies, exposed to the ideas of the revolution and the Magonistas, were already seeking to redefine themselves as bona fide labor unions. In California, the leaders of numerous immigrant groups, which represented some two thousand Mexican agricultural workers, formed the Confederación de Uniones de Obreras Mexicanas (CUOM) in 1928. Modeled after Mexico's largest labor federation at the time (the Confederación Regional Obrera Mexicana), CUOM proclaimed it would represent the "racial and patriotic principles" of the Mexican nationals working in the United States, strive to secure higher wages from employers, safeguard its members from duplicitous labor contractors, and recommend just emigration policies to the Mexican government. As Douglas Monroy discovered, CUOM's literature often reflected the influence of the Magonistas. "The exploited class," explained a CUOM broadsheet, "the greater part of which is made up of manual labor, is right in establishing a class struggle in order to effect an economic and moral betterment of its condition, and at last its complete freedom from capitalist tyranny."[6] Following CUOM's lead, some twenty-seven hundred Mexican agricultural laborers in the Imperial Valley formed La Unión de Trabajadores. These immigrant-led labor organizations were very difficult to sustain by agricultural workers, who were poorly paid, seasonally employed, and geographically dispersed and who had to cope with hostile growers, ranchers, and police officers who cracked down on their organizing efforts.[7] What is noteworthy about groups like CUOM and La Unión is that they demonstrate the degree to which Mexican immigrants, influenced by the radical heritage of the revolution, sought to unionize.

In the Midwest in the 1930s, immigrants formed radical Mexican nationalist societies like the Frente Popular Mexicano (on the Frente, see chapter 4). Prior to the rise of the Frente, middle-class Mexicans had established liberal associations in Chicago that carried out social-service projects among working-class migrants. The leaders of these liberal groups characterized themselves as Mexican nationalists, not as anarchists engaged in class struggle. Mexican liberals, however, imbued the broader Mexican population with an anti-imperialist sense of Mexican nationalism, but the liberals were not union organizers in any sense of the term. In the context of the Depression, a few liberals and many working-class Mexicans turned to radical Mexican nationalist politics, formed the Frente, and then offered the broader Mexican population of Chicago a Marxian analysis that assigned value and prestige to Mexican laborers. As the Frente elevated the status of Mexican workers in Chicago, it led them into local political activities, which exposed Mexicans to the CIO and the Communist Party of the United States (CPUSA).[8]

The severity of the Depression and the passage of New Deal labor legislation that granted industrial workers collective bargaining rights prompted a group of union leaders within the American Federation of Labor (AFL) to form an alternative labor federation, the CIO, which emerged between 1935 and 1938. The CIO was committed to organizing industrial workers regardless of skill level, and it eventually succeeded in establishing the first long-lasting industrial unions in the United States. The CIO's success derived from its organizing drives in electrical appliance and automobile plants and in the historically nonunion meatpacking and steel industries. CIO campaigns in meatpacking and steel were spearheaded by the Packinghouse Workers Organizing Committee (PWOC), precursor to the UPWA, formed in 1943, and the Steel Workers Organizing Committee (SWOC), forerunner of the USWA, established in 1942.[9]

In Chicago, radical Mexican nationalists joined the PWOC and the UPWA. The CIO created the PWOC in 1936, and the Mexican members of the Frente, the Lombardo Toledano Club (named after the president of the Mexican labor federation, the Confederación de Trabajadores de Mexico [CTM]), and the Lázaro Cárdenas Club all helped build the PWOC.[10] Recognizing their shared agenda, the Toledano and Cardenas Clubs merged with the Frente, and Frente leaders then directed all radical Mexicans to join the CIO's unions. The Frente activists who supported the PWOC included Refugio Román Martínez, Lupe Marshall, José Lázaro, and Venustiano Rodríguez. These radicals were later joined by Raymond Salinas, José T. Ramírez, José Mena, Gregorio Aguilera, and others. Union records reveal little about the backgrounds of these Mexican PWOC activists and their reasons for joining the CIO. However, through the membership rolls of Mexican immigrant societies, oral testimonies, and naturalization records, we can reconstruct the biographies of several key labor leaders and examine their characteristics in relation to those of the 1,411 working-class Mexicans who worked in meatpacking, steel production, and other industries in Chicago and applied for U.S. citizenship between 1900 and 1940.[11] What follows is a biographical analysis that begins with the life of Refugio Román Martínez, a radical immigrant who first became politically active during the revolution, arrived in Chicago in the mid-1920s, joined the Frente in the 1930s, and then became a CIO organizer for the PWOC and the UPWA.

Exploring the Premigration Histories of Mexican CIO Radicals

Refugio Martínez's politics were shaped by the economic nationalism and anti-imperialism of the revolution. Born in 1903, Martínez was raised in a working-class borough called Villa Cecilia, which was located on the outskirts of Tampico, Tamaulipas, a port city developed by the American-owned Atchison, Topeka and Santa Fe Railroad and the Standard Oil Company. In Villa Cecilia, Martínez attended school for three years and then, as a young man, began working as a tinsmith.[12] Like other manual laborers in Mexico, Martínez acquired only a few years of formal schooling, but he received an unorthodox education during the revolution that taught working-class Mexicans lessons in the contradictions of foreign capital investment.

Martínez's childhood overlapped with the final years of the Porfiriato, when Mexican citizens were becoming increasingly critical of the power and influence of American corporations in Latin America. American financiers first became interested in the city of Tampico because it was situated on the Gulf of Mexico, and they believed the city could serve as a commercial conduit to the Pacific Ocean. In the 1880s American banking interests and representatives of the Santa Fe Railroad arrived in Tampico and incorporated a subsidiary named the Mexican Central, which hired Mexicans to lay rail lines that would eventually link Tampico to the Pacific and the U.S. states of Texas and Arizona. As Mexican workers laid track for the Central, Robert Colgate of the Colgate-Palmolive Company and Mexican Telephone Company began hiring Mexicans to construct a binational communications network between Tampico and several U.S. cities. With the completion of these transportation and communication connections, American business-men began migrating into Tampico en masse, and they created an American enclave within the city.[13]

American businessmen and politicians often argued that it was in the national interest of the United States to invest in Mexico. Speaking to a group of journalists in 1881, Smith D. Atkins, an influential newspaper editor, explained U.S. investment in these terms: "The conquest of Mexico is a commercial, if not a political, necessity. That country will never be developed or governed until we take hold of it. If we put property there, we must protect it, and if we do not put property there, it will always be a standing menace to our civilization. The immense national wealth of Mexico only awaits American enterprise for its development."[14] Tampico became even more important to U.S. investors after the American fortune-hunter Edward Doheny struck oil near the city in 1902. Shortly after, the subsidiaries of Standard Oil and Royal Dutch Shell expanded their operations in the region, and they started shaping Tampico's economy as they superseded the influence of the Mexican Central railway. With the start of the First World War, U.S. military analysts pointed to the strategic significance of Tampico, recognizing that Mexico had become the world's second largest producer of oil.[15]

Throughout this period of Tampico's growth, Mexican politicians, businessmen, and some workers openly welcomed foreign investment into the city, believing it would lead to jobs, social services, and, generally, more opportunities. But sharp disputes developed between companies seeking to maximize their profits and Mexican workers who desired a high standard of living. In 1881 the Mexican employees of the Central Railway complained that they received lower wages than the American migrant workers who labored alongside them. The Central refused to negotiate with its Mexican workforce and imported a thousand white and black American laborers to circumvent Mexican grievances. Infuriated Mexicans rioted, and the Central called on Gen. Jesús Alonso Flores to restore order. U.S. companies defended their policies by claiming that Mexicans did not want to perform grueling work and were not fluent in the English language of the American managers working in Mexico. Mexican workers were learning important lessons from these experiences: U.S. companies were in Mexico to amass wealth, and Mexican government officials would defend foreign companies at the expense of Mexican citizens.[16]

Inspired by the start of the revolution, Mexican laborers launched a strike wave against foreign companies and American and European hegemony in Tamaulipas. In November 1910 workers in Villa Cecilia organized a demonstration in favor of the revolution. Four months later, they marched into

Tampico chanting revolutionary slogans and attacked the city's police department. In July 1911 three thousand stevedores struck against an American dock company, and five hundred workers shut down a refinery owned by a Standard Oil subsidiary. In March 1912 an anti-American rally was scheduled in Tampico, and the mayor received death threats for allegedly selling the city to foreigners. By 1917 Mexican citizens were mobilizing around the newly inaugurated Mexican Constitution, specifically Article 123, which legitimized the formation of unions and the right to strike under certain conditions. In this year alone some eight thousand Mexican oil workers went on strike against the British-owned El Águila refinery (also known as the Mexican Eagle Oil Company).[17]

While the specifics remain unknown, family lore holds that Martínez joined in these revolutionary demonstrations and, upon discovering that he was in grave danger, fled Mexico and immigrated to the United States. Martínez arrived in Laredo, Texas, in 1924, applied for permanent residence, paid a head tax, and legally crossed the border.[18] After working in Texas for a while, Martínez made his way to Chicago, where he found a job at the Swift & Company meatpacking plant.[19]

In Chicago, Martínez read the Spanish-language press regularly, and it seems that he passively supported the Mexican liberal-reform movement of the city but was too radical and too working class to join the liberals wholeheartedly. In the pages of the liberal press, Martínez would have read about U.S. interventions in Central America and about racial conflicts between Mexicans and white ethnics. At times, liberal writers also covered labor issues. Liberals endorsed the unionization of Mexican migrants, and they even hoped that the AFL would cooperate with unions in Mexico to organize some kind of a hemispheric labor federation. Many Mexican liberals were anti-imperialist, antiracist, and in favor of labor rights, but they also accepted the legitimacy of private property and the validity of market solutions to social problems, and they tended to believe that labor and capital could coexist in harmony under the right political leadership. More important still, formally educated liberals frequently argued that the world's most pressing social problems could be solved through education.[20]

Blue-collar immigrants like Martínez who had experienced the anti-imperialist and economic nationalist politics of the revolution arrived in Chicago in search of a working-class Mexican organization that would offer them a more radical analysis and transformative solution to class conflict. Martínez understood that in cities like Tampico, Americans acquired property, lived, worked, and profited, and were assisted by the Porfiriato.[21] By comparison, Mexican migrants lived difficult lives in the United States, whether they were in the fields or in the mills. Then, to add insult to injury, Americans felt they had the right to pressure Mexican immigrants to surrender their Mexican citizenship, while American corporate owners, managers, and personnel in Mexico were permitted to retain their U.S. citizenship. When laborers in Mexico went on strike to improve their conditions so they could avoid having to emigrate, they were violently repressed by their own ostensibly elected officials.[22] Mexican radicals like Martínez wanted to belong to a community that recognized the hypocrisy and injustice of the global capitalist economy.

Mexicans and the Communist Party of the United States

Compelled to labor in the United States because of the exploitative structure of the Mexican economy, Mexican migrants found themselves in a precarious position during the Depression. As Mexican migrants lost their jobs, some took advantage of their vulnerable and unemployed compatriots, while others like Martínez again joined in radical protest.

Faced with few options during the Depression, many unemployed Mexicans initially turned to Chicago's relief centers for assistance. By 1933 approximately 30 percent (some 4,272 persons) of the Mexican population of Chicago was using relief.[23] As the U.S. economy continued to contract, Martínez lost his job at Swift, and he began struggling to make ends meet. Evaluating his situation and that of his neighbors, Martínez learned that Mexicans who had acquired English-language skills were offering to help other migrants obtain relief for a "percentage" of their aid. Ashamed of these relief brokers who charged migrants "for everything they did," Martínez decided to learn how to "help the Mexican people . . . get relief," and his decision led him to the CPUSA.[24]

In Los Angeles and in other cities in the Southwest, the CPUSA and its left-wing affiliates sought to recruit Mexicans because they were perceived as the largest and most exploited group of laborers in the region, making them open to a Communist alternative to capitalism.[25] In Chicago, Mexicans represented a much smaller percentage of the total labor force of the city, and as a consequence, the CPUSA did not target them for recruitment. The few Mexicans who joined the CPUSA in Chicago in the 1930s did so largely on their own accord, and it appears they were attracted to the party because it was open to immigrants but led by politically experienced Americans who knew how to effectively obtain relief in Chicago. During the Depression, patriotic groups like the American Legion zeroed in on the noncitizen status of many Mexicans, tried to deny them relief, and later helped coordinate deportations.[26] The CPUSA, by contrast, assisted and defended immigrants and working Americans through its Unemployed Councils, which organized the unemployed to demand jobs, acquire relief, and stop evictions. Martínez first came into contact with the CPUSA in Washington Park, a radical hub in Chicago.[27] Martínez started attending CPUSA talks in the park, paid close attention when Communists discussed relief, and, before long, was approached by a Communist about joining the party. Considering his circumstances, Martínez decided he would join the CPUSA in order to become "closer with the people . . . who were active" in the "unemployed council where they had relief committees."[28]

Joining the CPUSA in 1932, Martínez began serving as a de facto social worker in Mexican neighborhoods, and through this work, he helped radicalize other migrants. More than two hundred Mexicans were in the process of applying for relief in the vicinity of the meatpacking plant where Martínez had once been employed.[29] On these city blocks Martínez collected the case histories of unemployed Mexicans and translated them for the CPUSA's Unemployed Councils, which then helped these migrants obtain relief. To broaden his base of support, Martínez organized a group of Mexicans into what he called an "educational club" that "[took] the cases of the Mexican workers without any charge and [fought] against those people who were trying to make a living off the unemployed workers."[30] At times Martínez had to confront city relief administrators and Mexican relief brokers when he believed they were taking advantage of migrants. These confrontations could turn violent, as when Unemployed Council activists clashed with relief administrators and police officers in 1932 and 1933.[31] On several occasions Martínez wound up in police custody, but he was always released without charges being filed against him.

In *Red Chicago*, Randi Storch found that Mexican immigrants in the Back of the Yards neighborhood "remembered the Mexican Revolution" and were often "more left-leaning and politicized than other workers." And yet, the CPUSA in Chicago could not retain the small numbers of Mexicans who joined the party.[32] The CPUSA's failure to hold onto Mexicans can be explained in part by the latent and, at times, explicit patriotism of both American and Mexican radicals in the 1930s. Although the CPUSA was founded by radical Americans who had largely rejected the ideology of nationalism in favor of international Marxism, at various times, American Communists struggled against their ingrained patriotic sentiments. Influential American Communists in the 1920s, like Bertram D. Wolf, strategized that they could win over "the American working-class" by teaching American workers about their so-called "native revolutionary traditions." For Wolf, this recruitment strategy involved highlighting the alleged similarities between the American Revolution and the socialist Russian Revolution. Other CPUSA members followed this trend, going so far as to characterize American Communists as the "proletarian 'Minute Men'" of their day.[33] Many Communists in the United States opposed this Americanizing trend, but these nationalist ideas never completely faded out. At the CPUSA's ninth convention in 1936, party leaders went so far as to proclaim, "Communism is Twentieth Century Americanism," and they decorated the convention hall with images of Thomas Jefferson and Abraham Lincoln.[34]

Martínez was attracted to the CPUSA because of its class-based support for workers of all nationalities, but within seven months of joining the party "there was a big fight" in his Communist unit, and a few American Communists concluded that Martínez should become a U.S. citizen if he was going to continue to reside in the United States. Martínez understood that becoming a U.S. citizen might facilitate his access to relief, but he was a proud Mexican national and thus chose to drop out of the CPUSA rather than surrender his Mexican citizenship.[35] Instead of following any formal procedure, however, he simply stopped paying the CPUSA his dues. Martínez had read the CPUSA's literature precisely. The "Programme of the Communist International," which outlined the conditions of party membership, stipulated that "membership in the Communist Party is open to all those who accept the programs and rules of the [CPUSA] and regularly pay Party dues."[36] Martínez had been paying the party about ten cents per month. Given that the CPUSA required its members to "regularly pay Party dues," Martínez reasoned that if he stopped making payments he could no longer be considered an official member of the party. He then could ignore his unit's directive, retain his Mexican citizenship, and continue working with the CPUSA-affiliated Unemployed Councils, which is exactly what he did.[37]

Within a few years, Martínez found a more permanent political home within the radical and Mexican nationalist Frente Popular Mexicano.[38] *Frentistas* were aware that Mexican liberals supported social welfare and even unionization, but middle-class Mexicans never addressed what radicals argued was the inevitability of class warfare.[39] Frente activists intentionally introduced Marx, socialism, and notions of class conflict to Mexican migrants but in a way that overlapped with their subaltern Mexican nationalism. Put another way, radical Mexican activists Mexicanized Marxism in order to sell Marx's theories to Mexican laborers who were already quite nationalist in their politics. As Michael Denning has shown, American Communists in the 1930s "Americanized Marxism" in an effort to recruit working-class Americans. CPUSA activists often conjoined Marx's criticisms of capitalist exploitation and inequality with the social reform arguments of Henry James and John Dewey in order to recruit American workers.[40] Mexican radicals carried out similar intellectual work, blending older Mexican liberal nationalist criticisms of U.S. corporate and government practices in Latin America with Marxian theory.

Immersed in this radical milieu, Martínez soon discovered a vocation that reflected his politics when he found employment as a PWOC union organizer. The PWOC attracted radical Mexicans like Martínez, Venturo Lázaro, and José Rodríguez and numerous American Communists, who now engaged each other in dialectical debate. While the Frente encouraged Mexican migrants to remain loyal to Mexico, the PWOC led migrants to develop deeper roots in the United States as Mexican workers established meaningful relationships with American unionists. For example, Martínez's new allies now included Herb March, a Jewish American member of the CPUSA; Frank McCarty, an Irish American who previously worked for SWOC; Sig Wlodarczyk, often described "as [the] Polish organizer" because of his broad network within the Polish community of Chicago; and Peter Davis, an African American labor militant who was fired from Armour for defiantly wearing a union badge to work.[41]

Martínez was initially hired part-time by the PWOC, but he quickly proved to be an invaluable asset to the union. His experience in meatpacking and his cultural capital (his bilingualism and membership in the Frente) granted him a particular kind of access to Mexican Chicago. PWOC members recalled that Mexican unionists held their meetings in Spanish, were almost all members of the Frente or other Mexican nationalist groups, and demonstrated "a high degree of loyalty to the union."[42] Over the following years, Martínez participated in several intense UPWA organizing drives. He was arrested and jailed on multiple occasions and consequently developed an admirable reputation as a unionist. As one white American unionist opined, "Brother Martinez . . . has done more than any other individual to bring the many Mexican workers in the Chicago packing houses into the CIO."[43] The UPWA agreed with this appraisal and sent Martínez to help win union campaigns in Kansas City, St. Paul, and Los Angeles.[44] In Kansas City Martínez partnered with Mexican UPWA members Seferino Montoya and Louis Medina in antiracist activities, "gather[ing] facts on [the] discrimination" that Mexicans experienced at several local factories. After he returned to Chicago, the UPWA appointed Martínez to the position of secretary and interpreter of the newly created Latin American Labor Committee, which was tasked with leading the union's new international work in Latin America.[45]

During the Second World War the UPWA established lines of communication with several unions in meatpacking and sugar-refining plants in Mexico, Puerto Rico, Cuba, and Argentina.[46] Martínez and other Mexican CIO members helped foster these hemispheric relationships and took advantage of the UPWA's interest in Latin America to create more opportunities for Latino unionists in the United States.[47] Drawing on his own growing prestige, Martínez helped Raymond Salinas, a member of Local 347, obtain a seat on the Back of the Yards Neighborhood Council, a community organization that engaged in neighborhood urban renewal projects.[48] Martínez's and Salinas's devotion to the CIO soon opened up opportunities within the UPWA for other Mexicans, who began to request and obtain administrative positions in the union. José Mena, a Mexican UPWA steward, started serving as a Spanish-language translator for the union, and UPWA member José T. Ramírez requested and won the chairmanship of the Spanish-Speaking Committee, tasked with creating forums where Latino labor leaders working in different cities could learn about each other's personal struggles and shared experiences in meatpacking. In recognition of the growth of its Latino membership, in the 1950s the UPWA asked Ramírez to contribute a Spanish-language column to the heretofore English-language periodical the *Packinghouse Worker*.[49]

Mexican nationalism united all of these unionists, but as radical labor leaders like Herb March understood, their nationalism was also their Achilles heel. American unionists often encouraged their European and Mexican immigrant members to become U.S. citizens.[50] Some believed that immigrants ought to naturalize if they were going to work in the United States, while radicals like March advised Mexicans to become U.S. citizens so they would have more legal protections. Mexican CIO radicals understood they would be safer organizing unions as U.S. citizens, and yet they typically refused to "change flags," as they described it.[51] March, a Communist and internationalist, was mindful of the limitations of nationalism in all of its iterations, and he worried that without U.S. citizenship, Mexicans would be targeted for deportation.[52] March's concern would prove prophetic for Martínez and other radical Latin American CIO leaders during the Cold War.

Although Martínez and other Mexican CIO radicals retained their Mexican citizenship, between 1900 and 1940, approximately 1,411 Mexicans who worked in skilled and unskilled blue-collar occupations in Chicago applied for U.S. citizenship.[53] In some ways, these immigrants were like Martínez and other radicals, but in several critical respects these were fundamentally different Mexican people. Like Martínez, the vast majority of working-class Mexican naturalizers were men in their early thirties who had lived in the United States for many years. Martínez was thirty-four in 1937 when he first began working for PWOC, but he had refrained from applying for U.S. citizenship since his arrival in the 1920s. Like many European immigrants, Mexicans often took years to decide whether or not to become U.S. citizens.[54] The vast majority (86 percent) of all Mexican naturalizers in Chicago were blue-collar workers (skilled, semiskilled, and unskilled), and Martínez had worked as an unskilled laborer in Texas and then as a semiskilled operative at Swift before becoming a union organizer. Fifty-five percent of Mexican naturalizers were unskilled workers, another 16 percent were semiskilled operatives in factories, and a noteworthy 14 percent were skilled craftsmen who worked as auto mechanics, electricians, machinists, and iron and steel molders, among other trades (see table 11). Martínez shared the gender, age, and blue-collar background of the vast majority of Mexican nationals who applied for U.S. citizenship in Chicago.[55]

What distinguished Martínez and other radical CIO unionists from these Mexican naturalizers were their regional backgrounds. Martínez had emigrated from the urban port city of Tampico in the border state of Tamaulipas. Port cities like Tampico and Veracruz were the organizing cores of the Partido Comunista Mexicano (PCM) in the 1920s, and in the 1930s these cities, along with Mexico City, became hotbeds of labor radicalism.[56] Frente activists largely emigrated from the Distrito Federal, Tampico, and other cities in Mexico. The number of Mexicans from the Distrito Federal and the border states who wanted to naturalize as U.S. citizens in Chicago declined in the interwar years as the number of Mexican naturalizers from the rural Bajío region of Mexico increased. Counting all of the working-class Mexican naturalizers in Chicago between 1900 and 1940 reveals that only twenty-two were from Tamaulipas, Martínez's birth state, while two hundred were from the state of Guanajuato, situated in the Bajío.[57] Tamaulipas's economy and political culture had been shaped by the economic nationalist and anti-imperialist politics of the revolution, often in reaction to the heavy-handed practices of U.S. and British corporations in the region. The political culture of the Bajío, by comparison, was influenced by small land-owners and their agricultural workers, many of whom had taken up arms as Cristeros against the anticlerical Mexican government in the 1920s. In Chicago, Martínez found his Mexican community in the Frente, while Mexicans from the Bajío in Northwest Indiana formed a traditionalist Catholic society, El Círculo de Obreros Católicos San José, that adamantly rejected radical Mexican politics. By the 1940s, Martínez was becoming a political minority within Mexican Chicago, and conservative traditionalist immigrants were settling in all around him.

Mexican Traditionalists Join the CIO in South Chicago and Northwest Indiana

Before the CIO formed the SWOC, Mexican immigrant Alfredo Ávila was already trying to organize an independent industrial union at the South Works plant of the Illinois Steel Corporation. Born in the city of Torreón in the border state of Coahuila in 1904, Ávila immigrated to the United States in 1923 and then settled in South Chicago, where he joined the roughly six thousand Mexicans who worked in the steel mills of Illinois and Northwest Indiana. In 1935, the year of the formation of the CIO, Ávila and his coworkers were represented by the Associated Employees of South Works, a company-sponsored union that had a poor reputation as an inauthentic "company union" that did not fairly represent steelworkers. The president of the Associated Employees, a Scottish immigrant named George T. Patterson, recognized the limitations of the union and began seeking support among steelworkers to form an independent union. Most steelworkers were cautious to back Patterson, but he found an immediate and committed ally in Ávila. Ávila quickly recruited Mexican immigrant Manuel García and twenty-five to thirty other Mexican immigrants to the cause.[58] Ávila, García, and their supporters understood the challenge before them: steelworkers had been defeated twice before in their attempts to form an independent union in 1892 and during the "Great Steel Strike" of 1919, when the mills recruited Mexican immigrants to replace striking steelworkers. Ávila and his allies were in a position to play key roles as Mexican organizers who could recruit other migrants to the SWOC while easing tensions among resentful white and black steelworkers who perceived Mexicans as "scabs" (workers who will take striking workers' jobs during a strike).[59]

Focused on winning over Mexicans, Ávila and García held union meetings in Spanish, wrote and distributed Spanish-language union literature, and organized cultural events to draw migrants into conversations about the value of joining SWOC. By July 1936, Ávila and Patterson had secured enough support among Mexican and white and black workers to obtain a CIO charter, which led to the creation of SWOC Local 65. South Chicago was an incredibly racially and ethnically diverse community in the 1930s.[60] To succeed in this diverse space, SWOC hired full-time organizers who self-identified as Mexican (Ávila), Polish (Stanley Baczsinski), Lithuanian (Charlie Jankus), Irish (Joe McNellis), American (James Stewart), and African American (Charlie Henry).[61] The PWOC would essentially copy this organizing strategy and hire Martínez to serve on its organizing committee in 1937. As one of the SWOC's ethnoracial organizers, Ávila created more opportunities for Mexican steelworkers by forming the SWOC Mexican Committee, which grew to include more than seventy-five active Mexican steelworkers.[62]

South Chicago was a more traditionalist community than the Back of the Yards, where Martínez was organizing meatpacking workers and where the Frente had established its first section. Mexicans in the Back of the Yards did not even attempt to start a Catholic church until 1945, while the Mexicans who settled in South Chicago began attending Mass at Our Lady of Guadalupe as early as 1924. Aware of these nuances, Ávila recruited Mexican steelworkers as they walked out of Mass at Our Lady, and this tactic produced results. Francisco A. Rosales and Daniel T. Simon reveal that while only 5 percent of the employees of South Works were Mexican, Mexican workers came to represent 11 percent of the SWOC's members.[63] SWOC officials identified Ávila as a leader and appointed him to the SWOC's executive board and bargaining committee.

The CIO's arrival in Chicago offered radical Mexican immigrants like Martínez and political moderates like Ávila the opportunity to recruit all Mexicans into one large federation: the CIO. Mexican immigrant societies rarely formed successful federations because Mexicans were so divided by revolutionary politics. Martínez and Ávila were organizing Mexicans in distinct political communities, but as numerous Mexicans joined the CIO, radical, moderate, and traditionalist migrants found themselves aligning within the same unionization campaigns. In May 1937 SWOC called a strike against the "Little Steel" companies and planned a major protest in front of the Republic Steel mill in South Chicago. Two months prior, after much negotiation and the threat of a strike, the SWOC won a union contract with the largest steel producer in the United States, the U.S. Steel Corporation. Rather than accept SWOC's success as a harbinger of the unionization of the steel industry, the Little Steel companies dug their heels in and refused to negotiate with the SWOC. The SWOC countered by calling a strike that shut down several small mills, but the strike failed to stop production at Republic, which maintained its operations by relying on its nonunion workforce.[64]

The SWOC supporters who attended the Republic Steel mill protest included Mexican immigrants Lupe Marshall (a Frente activist), Max Guzmán (a political moderate), Philip Morengo (also a moderate), and a contingent of Mexican traditionalists from East Chicago, Indiana.[65] Marshall entered the United States as a young girl in 1917 toward the tail end of the revolution. By the age of thirty-one she had married and started a family and was living on the Near West Side of Chicago. Describing herself as a "housewife" who was "very much interested in the Mexican people [and their] attitude within the organized labor movement," Marshall began volunteering at Hull House and then joined the Frente. In 1935 she was arrested at an anti-imperialist protest along with other radical Mexicans. Undeterred by the arrest, Marshall continued to participate in radical Frente activities and joined steelworkers and their families to picket the Republic mill.[66]

Mexican radicals were critical of U.S. corporations and the U.S. government, and their experiences in the U.S. labor movement only reinforced

their radical convictions. As Marshall and hundreds of steelworkers and
their wives and children approached the gates of the Republic mill to chant
union slogans they were met by a squadron of police officers. The officers
began exchanging words with those at the head of the protest, and it was
then that Marshall noticed "an officer directly in front of [her who] had his
gun out." "I [then] heard a dull thud toward the back of the—of my group,"
Marshall would later recall, "and as I turned around there was screaming
. . . and simultaneously a volley of shots. . . . I couldn't believe that they were
shooting." As gunshots rang out all around her, Marshall tried to stop a policeman from clubbing a steelworker. She "screamed at the policeman," but
then "somebody struck [her] from the back." "As I went down," continued
Marshall, "a policeman kicked me on the side [and] after he kicked me I tried
to get up, and he hit me three times across the back." After she was beaten to
the ground, Marshall was tossed into a patrol wagon along with sixteen other
bludgeoned steelworkers. Although her "head had been broken open" by an
officer's club, Marshall regained her bearings and began treating the wounded
protesters lying around her. In all, ten steelworkers were killed and dozens
were injured in what became known as the Memorial Day Massacre.[67]

The Mexican immigrants who supported the SWOC and were bloodied
alongside white and black Americans at the Memorial Day Massacre represented a cross section of the immigrant population, which included radical Mexican nationalists choosing to retain their Mexican citizenships and
politically moderate and traditionalist Mexicans who were in the process of
becoming U.S. citizens. In Chicago, Frentistas encouraged Mexicans to support the CIO, but they also asked them to decline U.S. citizenship. Farther
away from the radical influence of the Chicago Frente, Mexican immigrant
neighborhoods tended to be more traditionalist and more amenable to U.S.
naturalization.

As discussed in chapter 2, Mexican traditionalists in Northwest Indiana
had questioned the value of their Mexican citizenship and their loyalty to
the Mexican state during the anticlerical Calles presidency (1924–28) and
the Cristero Rebellion (1926–29). In East Chicago, traditionalists created a
conservative Mexican community that remained largely insulated from the
Mexican liberal and radical political movements of Chicago proper. Most
Mexicans in East Chicago were from the Bajío, and, as other scholars have
explained, the "Bajío had never been an area where the masses took up arms
to fight for the ideals of the Revolution."[68]

Traditionalist societies in Indiana like the Círculo and the Sociedad Mutualista recognized that Mexican steelworkers would benefit from unionization,
but they expressed their support only for unions that respected workers'

religious beliefs.[69] For example, the Círculo denounced the Industrial Workers of the World for their "red socialism and theoretical anarchism," which the Círculo accused of trying to "destroy every religious idea and especially that of the Catholic religion." Although the Círculo attacked the Wobblies, it endorsed the unionization policies of Mexican president Emilio Portes Gil (in office 1928–30), who had helped put an end to the Cristero Rebellion.[70] Under the right circumstances, traditionalists were in favor of unionization and were therefore receptive to the SWOC as an alternative to the Wobblies and other radical labor groups that were thought to be too closely associated with anarchism and Communism.

The majority of Mexicans who joined the SWOC in Northwest Indiana had been longtime members of immigrant societies. Some sixteen Mexican immigrant societies survived the Depression and still functioned in Northwest Indiana into the 1940s. The Mexican members of these societies who became SWOC activists included Basil Pacheco, Miguel Arredondo, Al Garza, Daniel Fernández, and Jesse Rocha, among others.[71] As these Mexicans signed up with the SWOC they began serving as intermediaries between their immigrant organizations and the SWOC, compiling work grievances and mitigating conflicts between Mexican laborers and white steel mill managers.[72] Basil Pacheco was an active member of the Sociedad Mutualista, and he joined SWOC Local 1010 at the Youngstown Sheet and Tube foundry in 1937.[73] Almost every member of Sociedad Mutualista worked at Youngstown, at Inland, or at Gary Works and Carnegie-Illinois Steel, and they all became union members.[74] These Mexicans understood the value in supporting the SWOC, which could enlarge the social welfare net their immigrant societies had established in the region. During the Depression, Pacheco had temporarily lost his job, and he had persevered by relying on the aid he received from the Sociedad Mutualista.[75] SWOC officials understood how important immigrant societies were to Mexican steelworkers and consequently worked closely with their leaders.[76]

Between 1936 and 1940, Pacheco and numerous other Mexican CIO traditionalists began applying for U.S. citizenship.[77] Almost all of these Mexicans had emigrated from the Bajío. The directory of Pacheco's Sociedad Mutualista reveals that 65 percent of the members were from the Bajío, only six members had emigrated from a border state, and no one had emigrated from Mexico City.[78] Assessing naturalization records in East Chicago, Indiana, Francisco Rosales determined that an incredibly high 14 percent of East Chicago's Mexican population naturalized between 1936 and 1945.[79] In Chicago, the Mexican rate of application for naturalization reached its high point of 9 percent in 1920 and decreased every year thereafter.[80] Between 1920 and 1940, Mexican

Chicago was shaped by liberal and radical Mexican nationalists from Mexico City, Tampico, and the border states, while East Chicago was a traditionalist Bajío community through and through and thus had a much higher rate of U.S. naturalization and Democratic Party participation.

After Pacheco became a U.S. citizen, he entered the world of American politics and followed a political curve similar to that of many Mexican Americans in the Southwest. Naturalized Mexican American laborers in East Chicago, like their counterparts in the Southwest, enthusiastically supported Franklin Delano Roosevelt, believing that the New Deal would provide them with more social services, steady employment, and the legal means to contest poor wages and working conditions.[81] In 1942 Pacheco joined the Democratic Party, and within two years he was rallying naturalized and U.S.-born "Mexican Americans" to reelect FDR.[82] The Democratic Party acknowledged Pacheco's service and his influence within the Latino community of Northwest Indiana and offered him a number of leadership roles.[83] For the rest of his life, Pacheco would serve as an active Democrat, devoting himself to labor and community issues that concerned him as an enfranchised Mexican American steelworker.[84]

While Pacheco became a U.S. citizen, he did not disassociate himself from his Mexican cultural roots. Pacheco remained active in the Sociedad Mutualista, continued to speak the Spanish language at cultural and political events, and still celebrated Mexican nationalist holidays. Pacheco embodied the political and ideological shift that had developed within the Bajío community of Mexican immigrants. Catholic Mexican traditionalists had decoupled Mexican citizenship from the Mexican state. Put another way, they had deterritorialized *mexicanidad*, celebrating the Mexican nation and their Mexican heritage, on the one hand, while encouraging Mexicans to become U.S. citizens and American political players, on the other.

As time passed and as the passionate and divisive politics of the revolution waned, ethnic Mexican societies in East Chicago began to consolidate under umbrella organizations that shared a commitment to the Catholic faith, offered ethnic Mexicans social welfare services, and promoted an understanding of Mexican nationalism severed from any allegiance to the Mexican government. In 1955 Pacheco was honored as a lifetime community activist by several Mexican organizations, and they appointed him to serve as the president of an umbrella group called the Comité Patriótico Mexicano (Mexican Patriotic Committee). Mexican revolutionary politics had shaped the Mexican immigrant communities of the United States in ironic and unintentional ways. Pacheco, a naturalized U.S. citizen and active Democrat, was now appointed to serve as the head of a society charged with organizing Mexican patriotic events.[85] Within a year, the Sociedad Mutualista had merged with several other organizations to form the Unión Benéfica Mexicana (UBM).[86] Rising to the vice presidency of the UBM in 1971, Pacheco had devoted his rich life to the ideals of Mexican Catholic unity and service. One of the UBM's contemporary signature projects involved building new Catholic churches in Mexico.[87] Mexican traditionalist political culture, which rejected the anticlericalism and radicalism of the revolution, had led Mexican Catholics like Pacheco to become proud and socially active Mexican Americans.

Conclusion

Historians Zaragosa Vargas and George Sanchez demonstrate that in Texas and California, Mexican Americans and some Mexican immigrants joined the CIO because they were motivated by the CPUSA, by FDR and the New Deal, and by their support of the United States in the Second World War.[88] "Ironically," Sanchez writes, "it was not the search for Mexican nationalism which engendered political radicalism for large numbers of Mexicans and Mexican Americans in the 1930s, but the forging of a new identity as ethnic Americans."[89] As Mexicans continued to become Americans in the Southwest, they joined the CIO and began investing in their lives on this side of the border.

In Chicagoland, radical Mexican immigrants, influenced by the Partido Comunista Mexicano (PCM), also joined the CIO, but they did so because they embraced the brand of radical Mexican nationalism promoted by Mexican *comunistas* and *cardenistas*. Radical Mexicans not only entered the CIO but became labor leaders who were asked to join organizing drives in other cities with Mexican populations, such as Kansas City, St. Paul, and Los Angeles. Mexicans like Refugio Martínez were attracted to the CIO because they had already been won over to a life of political activism and community organizing by their experiences in Mexico during the revolution and by the projects carried out by the PCM-affiliated Frente. These Mexicans fought for workers' rights in the United States and encouraged their countrymen to join the CIO, but they still implored them to remain Mexican citizens. There was an ideological tension between the Marxism and subaltern nationalism of radical Mexicans that reflected both an internationalist "workers of the world unite" ethos and a nationalist loyalty to Mexico that, in one sense, shackled Mexican radicals to their Mexican citizenship.

But radical Mexicans had come to believe they had the right to retain their Mexican citizenship while working in the United States because they understood what many Americans did not: U.S. citizens have a long history of living, working, and profiting in Mexico and other Third World nation-states, and they rarely renounced their U.S. citizenships. If the Americans managing businesses in Mexico were not becoming Mexican citizens, on what grounds should Mexican workers be forced to "change flags"?

Mexican traditionalists also joined the CIO in the 1930s, and many became union leaders, but, unlike the radicals, they applied for U.S. citizenship in significant numbers between 1931 and 1940. The majority of blue-collar (un-skilled, semiskilled, and skilled) Mexican naturalizers in Chicago in these years (about 49 percent) were from the Bajío, the heartland of traditionalist Catholic culture in Mexico. Only 21 percent of working-class naturalizers were from a border state, and only 9 percent were from the Distrito Federal during this period.[90] Mexican CIO radicals were typically from Mexico City, Tampico, and other cities in Mexico that had radical political cultures. It is critical to note, however, that Mexican CIO traditionalists were just as committed to the CIO as the radicals, as evidenced by the blood they shed alongside radical Mexicans and white and black Americans at the Memorial Day Massacre. Unlike the radicals, however, the traditionalists who joined the CIO began advancing their interests in the United States as naturalized U.S. citizens and New Deal Democrats. Traditionalists like Basil Pacheco followed the political arc of many naturalized and U.S.-born Mexican Americans in the Southwest. Pacheco participated in U.S. citizenship drives, rallied newly naturalized Mexican Americans to vote for FDR, and was a lifetime supporter of the Democratic Party, but he also remained active in Mexican traditionalist societies. Mexicans like Pacheco effectively decoupled Mexican nationalist pride from Mexican citizenship, commemorating Mexico, on the one hand, while concurrently encouraging migrants to become American citizens and Democratic Party members, on the other. As American politics turned to the right during the Cold War, Mexican radicals like Refugio Martínez who had chosen to retain their Mexican citizenship would experience a different fate in the United States, for they would be aggressively persecuted by the U.S. government.

6 The Cold War and the Decline of the Revolutionary Generation

> An order of deportation is not a punishment for a crime, but rather is simply a method of enforcing the return to his own country of an alien who has not complied with the conditions . . . to reside here [in the United States].
>
> —Order of deportation issued against Refugio Román Martínez, October 1951

On April 27, 1953, veteran union organizer Refugio Román Martínez received a letter from Marcus T. Neelly, the director of the Chicago area U.S. Department of Immigration and Naturalization Service (INS). The letter explained that on April 28, the following day, Martínez was to board a train for Laredo, Texas. Upon arrival, he was to report to an INS agent, who would process Martínez's deportation into Mexico.[1] Martínez was distraught. He had devoted years of his life to building the Congress of Industrial Organizations (CIO), and he was now going to be deported by the INS. Complicating matters, he had recently suffered a stroke and had informed the INS that he was unfit to travel.[2] What was he to do? If he complied with the INS, where would he live in Mexico, and how would he earn a living given his present condition? More important, what would happen to his wife and his two children, who were U.S. citizens? Ignoring his concerns, the INS deported Martínez. A week later, Martínez's lawyer and friend, Eugene Cotton, wrote to Neelly: "In order that your files may fully reveal the majesty and accomplishment of the law, you may appreciate being advised that [Refugio] died in Mexico last week."[3]

This final chapter assesses the decline of the radical wing of the revolutionary generation through the deportation and death of Refugio Martínez, who was introduced in chapter 5 as one of several radical Mexican nationalists who joined the Packinghouse Workers Organizing Committee (PWOC) in the 1930s and then continued to unionize meatpacking workers through the

United Packinghouse Workers of America (UPWA). Martínez entered the United States legally after the revolution. He organized the unemployed during the Great Depression, helped unionize workers in multiple cities through the PWOC and UPWA, and then was deported by the INS during the Cold War. The INS ostensibly deported Martínez because of his past involvement with the Communist Party of the United States (CPUSA), but the underlying motive for his deportation was his union organizing activities in the Chicago meatpacking industry. While other unionists endured police harassment, arrests, costly trials, and occasional beatings, radical Mexicans like Martínez were also investigated by the INS, which could result in deportation.

By the early 1950s, the decline of the New Deal coalition, the onset of the Cold War and McCarthyism, and the start of an economic recession that began with the end of the Korean War prompted the INS to carry out yet another mass deportation campaign aimed at Mexican immigrants. Between 1951 and what the INS termed "Operation Wetback" in 1954, the U.S. federal government deported more than one million Mexicans. During these Cold War deportations, radical Mexican nationalists found themselves in a vulnerable position. The passage of the McCarran Act of 1950 and McCarran-Walter Act of 1952 added to their distress because these laws projected a Cold War fear of subversion onto immigration policy, establishing that legally residing immigrants who had at one time participated in so-called subversive activities could now be deported for their past behavior. As a radical Mexican labor leader, Martínez was investigated by the Chicago Police Department, the FBI, and the INS, which defined him as a dissident and deported him.

This biographical study of Martínez's struggle with the INS reveals how the Cold War deportations settled the contest between the radicals and traditionalists in favor of the traditionalists. From the Southwest to the Midwest, Mexican and Latino CIO radicals were disciplined and deported by the INS, while Mexican CIO traditionalists, who had already applied for U.S. citizenship in significant numbers, were largely ignored by the INS. Traditionalist community leaders were therefore left in the position to have the greatest influence on the rising generation of young Mexican Americans who witnessed the persecution and deportation of the Mexican CIO radicals who had chosen to retain their Mexican citizenship while organizing unions in the United States. George Sanchez and other historians have shown that in the southwestern United States, young Mexican Americans developed ambivalent American identities after witnessing the Depression-era deportations. In the Chicago region, the Cold War deportations cemented what young ethnic Mexicans and their traditionalist parents had learned during the Depression: U.S. citizenship was not a privilege but a necessary legal shield against deportation.

Disciplining Latino CIO Radicals from the Southwest to the Midwest

During the Cold War, the INS initiated an aggressive operation against Latina/o CIO radicals. The INS did not try to deport every radical, but its public and relentless persecution of key immigrant labor leaders served as an ominous warning to other immigrants interested in supporting the American labor movement. In 1948 the INS launched an investigation of Guatemalan immigrant Luisa Moreno, a well-respected official in the CIO's United Cannery, Agricultural, Packing and Allied Workers of America (UCAPAWA).

Like Martínez, Moreno had become a radical activist well before joining the CIO. Born in Guatemala, Moreno immigrated to Mexico City and began working as a journalist. While in the Distrito Federal, she married a Mexican artist, and the young couple then moved to New York City, where they started a family. In New York, Moreno became involved in Latino antiracist protests against police brutality. A local community activist named Gonzalo González had been organizing pickets in front of theaters that showed films that denigrated Latin Americans. During one picket, policemen came in and attacked González and other protesters. They brutally billy-clubbed González and fractured his skull, killing him. Incensed, Moreno joined with Puerto Rican, South American, and Central American immigrants to protest González's death.[4]

As Moreno became more politically active, she and her husband developed marital problems. They separated, and Moreno started working as a seamstress to support herself and her young daughter. Frustrated by the low wages and sweatshop conditions in the needle trades, Moreno joined the Needles Trades Workers Industrial Union, an affiliate of the Trade Union Unity League, which was a labor federation started by the CPUSA. Through the Needles Trades Union, Moreno befriended several Communists, joined the CPUSA, and then was hired on as a union organizer. Moreno developed a reputation for her ability to unionize Latinos, and the American Federation of Labor (AFL) took notice and recruited her to unionize Latina and African American women in tobacco production in Florida. After the CIO was formed in 1935, Moreno was drawn to its professed commitment to the rank and file. She soon joined the CIO's UCAPAWA, which dispatched her to Texas and then to Southern California to organize Mexican women pecan shellers. By 1938 Moreno was an experienced union organizer, and she was well acquainted with the challenges Spanish-speaking women faced in industrial settings and in American unions. She wanted to create an organization devoted to Latino workers and specifically to Latin American immigrants.

Calling on her contacts in the CIO, CPUSA, and other progressive groups, Moreno helped found El Congreso del Pueblo de Habla Española (El Congreso).[5]

As Mario Garcia's insightful work has demonstrated, Moreno was able to take advantage of the broad social movements that had developed in the 1930s around the issues of joblessness, social welfare, and anti-Fascism. She therefore succeeded in organizing El Congreso chapters in Southern California, Texas, New Mexico, Arizona, and Colorado. Declaring that El Congreso would improve the lives of all Spanish-speaking people in accord with the principles of the U.S. Constitution, Moreno received support from the CIO; progressive groups such as the Women's International League for Peace and Freedom; intellectuals like George I. Sanchez of the University of New Mexico and Carlos Castañeda of the University of Texas; and leftist Hollywood producers, writers, and actors such as Melvyn Douglas of the Screen Actors Guild and John Bright of the League of American Writers. When El Congreso organized its first assembly in Los Angeles, delegates from seventy-three ethnic Mexican societies were present. Their collective membership was estimated at seventy thousand persons. At the following first national convention of El Congreso in Los Angeles in 1939, some fifteen hundred attendees participated in sessions on Latinos and the labor movement, civil rights and discrimination, education and culture, U.S.-Mexico relations, Depression-era relief, and immigrant rights. During the conference, participants waved banners that read "Citizens and Non-Citizens Unite Together" and "In Defense of Our Homes We Struggle Against Deportations."[6]

As a radical immigrant, Moreno was unwavering in her support of immigrant rights and grounded her position in Marxian theory, which held that Mexican immigrants were owed rights based on the wealth they generated for American businesses. Moreno would often repeat, "These people [Mexican immigrants] are not aliens—they have contributed their endurance, sacrifices, youth and labor to the Southwest. Indirectly, they have paid more taxes than all of the stockholders of California's industrialized agriculture, the sugar beet companies and the large cotton interests that operate or have operated with the labor of Mexican workers."[7] Moreno's passionate immigrant rights activism attracted U.S-raised and U.S.-born ethnic Mexicans who sympathized with Mexican nationals on a kinship level.

Through El Congreso, Moreno befriended Mexican immigrant Josefina Fierro, a tireless community activist, and Bert Corona, a gifted Mexican American labor organizer who worked for the CIO's International Longshoremen's and Warehousemen's Union (ILWU). Fierro was born in Mexicali, Mexico. Her father fought in Pancho Villa's northern army during the revolution, and her maternal grandmother and mother were Magonistas. Through her parents, Fierro was raised in a proud Mexico-centered radical culture. As Fierro would explain of her mother, "She taught us to fight discrimination. She taught us to organize [and] that it wasn't a shame to be Mexican."[8] While attending college, Fierro worked in a club and met the Hollywood screenwriter John Bright. They later married, and Bright introduced Fierro to the "Hollywood Left." Drawing on the financial support of her husband and his contacts, Fierro started organizing protests against companies in Los Angeles that discriminated against Mexican workers. Her activism led her to join El Congreso, through which she rose to the position of executive secretary.[9]

Like Fierro, Bert Corona was influenced by the radical politics of the revolution. Corona's father was also a follower of Pancho Villa, and he remained politically active in Mexico after the revolution. Corona's father had taught the young Bert that ordinary people needed to organize their communities to defend their interests. Corona's mother was a middle-class Mexican Protestant who believed in the democratic ideals of the revolution, and she was very supportive of her husband's community activism. At times, the Coronas lived on both sides of the U.S.-Mexico border. While embroiled in a political campaign in Chihuahua in 1924, Corona's father and a group of his supporters were assassinated. This tragedy had a profound impact on Bert, who saw his father as a champion of social justice. The Coronas moved to Texas and then to Los Angeles, where Bert joined various political causes. While working in a factory in L.A., Corona was recruited into the emerging ILWU. Corona was incredibly charismatic and innovative in his organizing techniques, and he contributed significantly to the growth of ILWU Local 26, which unionized more than six thousand workers between 1939 and 1941. Through the ILWU, Corona befriended Moreno and Fierro and then joined El Congreso.[10]

El Congreso brought Moreno, Fierro, and Corona together with Humberto Silex, a Nicaraguan immigrant and a dynamic leader in the CIO's International Union of Mine, Mill, and Smelter Workers (IUMMSW), and with Refugio Martínez of the CIO's PWOC. Silex was born in Managua in 1903. He legally immigrated into the United States in 1921 and worked in Texas, Missouri, and then Chicago. While in Chicago, Silex was disturbed to read about the U.S. occupation of Nicaragua. As Silex recalled, "I remember . . . reading once in a newspaper [in Chicago] that the U.S. Marines had destroyed Chinandega, a village in Nicaragua, with bombs from the air—the first time this was done anywhere."[11] When Silex heard that Socrates Sandino (Augusto Cesar Sandino's brother) and other Nicaraguan nationalists were in Chicago organizing fundraisers, he attended their events and donated what little money he had to bring an end to the U.S. occupation. From Chicago, Silex returned to Texas, settled down in El Paso, and married a Mexican woman who was from the border state of Chihuahua. Their first child was born in Juárez, Mexico. To support his new family, Silex began working at the American Smelting and Refining Company and was quickly reminded that in Texas, Mexicans "worked like slaves and were ill-treated and discriminated against everywhere."[12] Determined to improve the quality of life of Spanish-speaking workers, Silex reached out to the CIO and founded IUMMSW Local 509 in El Paso and then built the local from the ground up. Between 1942 and 1945, Silex served his local as an organizer, secretary, treasurer, and then president. He then was asked to represent the union as a national representative for district 2, which had jurisdiction over the majority of the states in the Southwest. Silex led the IUMMSW through a number of successful strikes against ASARCO and Phelps Dodge.[13]

Silex succeeded in winning strikes where American unionists often failed because he established a working relationship with the Cárdenas-affiliated Confederación de Trabajadores de México (CTM) in Ciudad Juárez, which cajoled, intimidated, and prevented Mexican workers from crossing the border and strikebreaking in El Paso. On several occasions Silex traveled to Juárez to meet with CTM president Vicente Lombardo Toledano and to participate in demonstrations of binational labor solidarity. During one of these events, Silex and five hundred members of the IUMMSW crossed into Juárez and joined more than ten thousand CTM members in a massive labor parade. Silex was a known radical who frequently denounced Fascism, and when he was given the opportunity to address the parade, he passionately declared, "The workers of North America are united with our working brothers in Mexico in the great fight that humanity wages against its greatest enemy, international fascism."[14] While Nazi Germany and Fascist Italy had been defeated during the war, Silex and other Latino unionists often reminded their coworkers that Fascists had won the war in Spain. Silex would often take these types of opportunities to start conversations about Fascism. Like other radical Latinos, Silex believed that the superexploitation of Latinos and African Americans in the United States was made possible by a culture of Fascist-like racism. For Silex and other IUMMSW activists, many Americans subscribed to jingoistic beliefs about the United States that were Fascist in the way they were rooted in notions of white supremacy. As a fellow IUMMSW organizer would explain after a successful strike, "The victory of the Phelps Dodge workers under the CIO banner will be a blow in the face of all the fascist-minded employers who utilize racial and national discrimination as a means of paying starvation wages."[15]

In 1949 the Mexican immigrant and Mexican American members of the IUMMSW joined with El Congreso activists in Phoenix, Arizona, and created the Asociación Nacional México-Americana (ANMA), which stood for "the protection of the civil, economic, and political rights of the Mexican people in the United States."[16] Like El Congreso, ANMA was started by Latinos who were closely connected to Mexican immigrants. ANMA held multiple conventions throughout the Southwest, and during its first national gathering in Los Angeles in 1950, ANMA announced it would unify Mexican immigrants and Mexican Americans, aggressively challenge deportations, and develop what ANMA called the "Mexican connection," what ANMA members described as the "organic ties" that Mexican Americans felt toward the Mexican nation.[17]

Between 1949 and 1953, ANMA engaged in various political struggles. In 1950 ANMA activists joined the broader American peace movement in opposition to the Korean War (1950–53). ANMA compiled Mexican casualty statistics from World War II and the Korean War to reveal that ethnic Mexicans shouldered an unfair share of the costs of U.S. wars. Although Mexican Americans represented only 17 percent of the population of Texas, they stood for 30 percent of the state's casualties during the Korean War, and these unfair and lopsided casualty rates were similar in other southwestern states. Challenging racial discrimination, the ANMA organized antiracist protests against newspapers, radio shows, and advertisers that depicted Mexicans and Latinos in stereotypical ways. In some cases, the ANMA succeeded in pressuring corporate donors to pull their sponsorships. ANMA activists also confronted racism within the criminal justice system. ANMA chapters in Los Angeles, in Sonora, Arizona, and in Fierro, New Mexico, led protests against the deaths of Mexican nationals and Mexican Americans at the hands of police officers. Understanding that the vast majority of ethnic Mexicans in the United States, regardless of their citizenship status, were working-class people, the ANMA petitioned the United Nations Commission on Human Rights to investigate the labor abuses of Mexican farm workers and pressured CIO unions to organize all ethnic Mexicans. When addressing Mexican American civil rights, the ANMA persistently internationalized the discussion, arguing that anti-Mexican racism was directly related to U.S. imperialism in Mexico and Latin America.[18]

Over the course of the Cold War, the INS marked ANMA activists and Latino labor leaders for deportation. In 1952 J. Edgar Hoover ordered the FBI to assess the citizenship status of ANMA organizers, while the INS independently investigated the backgrounds of the "subversive resident aliens" who attended ANMA events.[19] The attorney general of the United States classified the ANMA as a subversive organization, and INS and FBI harassment jointly contributed to the ANMA's collapse. In Southern California, Luisa Moreno had been unionizing cannery workers through UCAPAW Local 64 and was starting to investigate cases of police and military abuse of Mexicans who lived near U.S. military bases in San Diego. Moreno made powerful enemies in San Diego, including California state senator Jack B. Tenney, who described Moreno as a "parasitic menace" and had her investigated as a security threat to the United States.[20] After a three-year investigation, the INS deported Moreno in 1950. When Fierro de Bright learned she was also under investigation and was going to be arrested and interrogated, she fled to Mexico. The INS tried to deport Humberto Silex on the grounds that he had a subversive relationship with CTM president Lombardo. The IUMMSW used its legal resources to back Silex, and the union managed to stop Silex's deportation. Bert Corona was also investigated, and he avoided deportation by proving he had been born in Texas.[21] Other Latino CIO unionists were less fortunate. Armando Dávila, Frank Martínez, Frank Corona, Tony Salgado, and Fred Chávez were all investigated by the INS.[22] In some cases, Mexican unionists like Davila, a leader in the United Furniture Workers, were deported quickly. In others, the INS repeatedly arrested and interrogated radical Mexican unionists for years before finally deporting them.

The deportation experience of the UPWA's Refugio Martínez reveals both the resiliency of radical Latino unionists and the antiunion motives of the U.S. government in pursuing these labor and community leaders. The INS only began to investigate Martínez after he gained a prominent reputation as a CIO organizer. He had been questioned in the early 1930s as a community activist, but it was his union organizing that drew the ire of the Chicago police department and the INS. Martínez's ordeal began back in 1938, when he and other PWOC activists stood at the gates of the Swift and Armour meatpacking plants, pleading with workers to join the CIO.[23] Several days prior, Martínez had been arrested on charges of "disorderly conduct" while leafleting in the stockyards. Undeterred, Martínez returned to the plants and was arrested again. Twice arrested, Martínez boldly refused to stop organizing. While Martínez was speaking to a group of workers about the CIO, he was apprehended yet again by the police. According to Refugio, the police officers became "vile" because they had "come in quite late. I was rid of the leaflets already." The officers hauled Martínez to a police station, threatened to beat him, and informed him they were going to call the INS because they had discovered that he was not a U.S. citizen.[24] Given that no law barred noncitizens from union organizing, the officers were acting less on the letter of the law and more on their own nationalist, racialist, and antiunion convictions.

Several hours later, INS agent John J. Marsh arrived at the police station. Marsh quickly attempted to establish that Martínez was unworthy of U.S. residency, a charge that was easy to corroborate, given that Martínez embodied the kind of immigrant that the INS had historically tried to exclude from the United States. While living in the United States, Martínez had accepted welfare, had a child out of wedlock, and participated in leftist political activities. Now he was working as a union organizer. The INS typically refused to admit an immigrant if it believed that he or she could become a public charge. With the onset of the Depression, the State Department took the proactive initiative of denying visas to immigrants on the grounds they were an impending LPC, "likely to become a public charge."[25] U.S. government agencies did not recognize the irony in defining immigrants as both laborers who generated incredible wealth for U.S. companies and laborers thoroughly unentitled to public assistance.

After confirming that Martínez had indeed accepted welfare during the Depression (his first offense against the U.S. state), Marsh turned to intimate matters, questions that highlighted the normative dimensions of U.S. immigration policy. Marsh learned that Martínez had an "illegitimate daughter" with a "common law wife."[26] The Immigration Service, the predecessor of the INS, had deported immigrants who violated middle-class sexual norms such as having children out of wedlock.[27] Marsh was subtly but methodically building a deportation case against Martínez. After Martínez answered another question about his daughter, Alexandra, a "plain-clothes [police] officer" began "heckling" him, calling Alexandra a "bastard child." Martínez sassed the officer right back and was immediately grasped by three policemen, who began roughing him up. Martínez pleaded with Marsh, asking him to "stop those people from doing all those things." Marsh apologized for their behavior but proceeded with the interrogation.[28] Through this time-tested method (some officers act civilly, while others behave aggressively), Martínez was being worn down.

After Martínez had been rattled by the police, Agent Marsh tried to trap Martínez into perjuring himself. The INS had considerable state resources at its disposal, and Marsh was already aware that Martínez had been a member of the CPUSA.[29] During the early years of the Depression, Martínez had joined the party and worked with the CP-affiliated Unemployed Councils of Chicago. Martínez had even been questioned by the FBI about these activities. Finding no cause to charge him with a crime, the FBI had released him but continued to monitor his activities. Marsh had access to Martínez's FBI file, and he used it in an attempt to catch Martínez in a lie. Marsh began, "Have you ever been a member of the Communist Party at any time?" "Yes," answered Martínez, and he explained that he had joined the party in 1932 but had "dropped out three years ago." Marsh then asked Martínez if he had read the "Programme of the Communist International," which described the party and outlined the conditions of party membership. "I've read it," replied Martínez. Marsh quoted from the document: "The Communists disdain to conceal their views and aims. They openly declare that their aims can be attained only by the forcible overthrow of all the existing social conditions. Let the ruling class tremble at a Communistic revolution. The proletarians have nothing to lose but their chains. They have a world to win." "Have you ever read that paragraph before?" taunted Marsh. "No," answered Refugio, definitively. Marsh continued, "Have you ever read the constitution and rules of the Communist International?" "Yes, I think I read it," admitted Martínez. Marsh read paragraph 3, which stated that one could only be a member of the CPUSA if one paid party dues.[30] Martínez acknowledged that he remembered reading this section of the "Programme."

If Marsh could maneuver Martínez into admitting that the CPUSA advocated overthrowing governments, Martínez would be in violation of several U.S. laws. So Marsh now pressed Martínez, forcing him to explain what the CPUSA meant when it claimed that its "aims" could be attained "only by the forcible overthrow of all the existing social conditions." Thoughtfully, Martínez answered that he had always interpreted the CPUSA's aims "according to the provisions in the [U.S.] Constitution." Marsh now challenged Martínez, how then do you "interpret the last paragraph on page 34 of the pamphlet, which I quoted and you read . . . 'The Bourgeoisie resorts to every means of violence and terror'?" "Concentration camps [and] refusal of Democratic rights," retorted Martínez. "Why [then] did you leave the Communist Party?" explored Marsh. "No reason, I just left on my own accord," said Refugio. "You still believe in the principles of the Communist Party?" questioned Marsh. "Yes," affirmed Refugio. Undoubtedly struck by Refugio's admission, Marsh probed deeper. "Do you believe in the overthrow of the US Gov[ernmen]t by force?" "No," avowed Refugio. "I believe in the evolution of Society or by the will of the people according to the Constitution."[31]

A seasoned political activist, Martínez was attempting to play on the patriotic sensibilities of his captors by reframing himself as a democratic political activist who believed the U.S. Constitution and U.S. democratic culture were outgrowths of the "will of the people." Martínez, like many radicals, saw the value in the rule of law and in constitutional rights and aspired to create a more democratic American society, but he also belonged to organizations that defined the United States as an empire and not as a democracy. In addition to joining the CPUSA, Martínez was a leader in the Frente Popular Mexicano, a radical Mexican nationalist organization that characterized the United States as a country that practiced imperialism, but he was not about to share this critical and nuanced interpretation of the United States with the INS. Martínez needed to protect himself; he needed to "wear the mask," for he understood that most Americans did not define the United States as an empire.[32] Martínez was eventually released, but the INS nevertheless flagged him as a dissident and began taking steps to deport him. He had been arrested first as an Unemployed Council activist and then as a union organizer, but the police could never charge him with a serious crime. They consequently called in the INS, which specialized in prosecuting noncitizens.

As the United States prepared to enter World War II, the federal government augmented its security measures and transferred the INS from the Department of Labor to the Department of Justice (DOJ). Congress then passed the Alien Registration Act (the Smith Act) and the Nationality Act of 1940. The former required noncitizens to register with the INS and stipulated that immigrants who conspired to overthrow governments could be imprisoned; the latter denied citizenship to immigrants who violated the Smith Act. The Smith Act largely amended the antianarchist Dillingham-Hardwick Act of 1918, which had been used to arrest thousands of European immigrants during a period of labor militancy in the years after World War I.[33] A wave of union organizing had swept across the United States during the Depression, and the federal government was recalibrating immigration and naturalization laws to punish and, if needed, to deport radical immigrants.

Martínez and the other Latin American migrants who helped build the CIO made considerable sacrifices for the American labor movement. The UPWA noted that Martínez "figured prominently in the early organizing days of the PWOC" and helped establish the UPWA in Chicago, Kansas City, St. Paul, and Los Angeles. In short, "Brother Martinez ha[d] rendered excellent service to the packinghouse workers and made an excellent contribution in the building of our organization."[34] Yet after ten years of union work, Martínez did not own a home in the United States or in Mexico and possessed less than $2,000 in valuable assets. His modest earnings and long work-related trips, which could keep him away from his family for months at a time, took a financial and emotional toll on him and his loved ones.[35] In 1941 the DOJ issued a warrant for Martínez on the grounds that he was in violation of the Smith Act because he had once been a member of the CPUSA.[36] Martínez's family, already distressed by the demands of his union work, became overwrought by this development.

A Modern Inquisition

The INS interrogated Martínez multiple times between 1946 and 1948, and these investigations reveal that the INS did not need to collect much evidence in order to deport and devastate the lives of immigrants.[37] Although the INS had uncovered no substantial evidence against Martínez, the agency continued to pursue him for his alleged past membership in the CPUSA. Lacking evidence but possessing legal and punitive power over noncitizens, the INS attempted to pressure Martínez into admitting his ostensible crime, his radical politics, his modern-day heresy against the U.S. government. When Martínez's hearings are assessed together, they suggest that the INS also sought to coerce him into incriminating his supporters, most notably, other members of the UPWA.

During his hearings Martínez often represented himself, and he was frequently questioned by INS agents Ralph W. Lockwood and Irving I. Freedman. As it became clear that the INS was going to continue to arrest and interrogate Martínez, the UPWA hired a defense attorney named Jack Freeman to represent Martínez. When Freeman began defending Martínez, he understood that Martínez's politics were on trial, and he therefore set out to establish that Martínez was no security threat to the United States. "During the time that you were a member of the [Communist] party," Freeman asked Martínez in front of several INS agents, "did you ever engage in military drilling?" "No," answered Martínez. Freeman asked Martínez if he ever engaged in "making hand grenades or bombs," in "activity of or attempting sabotage," in "firing firearms," or in "learning or teaching others how to assassinate public officials of the United States." "No, sir," Refugio consistently replied.[38]

Freeman then attempted, albeit unsuccessfully, to insert the politics of race into Martínez's case. INS officials allowed Freeman to all but mock them and the charges of subversion against Martínez, but they would not allow him to discuss racism. Freeman began this line of defense by asking Martínez to explain why he believed he had been investigated as a union organizer. Martínez claimed he could not say. Freeman offered Martínez a rationale: "Is it merely because you were a Mexican?" "I suppose," responded Martínez. An INS agent quickly objected to this line of questioning and was sustained by the INS presiding inspector, who served in the role of judge during the INS hearings. The INS had incredible leeway and authority to arrest, prosecute, and judge noncitizens, and it promptly established that questions about race would have no place in Martínez's hearings.[39]

INS agents Lockwood and Freedman must have realized that their investigation was coming up short. They had thus far revealed nothing that the agency did not already know, so the agents fell back on the broadly deportable offense of "likely to become a public charge." The INS had established that Martínez had received welfare during the Depression, and now they wanted to show that his poverty defined him as a neglectful parent. INS agents asked Martínez several questions about his family, and Martínez divulged that his wife had recently fallen ill, and, for a time, he had been forced to place his two children in the care of a family that resided in Kansas City. Agent Lockwood focused in on the public welfare issue at hand, namely, monetary child support. "Did you contribute to the support of your children while they were in Kansas City?" inquired Lockwood. "Yes," said Martínez. "How much?" challenged Lockwood. "[A]round $10 a week for each child, as I stated before," specified Martínez, clearly irritated by the implications of the question. "Twenty dollars a week for the two children?" scoffed Lockwood. "Yes," asserted Martínez.[40]

During these interrogations, Martínez was frequently reminded of his wife's illness and of his two daughters, who had lived apart from him for some time. Questions about the welfare of his children and the entire process of interrogation were starting to undermine Martínez's mental health, and the INS took this opportunity to tie his current union work to his past CPUSA activities. Inquiries about the union always seemed to unnerve Martínez, for over the course of his hearings he tried to protect his radical labor allies from the INS. After the INS agents reestablished that Martínez possessed a lengthy arrest record, Martínez attempted to explain that he had been arrested as an Unemployed Council activist, but the majority of his arrests occurred as a result of his "activities in the union, distribution of leaflets, something of that sort." Sensing Martínez's fatigue, Lockwood showed Martínez an FBI dossier in his name: "I present for your examination a report from the Federal Bureau of Investigation . . . in the name of Refugio Roman Martínez." Intending to shock Martínez with the file, the INS officers now aimed their questions at the more important prize. "Was the PWOC a member of the Communist Party?" asked Agent Lockwood. "No," avowed Martínez, "it was a committee of the Packinghouse Workers of America." Martínez was clearly troubled by this question. "Was the Unemployed Council part of the Communist Party?" asked Agent Freedman. "The only thing I know, most of the people, the ones who really was fighting for the interest of the people," answered Martínez. "I am asking," demanded Agent Freedman, irritated by Refugio's convoluted answer, "was the Unemployed Council a part of the Communist Party?" "No, I don't know," groaned Refugio. Freedman now needled Martínez: "Which people were helping the unemployed, the Unemployed Council or the Communist Party?" "The Unemployed Councils," confirmed

Refugio, trying to shift the conversation away from the PWOC. "You say you joined the [CPUSA] because they were helping the unemployed—they were the only ones that did not take any money?" tested Freedman. "The other people within the Unemployed Council," Refugio tried to explain, "were those who were branded as Communists, most active people, and among them one approached me to join."[41] Refugio rambled on, then broke under the pressure:

> The charge I am charged for, I did not believe in; I did not deny I was a member of the Party. . . . [S]econdly, I got children born in the United States. I got a wife, she is sick, I am supporting the wife and children. . . . I think I am capable of doing better for the United States than I can do in Mexico. I am lawfully admitted and have lived in this country for the last 22 years. . . . I am willing to prove my loyalty through my activity. . . . I hold a pretty good position in the Mexican colony [and] can get persons to testify in my character.[42]

The INS listened to Refugio's exasperated plea and then concluded the hearings. After several lengthy interrogations, the INS was still essentially accusing Martínez of nothing more than a past membership in the CPUSA, a charge Martínez had disclosed to the INS. After the 1948 hearing, the INS added that Martínez had once distributed CPUSA literature, a charge the INS appears to have extrapolated from Martínez's union leafleting. By the INS's own account, Martínez had not been a member of the CPUSA for a decade, he had never perjured himself, and yet the INS still ordered "the alien be deported to Mexico."[43]

Reconsidering Becoming American

As it became clear that Martínez was to be deported, his radical and multiracial American community came to his defense.[44] In Chicago, Martínez was supported by Mexican nationals, Mexican Americans, white Americans, progressive organizations, and his union, the UPWA. Mexican Americans backed Martínez because they were connected to Mexican nationals through familial bonds. Mexican Americans could not easily accept that immigrants constituted their primary obstacle to higher wages and improved working conditions. In many ways, Mexican Chicago was more intimately connected to Mexico than many of the Mexican-origin communities of the Southwest. Mexicans had migrated to Chicago during the early twentieth century; by contrast, Spanish-speaking communities had emerged in the Southwest as early as the seventeenth century. Mexican Americans had come of age in several states in the Southwest by the 1920s, whereas an influential Mexican American leadership would not develop in Chicago until the 1940s. By these years in the Southwest, a Mexican American generation was actively competing with immigrants for jobs, resources, and even the cultural representation of the ethnic Mexicans of the United States. Consequently, while some ethnic Mexican organizations in the Southwest, such as the ANMA, defended immigrants, organizations led by Mexican Americans, such as the League of United Latin American Citizens (LULAC), were more ambivalent about Mexican nationals and, at times, accepted and even endorsed their deportation.[45]

Mexican Americans in the Chicago area typically united with and defended immigrants, in part because most Mexican Americans had been raised by two Mexico-born parents. Between 1900 and 1940, roughly 863 married Mexican immigrants applied for U.S. citizenship in Chicago, and 77 percent of these Mexican naturalizers had married a Mexico-born spouse (see table 13 in the appendix). In total, the Mexicans who married other Mexicans tended to have more children than those who married Americans, European immigrants, and non-Mexican Latin Americans. While some 218 marriages between two Mexican nationals raised three to five children in Chicago, only 14 marriages between a Mexican immigrant and an American-born spouse did the same (see table 14 in the appendix). Out of a total of 623 children who were born to Mexican naturalizers, 48 percent of these children were born in Illinois and had been raised in Mexican Chicago surrounded by Mexican nationals. Another 30 percent of these children were born in Mexico but were raised in Chicago (see table 15 in the appendix). These Mexican American children could empathize with immigrants because of their family affinities, but they also characterized themselves as Americans because they had been raised in the United States and were, in many ways, loyal U.S. citizens.

Young Mexican Americans who advocated immigrant rights were often the children of immigrants and expressed emotional pain and frustration when discussing the deportations of Mexican nationals. As a teenager, Mexico-born but U.S.-raised John Gutiérrez witnessed Mexican deportees herded into railroad boxcars during the Depression. Bob Flores was only seven years old during the Depression-era deportations but remembered the anguish he felt when he saw his grandmothers deported. "The train was full," evoked Flores. "There were people lined up by the train, very emotionally upset. I watched both grandmothers . . . [Flores went silent at this point during the interview]."[46] Jesse Villalpando was a toddler when city officials came to escort his mother to a deportation train. Villalpando recalled his mother telling him how she frantically fought off the city officials who came to deport her, demanding she be allowed to remain in the United States, given that her two sons were U.S.-born Americans. Unsure as to how to deal with this strong-willed Mexican woman, the officials simply left and never returned.[47] These deportation experiences deeply affected young Mexican Americans into the Cold War years.

In the 1950s, John Gutiérrez, now an active member of the United Steel-workers of America, was walking near his home in East Chicago, Indiana, with an Italian American coworker when two "fellows in suits stopped me," recalled Gutierrez. They identified themselves as "Immigration [agents]" and then curtly demanded, "Let me see your papers." As a veteran of the Second World War, Gutierrez was appalled by their request. His coworker, shaken by the agents' behavior, simply uttered, "I'm Italian," at which point they released him but continued to detain Gutierrez. Gutierrez was eventually permitted to leave, but he was "really bothered by the fact that they [the agents] only detained me and not my Italian friend." Gutierrez would later learn of Martínez's case and that of other Latino labor leaders, and he would try to stop their deportations.[48]

While these Mexican Americans stood with immigrants, as Mexican Chicago transitioned into the hands of the second generation, they largely abandoned the anti-imperialist and Marxian arguments in defense of immigrant rights that the radical wing of the revolutionary generation had expressed in the 1930s. The political activities of the Mexican Civic Committee illuminate this point. Founded in Chicago in the early 1940s by self-identified "Mexican Americans," the committee's mission was to integrate ethnic Mexicans into "the social and economic life of America." The committee's community ties to Mexican nationals obliged it to defend immigrants, but it did so largely through a discourse of American patriotism. When the committee learned of Martínez, members came to his defense, distributing literature that argued that Martínez's deportation endangered "the democratic rights of the American people." After all, the committee argued, the United States was founded on the principles of "Freedom" and "Liberty" and had a history of openly embracing immigrants. "Isn't this the America our ancestors came to," asserted the committee, "looking for Freedom of speech, and Freedom of religion? It seems we have forgotten what the Statue of Liberty represents." Disregarding the long history of racially restrictive U.S. naturalization and immigration acts, from the Naturalization Act of 1790, which limited naturalization to persons deemed "white," to the explicitly racialist Chinese Exclusion Act of 1882, the committee reinforced a race-neutral myth of American immigration policy as it rallied Americans to support Martínez.[49]

Throughout the Cold War, however, radical immigrant unionists in Chicago received more overall assistance than what was offered to radical immigrant unionists in the Southwest.[50] The Mexican Midwest identified with Mexicans and Mexico, and in multiethnic cities like Cleveland and Chicago, white American liberals had founded organizations and settlement houses to help transition immigrants into American society. As settlement house activists and the Chicago division of an organization called the American Committee for the Protection of the Foreign Born heard about Martínez, they began raising funds to defend him and several European immigrant CIO organizers who were also under INS indictment. The American Committee appears to have been founded by Communists, but it was sustained by liberals who supported immigrant rights. In order to attract broad public support, the American Committee avoided discussing U.S. interventions in Latin America and class arguments about the Mexican people's contributions to the U.S. economy. Instead, the American Committee defended immigrants through a discourse of American nationalism, going so far as to redefine Martínez as one of many "Mexican-American . . . victims of the Justice Department's deportation drive."[51] Faced with the reality that thousands of Mexican and European immigrants were working and living in the United States but had not yet applied for U.S. citizenship, the American Committee tactically chose to characterize these immigrant workers as "Americans" in its literature while concurrently acknowledging their "non-citizen" status. The UPWA followed a similar public strategy, describing Martínez as an "AMERICAN [emphasis in original]" who had "proven himself a good American by his devotion toward a better world for everyone."[52] Unfortunately, the INS did not share this global and more inclusive "citizen of the world" definition of Americanness.

The calculated rhetoric of the Mexican Civic Committee, the American Committee, and the UPWA, all representative of the immigrant rights community of the late 1940s and 1950s, reflected the contradiction between globalization and nationalism that continues to challenge immigrant rights activists to this day. On one level, members of the immigrant rights community recognized that an integrated and asymmetrical global capitalist economy compelled people to migrate. On the other hand, they rarely considered the ways specific U.S. foreign practices in Latin America prodded Latin Americans to immigrate to the United States. The antiradical and jingoistic culture of the Cold War further complicated the work of American immigration activists, who now had to conceive of ways to publicly support foreign nationals in the United States while steering clear of all radical and internationalist arguments, which were deemed too un-American for the general public in light of the conservative political climate of the country.

Liberal Americans ultimately argued that immigrants were owed support because they were helping to build the CIO, one of the pillars of the New Deal.

The liberals who advocated this perspective recognized the contribution of noncitizens to the CIO, but they inadvertently depreciated the labor of the hundreds of thousands of Mexican immigrants who remained unincorporated by the CIO. These Mexican nationals may not have been CIO members and New Deal voters, but they were harvesting the crops and producing the goods that Americans consumed and that added to the wealth of the U.S. economy. More problematic still, the liberal defense of immigrants coupled immigrant rights to FDR and the Democratic Party, which led immigrant rights activists to generate countless criticisms of post-FDR Republican politicians, all of which circumvented discussions about American corporate and government policies in Latin America, policies and practices that exiled Mexicans, Puerto Ricans, Central Americans, and others out of their countries of origin.[53]

These criticisms aside, progressive Americans passionately defended Martínez and other immigrants during the Cold War, and without their support, these immigrants would have been practically unable to legally defend themselves against the U.S. government. In 1948 the UPWA hired Eugene Cotton to serve as its general counsel and then asked him to build a second legal case in defense of Martínez. From the start, Cotton advised Martínez to apply for U.S. citizenship, and Martínez, now desperate, conceded. The INS promptly rejected Martínez's application and then served him with a notice of deportation. The INS had uncovered no substantial evidence against Martínez. It was essentially prosecuting him by criminalizing his past behavior. In fact, Cotton's amended complaint to the U.S. District Court in Chicago explained that the charges against Martínez violated the ex post facto provisions of the U.S. Constitution. The INS was prosecuting Martínez for violating the 1940 Smith Act in 1932. Two years later, Cotton received a reply from the U.S. District Court explaining that Martínez's deportation was not an ex post facto violation, because this constitutional provision had "no application to deportation proceedings for the reason that an order of deportation [was] not a punishment for a crime, but rather [was] simply a method of enforcing the return . . . of an alien" to his or her country of origin.[54] Disingenuously, the court claimed that Martínez was not being disciplined for either his past CPUSA membership or his current union organizing. He was simply being "return[ed]" to Mexico.

The Bracero Program and the Cold War Deportations

Martínez's former attorney had defended him in the waning years of the New Deal and its liberal political culture. Eugene Cotton was defending Martínez in the 1950s, a conservative decade marked by extreme American nationalism and anti-Mexican nativism. The public critique of Mexicans that developed during the Cold War was, in part, an outcome of the Bracero Program (1942–64), which increased the number of authorized and unauthorized Mexican entries into the United States. Large-scale farms in California began calling for the importation of Mexican contract workers with the start of the Second World War. The farmers claimed they were going to face labor shortages when war production pulled farmworkers out of agricultural fields and into war industries. Conceding to these requests, the United States started a labor-contract program with Mexico that was supposed to expire with the end of the war but instead lasted for twenty-two years. In total, the program offered Mexican workers more than 4.5 million labor contracts, and over its duration, more than 2 million Mexicans entered the United States as legally contracted bracero workers.[55]

The Bracero Program affected Mexican immigrant communities and the political climate of the United States in several far-reaching ways. To begin, bracero workers represented yet another generation of Mexican immigrants. Braceros were typically young men between the ages of seventeen and twenty-two (women were excluded from the program). The majority had not participated in the revolution, most were not invested in revolutionary politics, and most were too young to have even experienced the radical Cárdenas presidency. The majority of braceros had come of age in a relatively conservative Mexico that witnessed the decline of *cardenismo* after 1940 and the rise of the PRI political party under the presidency of Manuel Ávila Camacho, a professed Catholic and staunch anti-Communist. While many braceros did not personally experience the Cristero Rebellion (1926–29), the majority of braceros emigrated from the traditionalist agricultural Bajío region of Mexico. Between 1942 and 1954, 74 percent of braceros emigrated from the Bajío (from the states of Jalisco, Michoacán, Guanajuato, and Aguascalientes) and the adjacent states of Zacatecas and Durango. Between 1951 and the end of the Bracero Program in 1964, less than 1.5 percent of braceros emigrated from the more liberal and radical Distrito Federal.[56] Entering the United States as contract workers, braceros focused their time and energy on earning and saving wages as opposed to building political communities and social movements. Deborah Cohen found that many braceros aspired to "become modern workers," and during their return trips to Mexico they "showed off clothes, electronics, and information that conveyed a modern knowledge."[57] Generally speaking, it appears that most braceros eschewed social transformative politics and instead focused on accumulating enough capital to buy land or to start a business upon their return to Mexico.

Braceros may not have been a part of the revolutionary generation, but they were by no means "cheap and docile workers." While much of the data that we have collected on braceros remain incomplete, in just a two-year period out of the program's twenty-two-year history, braceros filed more than eleven thousand formal complaints against U.S. employers, and each complaint often included the grievances of dozens of signatories. U.S. growers did not always comply with the program's stipulations. Some growers underpaid braceros, illegally deducted money from their wages, placed them in occupationally hazardous situations, offered them substandard housing and rations, and, at times, physically assaulted them. Braceros responded by filing complaints, organizing work stoppages and strikes, and "skipping" on their contracts, that is, walking out of the fields in search of fairer, safer, and more remunerative work elsewhere. In doing so, these braceros became "illegals" or "wetbacks," as they were called by their detractors.[58]

The braceros who became "illegals" added to the growing undocumented Mexican population of the United States, which increased in size every single year over the course of the Bracero Program.[59] As Mexicans from the Bajío and other agricultural regions migrated to bracero recruitment centers located along the U.S.-Mexico border, they often had difficulty securing bracero contracts because the process involved passing security clearances and health inspections and paying numerous fees and bribes. The migrants who arrived at the border and were stymied by this bureaucracy increasingly crossed the border illegally. The U.S. government understood that this was happening, and, in many ways, it facilitated these illegal entries. U.S. growers wanted access to superprofitable (so-called cheap labor), mobile, and nonunion laborers, and they were accustomed to employing Mexicans when they needed them. Prior to the Bracero Program, conscientious Border Patrol agents in Texas and Arizona complained and even testified under oath during congressional hearings that they were pressured by agribusiness interests to suspend their apprehension duties during harvest times. With the start of the Bracero Program, the Border Patrol institutionalized a catch-and-release approach to undocumented immigration that acceded to the needs of growers. When workers were needed on large farms during harvests, apprehended undocumented immigrants would be taken to the border, asked to walk across to Mexico and then back again into the United States, and then promptly processed as new braceros. The INS referred to this process as "drying out wetbacks." Critics of the Bracero Program spotlighted these problematic procedures and charged that the federal government was, intentionally or not, facilitating the entry of "illegal aliens." After the war, Congress became divided between senators and congressmen from the Northeast and Midwest who argued in favor of border enforcement and an end to the Bracero Program and those from California, Arizona, and Texas whose agricultural constituencies wanted the federal government to continue to support their historic access to Mexican labor. The Cold War reconciled this division between congressmen at the expense of the braceros but in ways that satisfied the needs of various special interest groups in the United States. Congress chiefly determined that the Bracero Program would continue to serve the interests of agribusinesses. The United States Employment Service and the Department of Labor would continue to recruit Mexican laborers, while the INS would receive substantial congressional support to deport the "illegal aliens" or "wetbacks" entering the United States.[60]

As the comprehensive work of Juan R. Garcia demonstrates, during the Second World War and into the Cold War, national security concerns dovetailed with arguments in favor of border security and immigration restriction. After the U.S. economy entered into a recession at the end of the Korean War in 1953, politicians who were typically uninterested in immigration began demanding that the INS secure the border and deport "aliens" who were argued to be both security risks and unlawful workers who competed with Americans for jobs. U.S. attorney general Herbert Brownell came to this position after touring the Southwest. Brownell was initially unconcerned by the "wetback problem," but while he traveled through the border states, he spoke with mayors, judges, district attorneys, police officers, welfare agents, and health officials who repeatedly claimed that "illegal aliens" were a drain on their resources. While accompanying Border Patrol officers in California, Brownell witnessed two large groups of Mexican migrants crossing the border illegally. The migrants were promptly arrested, but the experience unsettled Brownell, who was shocked by just how unprotected and porous the U.S.-Mexico border was.[61] Brownell returned to Washington with a newfound sense of urgency and called on Gen. Joseph Swing of the Sixth Army in California to assist him in putting a stop to the "illegal invasion of . . . 'wetbacks.'" Swing was appointed commissioner of the INS and in military fashion committed himself fully to the task at hand.[62]

Swing had deep connections in Washington and a complicated personal history with Mexico. He was a close friend of President Dwight D. Eisenhower, who had been Swing's classmate at West Point. Throughout Swing's tenure as commissioner of immigration, he would call on the president and receive the support of the White House. On another personal level, when Swing had first joined the army, he had been ordered to serve in Gen. John Pershing's expedition into Mexico, the failed expedition that had tried to capture the Mexican revolutionary Pancho Villa. Apparently, this experience may have led Swing to develop an antipathy toward Mexicans. In any case, Swing's contemporaries described him as a tough and serious man, and numerous officials in Washington were confident he would succeed in securing the border.[63]

After Swing took over the INS, he quickly militarized the agency. Swing recruited Gen. Frank Patridge and Gen. Edwin Howard to serve as INS consultants, and they reorganized the Border Patrol along military lines, engendering an esprit de corps among officers that involved establishing clearer chains of command and standardizing the uniforms of Border Patrol agents so they would be perceived as a force apart from the "aliens" and the U.S. citizens the agents would be engaging. When new positions and departments were needed, Swing simply created them, and he had the support of the attorney general and the president to do so. Swing formed the INS Mobile Task Force, akin to a Special Forces unit—a tight team of twelve officers equipped with modern weapons, jeeps, trucks, and buses. Unfettered by jurisdictional boundaries, the Special Mobile Force, as it became known, was expected to be aggressive in its pursuit of "illegals." To aid the Special Mobile Force, Swing created new INS divisions such as the Border Patrol Air Transport Arm, which collected aerial intelligence along the entire border. The INS had traditionally used buses and trains to deport Mexicans. Under Swing, the INS acquired planes and boats to deposit migrants eight hundred miles into Mexico's interior and to transport Mexicans from the Midwest to INS rendition points in Texas, where they would be interrogated and processed for deportation. A few of these changes in the organizational structure of the INS had been initiated by former commissioners, but Swing had the clout and connections to see numerous proposals through, and he transformed the INS into a powerful agency.[64]

In June 1954 Attorney General Brownell and Commissioner Swing announced their capstone, a massive deportation drive that they named Operation Wetback. Classified INS proposals outlined a partnership with the United States Army that would involve the use of more than four thousand U.S. troops who would engage the "aliens" on U.S. soil. In the end, the INS boosted measures it had been implementing since 1951. Essentially, the INS partnered with state and city officials and numerous police departments that enthusiastically supported the INS. Police departments even proposed dragnets that the INS had to respectfully decline because the proposals were too constitutionally suspect and could draw negative publicity. Working closely with the police, the INS was able to carry out multiple, concurrent, and well-publicized raids in heavily concentrated Mexican neighborhoods in pursuit of undocumented immigrants or, as the INS described them, "aliens of the most dangerous and subversive classes" who were "endangering the national security" of the United States.[65] By year's end, the INS claimed to have deported 1,075,168 immigrants. Scholars argue that the INS inflated its Cold War deportation figures to dramatize its power and effectiveness. Perhaps it did, but starting in 1951, when the INS began carrying out more frequent deportation raids, and through Operation Wetback, the INS deported well over one million Mexicans.[66]

Various authorities estimated that between nine and fifteen thousand undocumented Mexicans lived in Chicago in the early 1950s, and with the start of the Cold War deportations, the Chicago office of the INS began deporting about three hundred Mexicans per month. "Because Uncle Sam is trying to send these wetbacks home as swiftly as possible," noted a journalist for the *Chicago Sun-Times*, "they [Mexicans] [now] live in constant fear."[67] Indeed, opportunistic employers capitalized on this culture of fear and began threatening their militant Mexican and Latino workers with deportation. During the Cold War deportations, all Latinos became suspect. With the start of the Second World War, the United States established the Bracero Program with Mexico and had created several other labor-recruitment agreements with Puerto Rico that led to the growth of the Puerto Rican population of Chicago. As Lilia Fernández has elegantly discussed, while some fifteen thousand braceros were incorporated into Chicago between 1943 and 1948, thousands of Puerto Ricans were concurrently recruited into the agricultural fields of the Midwest and into foundries and domestic lines of work in Chicago proper. During the 1950s Puerto Ricans recalled being pulled out of their cars by police officers who would brazenly ask them if they were "wetbacks." Since Puerto Ricans had been made U.S. citizens by the U.S. government in 1917, the vast majority of Puerto Ricans avoided deportation.[68]

The Mexican migrants defined as "illegals" by the U.S. government—which included braceros who had "skipped" on their contracts and migrants who crossed the border without authorization—were in a completely different legal category. As thousands of undocumented Mexicans were arrested, interned, and effectively deported from Chicago, Eugene Cotton prepared Martínez for an appeal to the U.S. Supreme Court. In light of the deportations occurring across the country, Martínez's case appeared bleak, and the strain on him proved too severe. In December, Martínez suffered a stroke that left him partially paralyzed and almost mute. His case eventually came before the Court, and it arrived at a split decision, upholding the lower court's 1951 ruling in favor of deportation.[69] As Martínez's case began to make mainstream headlines, the United States Court of Appeals ruled that immigrants were specifically not shielded by ex post facto constitutional provisions because the Internal Security Act of 1950 established that immigrants could be deported if, after entry into the United States, they had been "at any time thereafter a member" of the Communist Party.[70] Martínez received a final order of deportation and went to see his two daughters for what would be the last time in his life. The following day, Refugio was deported, and within a week he had died.[71]

Conclusion

Refugio Román Martínez's deportation during the Cold War is illustrative of the broader persecution of the radical nationalist wing of the revolutionary generation. Latina/o immigrant unionists like Luisa Moreno, Josefina Fierro, and Humberto Silex and the many Mexicans who organized workers alongside them were arrested, interrogated, and sometimes deported by the INS. Radical Latina/os paid a serious price for helping to build the U.S. labor movement while retaining their foreign citizenships. Some, like Silex, successfully defended themselves; others, like Moreno and Martínez, were deported. Martínez crossed the border legally, was never convicted of a crime in the United States, was never charged with perjury by the INS, but was prosecuted for some twelve years before he was ultimately deported as a dissident.

Martínez's deportation was made possible by an entrenched culture in the United States that defined Mexicans as a deportable people. Mexicans were recruited into the United States during World War I and World War II but then expelled from the country after the recessions of 1920, 1929, and 1953. Martínez was expelled between 1951 and 1954, during the Cold War deportations, when tens of thousands of Mexican people (objectified as "wetbacks") were forced out of the United States while the U.S. government continued to "import" tens of thousands of Mexican people (objectified as "braceros"). This process of cyclically importing and deporting Mexican workers dehumanized the ethnic Mexican people of the United States and normalized the mistreatment of Mexicans as a commodified and disposable people.

In Chicago, young Mexican Americans defended Mexican nationals because they were personally connected to them through kinship bonds. Many if not most Mexican Americans in Chicago were the children of two Mexico-born parents, and these young Americans knew Mexican nationals as family members, neighbors, coworkers, and CIO brothers and sisters. As the U.S.-born and U.S.-raised Mexican Americans adopted an ethnic identity as Americans, they continued to defend immigrants but abandoned the anti-imperialist and Marxian arguments in favor of immigrant rights that radical Mexican immigrants had once expressed. Mexican Americans in Chicago and in Los Angeles developed "ambivalent American" identities because they experienced not one but several mass deportation campaigns and learned that in times of economic and political crisis, all ethnic Mexicans could be targeted for deportation.[72]

Conclusion

During the first half of the twentieth century, Mexican Chicago was profoundly shaped by the ebbs and flows of Mexican revolutionary politics. In many ways, Mexican Chicago was closer to Mexico than many of the ethnic Mexican communities of the Southwest. Mexicans arrived in Chicago in the wake of the revolution, while Spanish-speaking communities had developed in the Southwest during the colonial era. The U.S. practice of expelling Mexicans from the United States, a phenomenon that began in the early nineteenth century, impeded the formation of a Mexican American community in the Southwest, but Mexican American leaders had emerged in some southwestern states by the 1920s. A Mexican American leadership did not develop in Chicago until the 1940s. Mexican Chicago was founded and led by Mexican nationals in a way the ethnic Mexican communities of the Southwest were not.

The Mexicans who settled in Chicagoland were a diverse lot to be sure, but initially they all defined themselves as patriotic citizens committed to the Mexican nation-state. Mexican liberals like Julián Mondragón, F. Patrón Miranda, and Antonia Aguilar and radicals like Nicholas Hernández, Jesús Flores, and Mrs. García believed in the transformative potential of the revolution. For the liberals, the revolution would secularize Mexico, expand educational opportunities, and create a more cultured and cosmopolitan citizenry. For the radicals, revolutionary politics, exemplified by the policies of Lázaro Cárdenas, had the capacity to fundamentally transform the quality of life of the Mexican working class. Radical revolutionary politics could empower Mexican workers whose hard labor produced the goods and services that Mexico, the United States, and the global capitalist market consumed. The radicals dreamed of re-creating a Mexico that would offer ordinary Mexican citizens a high standard of living and thus the choice to remain in their own country of origin.[1] All the while, traditionalists such as Benjamin Figueroa, Ignacio González, and Rosaura Herrera who were faithful Catholics devoted to the church tried to contain the anticlericalism and radicalism unleashed by the revolution. These Mexicans had an earnest sense of morality, and they did not want to forsake the Catholic and empathetic ethic they believed defined *mexicanidad*.

Middle-class Mexican liberals established the nationalist foundations of Mexican Chicago in the 1920s. The liberals created a community and a reform movement that celebrated the anticlerical and liberal Mexican nation-state and the Mexican people's indigenous and *mestizaje* heritage. These Mexicans criticized U.S. racial discrimination, devalorized whiteness, and denounced U.S. imperialism in Latin America, and they were compelled to take an unwavering position against U.S. interventions by their Central American and Caribbean allies. Through various social service projects, Mexican liberals drew working-class migrants into their nationalist movement and succeeded in dissuading many migrants from surrendering their Mexican citizenship.

During the Depression, the liberal movement collapsed, and Mexican politics turned to the left. President Lázaro Cárdenas's awe-inspiring redistributive policies exhilarated radicals in Mexico and in Chicagoland. Radical Mexicans formed organizations like the Frente Popular Mexicano and recruited, trained, and encouraged migrants to become community activists and then CIO unionists. The Frente, however, also implored migrants to remain loyal to the Mexican state. The radicals largely ignored the identity, mestizaje politics of the liberals but appropriated their anti-imperialism and then provided Mexican laborers with a way to rationalize their right to live and work in the United States as Mexican citizens. Today, South and East Asian and African immigrant rights activists in the European Union chant, "We are here because you are there!" (i.e., "We [Third World migrants] are here [in Europe] because you [First World citizens, corporations, and empires] are there [in the Third World]"). Radical Mexican immigrants did not articulate their right to work and live in the United States as forcefully and as lyrically, but they were cognizant of U.S. imperialism and its implications and recognized that U.S. corporations in Mexico were treated with *cariño* (love and affection) by the Mexican state, while Mexican workers were "exploited" on both sides of the U.S.-Mexico border. Radical Mexicans declined U.S. citizenship because they were "subaltern nationalists" who believed that U.S. corporate and state practices in Mexico ought to grant Mexican citizens the right to migrate and work in the United States without being criminalized or pressured to naturalize.[2]

The Calles and Cárdenas presidencies in Mexico in the 1920s and 1930s reinforced the Mexican nationalism of the liberals and radicals in Chicago, while these same presidencies repulsed traditionalists from the Mexican state. As traditionalist leaders distanced themselves from postrevolutionary Mexico, they began offering Mexican Catholics a deterritorialized interpretation of Mexican identity that characterized Mexicans as a supranational Catholic people. The anticlerical Calles presidency and Cristero Rebellion bolstered the traditionalists' Catholicism, and many began to define the United States as a religious sanctuary that would protect Mexican Catholics from the punitive reach of the anticlerical Mexican government. The deportations of the Depression and Cold War eras only underscored the ways Mexican citizenship could cost traditionalists their U.S.-based Catholic communities. In the end, Mexican liberals and radicals were simply too disenchanted by U.S. imperialism and racism to accept U.S. naturalization, while Mexican anticlericalism and radicalism and American nativism convinced traditionalists that it was in their best interest to become American citizens.

In Texas, New Mexico, California, and other southwestern states, U.S.-born and naturalized Mexican Americans formed new organizations that went on to create the Mexican American civil rights movement. Within this Mexican American generation, those who were politically moderate and right of center in their beliefs often sought equality with white Americans by emphasizing their quasi status as white persons, their U.S. citizenship, and their opposition to "illegal" immigration from Mexico. Progressive Mexican Americans, by comparison, "struggle[d] for fundamental civil rights, ethnic respectability . . . and effective political representation" as cultural pluralists who affirmed their Mexican heritage while fighting for their place in the United States as ethnic Americans.[3] In Chicagoland, Mexican American civil rights groups like the Mexican Civic Committee (MCC) followed this more progressive course. Mexican Americans in Chicago advanced their interests as American citizens, but many continued to defend immigrants. Frank Paz, who served as the president of the MCC, witnessed the rise of the Frente Popular Mexicano when he was a young boy, and under his leadership the MCC remained supportive of immigrant rights.[4] Progressive Mexican Americans in Chicago, however, like their counterparts in the Southwest, typically avoided the anti-imperialist and Marxian arguments in defense of immigrant rights that radical Mexican nationalists had conveyed in previous years. The political culture of liberal and radical Mexicans was simply too critical of the United States for many Mexican Americans who were genuine American patriots.

In the 1960s, during the Vietnam War and the farmworkers movement, a new generation of Mexican Americans would take leadership and return the ethnic Mexican communities of the United States to their revolutionary roots. From Los Angeles to Chicago, young Chicanos gave new meanings to the mestizaje and anti-imperialist politics of the Mexican liberals and the Marxian labor rights arguments of the radicals. Chicana/os were certainly influenced by the African American civil rights movement, but they were not, as some scholars claim, simply "follow[ing] the leads of blacks instead of whites."[5] The Chicana/os were advancing criticisms of the United States that had been expressed for generations within their own transnational Latino communities. As Lorrin Thomas has argued, "Most narratives of the heterogeneous terrain of sixties radicalism presume that Black Power was the progenitor of radical politics in the United States, a singular force in the radicalization of other identity-based activist groups. . . . In fact, the long history of radical nationalism and anti-imperialism in twentieth-century Latin America, which formed the ideological roots of both Puerto Rican and Chicano nationalists, was also essential in shaping black nationalists' ideas by the mid-sixties."[6] Chicano activists drew on their own people's history of thinking transnationally while acting locally, and they organized a broad social movement against anti-Mexican racism and U.S. imperialism. Chicana/os, in collaboration with Puerto Rican and Black Power nationalists, created opportunities for an entire generation of Mexican Americans.[7]

Nearer to our present, in March 2006, ethnic Mexicans in Chicago led a series of massive immigrant rights demonstrations against the Border Protection, Anti-terrorism, and Illegal Immigration Control Act, which sought to classify undocumented immigrants as felons while criminalizing U.S. citizens who "aid" the undocumented. Some three hundred thousand ethnic Mexicans protested the bill in Chicago, more than five hundred thousand demonstrated in Los Angeles, and another three to five hundred thousand protested in Dallas. These demonstrations were accompanied by acts of civil disobedience in more than one hundred cities across the United States. After the March "megamarch" in Chicago, immigrant rights organizers gathered at Haymarket Square (where radical German immigrants had convened in favor of the eight-hour work day in the 1880s) to propose a larger march on May 1. With the support of the SEIU, UNITE-HERE, other progressive unions, and a few Catholic churches, more than four hundred thousand ethnic Mexicans and their allies marched on May Day, recognized outside of the United States as a radical holiday because this day was chosen as the

International Workers' Day by the socialists and communists of the Second International in 1889.

The leaders of the immigrant rights movement in Chicago included Jorge Mújica, a *capitalino* (a person from Mexico City) and self-declared socialist, and the founders of several Bajío hometown associations, including those of Casa Michoacán. Socialist capitalinos like Mujica now work closely with devout Mexican Catholics from the Bajío who were pivotal in organizing the megamarches. Ethnic Mexican activists from Chicago flew to Mexico City to seek support, as they had in the 1990s, when they secured assistance from progressive Mexican politicians like Lázaro Cárdenas Batel, the grandson of former president Lázaro Cárdenas.[8] An array of activists helped plan the marches, and they held regular meetings at Casa Michoacán, where as a graduate student I was asked to talk about the lost history of Mexican immigrant activism in Chicagoland. In recognition of the size of the first megamarch, Jorge Mújica informed the press, "Chicago seems to be for many reasons the political capital of immigration. There may be more immigrants in California or the border states, but Chicago is the place where lots of ideas came together."[9] Indeed, Chicago has been the political capital of Mexican immigrants since the 1920s, but in the contemporary period, Mexican radicals and traditionalists were now banding together in authentic coalitions. The U.S. government's long history of treating Mexicans as a deportable people was accomplishing what the Mexican state never could: the U.S. government had created a (trans)national Mexican community "capacious enough to allow the [Aztec] eagle and the [V]irgin [of Guadalupe] to coexist peacefully"—for the time being.[10]

Appendix

On Naturalization Records

One of the most influential studies of Mexican identity and assimilation is *Becoming Mexican American: Ethnicity, Culture, and Identity in Chicano Los Angeles, 1900–1945* by George J. Sanchez. In this landmark monograph, Sanchez surveyed the records of 2,238 Mexicans who applied for U.S. citizenship in the Federal District Court of Los Angeles before 1940.[1] To assess Mexican politics and assimilation in the Chicago area, I collected the records of every Spanish-speaking immigrant who applied for U.S. citizenship in the Federal District Court of Chicago between 1900 and 1940 and the Circuit Court of Cook County between 1906 and 1929. Through these applications for naturalization, I created a naturalization census of 3,110 Spanish-speaking immigrants (1,982 federal records and 1,128 county records). To date, this is the largest and most inclusive historical census of Hispanic naturalization in the United States.

While the majority of Mexican immigrants in Los Angeles and Chicago never applied for naturalization, 1,893 Mexicans applied for U.S. citizenship in Chicago between 1900 and 1940. Naturalization records are incredibly valuable in ascertaining the characteristics of the Mexicans who chose to establish themselves in the United States. Censuses, parish registers, city directories, and marriage licenses can tell us much about the Mexican population of a particular place and time, but these sources rarely distinguish between Mexicans who were sojourning in the United States and those who were seeking permanent residence. U.S. and Mexican government records reveal that Mexican immigrant communities were in an incredible state of flux during the first half of the twentieth century. More than one million Mexicans entered the United States between 1900 and 1929. Thousands of Mexicans repatriated during the recession of 1920; more than half a million Mexicans repatriated or were deported during the Great Depression;

and more than one million Mexicans were deported during the Cold War. Mexican government sources allude to an even higher volume of to-and-from migration during these years. For example, while the U.S. government claims that only 3,572 Mexicans left the United States for Mexico in 1920, Mexican sources cite an astounding 105,834 Mexican returnees in this same year.[2] Unlike most sources that do not distinguish between Mexican sojourners, repatriates, and deportees, naturalization records provide researchers with detailed information about the subset of the total Mexican population that was seeking to permanently settle in the United States.

Table 1 State of origin of Mexican naturalizers in Chicago, 1900–1940

Mexican states	Percent (number)
Guanajuato	16.7 (274)
Distrito Federal	14.4 (237)
Jalisco	13.2 (217)
Michoacán	10.0 (164)
Nuevo León	6.2 (102)
Chihuahua	5.7 (95)
Zacatecas	5.4 (89)
Coahuila	4.5 (74)
San Luis Potosí	4.3 (71)
Durango	3.8 (63)
Aguascalientes	2.0 (34)
Tamaulipas	1.7 (29)
Puebla	1.7 (28)
Veracruz	1.6 (27)
Oaxaca	1.2 (20)
Yucatán	0.9 (16)
Sonora	0.9 (15)
Mexico State	0.8 (14)
Querétaro	0.7 (13)
Hidalgo	0.7 (12)
Chiapas	0.6 (11)
Nayarit	0.4 (7)
Tabasco	0.3 (6)
Baja California	0.2 (4)
Colima	0.2 (4)
Morelos	0.2 (4)
Guerrero	0.2 (3)
Campeche	0.1 (2)
Sinaloa	0.1 (2)
Tlaxcala	<0.1 (1)
Baja California Sur	0.0 (0)
Quintana Roo	0.0 (0)

Note: This table includes 1,638 Mexican naturalizers, 140 of whom are Mexican women. This table excludes Mexican naturalizers who did not list a state of origin on their naturalization applications. Percentages may not sum to 100 percent because of rounding.

Table 2   Ports of entry of Mexican naturalizers to Chicago

U.S. ports	Mexican border town	Percent (number)
Land ports		
Laredo, TX	Nuevo Laredo, Tam.	55.7 (696)
El Paso, TX	Ciudad Juárez, Chih.	27.0 (338)
Eagle Pass, TX	Piedras Negras, Coah.	6.8 (86)
Brownsville, TX	Matamoros, Tam.	2.4 (30)
Hidalgo, TX	Reynosa, Tam.	0.6 (8)
Del Rio, TX	Ciudad Acuña, Coah.	0.5 (7)
Detroit, MI	—	0.4 (5)
Nogales, AZ	Nogales, Son.	0.4 (5)
Rio Grande City, TX	Ciudad Camargo	0.3 (4)
Dallas, TX	Tam.	0.2 (3)
Douglas, AZ	—	0.2 (3)
Calexico, CA	Agua Prieta, Son.	<0.1 (1)
Chicago, IL	Mexicali, Baja Cal.	<0.1 (1)
Columbus, NM	—	<0.1 (1)
Fort Worth, TX	Puerto Palomas, Chi.	<0.1 (1)
Kansas City, MO	—	<0.1 (1)
Naco, AZ	—	<0.1 (1)
Noyes, MN	Naco, Son.	<0.1 (1)
Port Huron, MI	—	<0.1 (1)
Portal, ND	—	<0.1 (1)
Presidio, TX	—	<0.1 (1)
Roma, TX	Manuel Ojinaga, Chi. Ciudad Miguel Alaman, Tam.	<0.1 (1)
Sea ports		
New York, NY	—	1.9 (24)
New Orleans, LA	—	1.1 (14)
Los Angeles, CA	—	0.2 (3)
Houston, TX	—	0.1 (2)
San Francisco, CA	—	0.1 (2)
Tampa, FL	—	0.1 (2)
Texas City, TX	—	0.1 (2)
Galveston, TX	—	<0.1 (1)
Key West, FL	—	<0.1 (1)
Port Arthur, TX	—	<0.1 (1)
Total listed ports of entry	1,248	

Note: This table excludes Mexican naturalizers who did not list a port of entry on their naturalization applications. A dashed line indicates an empty cell. Percentages may not sum to 100 percent because of rounding.

Table 3 The migrant journey of Mexican naturalizers to Chicago, 1900–1940

Mexican naturalizers	Migration directly from town or city of birth	Migration from state of birth (but not same birth town or city)	Migration from region of birth	Migration from regions north of region of birth	Migration from regions south of region of birth
100% (1,503)	39% (584)	17% (256)	11% (168)	26% (390)	7% (105)

Note: This table excludes Mexican naturalizers who did not list a place of birth on their naturalization applications.

Table 4 Regional origins of Mexican naturalizers in Chicago who crossed into the United States as children and as adults, 1900–1940

Nationality (sample size)	Border states and northwestern Mexico	Central Mexico	Bajío	North-central Mexico	Southern Mexico	Western Mexico
Mexican, 1900–1920 (166)[1]	36% (60)	27% (44)	19% (32)	8% (13)	8% (13)	2% (4)
Mexican, 1921–30 (500)[2]	23% (115)	26% (130)	37% (186)	7% (37)	6% (29)	1% (3)
Mexican, 1931–40 (923)[3]	21% (196)	12% (114)	50% (461)	12% (109)	4% (40)	1% (3)
Total Mexican, 1900–1940 (1,638)[4]	23% (384)	18% (296)	43% (702)	10% (160)	5% (85)	1% (11)

Note: This table excludes naturalizers who did not list a region of origin on their naturalization applications. My tables divide Mexico's political geography in the following order: the border states and northwestern Mexico include Baja California, Baja California Sur, Chihuahua, Coahuila, Durango, Nuevo León, Sonora, Sinaloa, and Tamaulipas; the Bajío includes Aguascalientes, Guanajuato, Jalisco, Michoacán, and Querétaro; north-central Mexico includes San Luis Potosí and Zacatecas; western Mexico includes Colima and Nayarit; central Mexico includes the Distrito Federal, Hidalgo, Mexico State, Morelos, Puebla, and Tlaxcala; and southern Mexico includes Campeche, Chiapas, Guerrero, Oaxaca, Quintana Roo, Tabasco, Veracruz, and Yucatán.
1. This sample includes two Mexican women.
2. This sample includes twenty-nine Mexican women.
3. This sample includes 117 Mexican women.
4. This sample includes 158 Mexican women and 49 Mexicans who applied for naturalization in Chicago but whose specific year of application between 1900 and 1940 could not be determined.

Table 5   Regional origins of Mexican naturalizers in Chicago who first crossed into the United States as adults, 1900–1940

Nationality (sample size)	Border states and northwestern Mexico	Central Mexico	Bajío	North-central Mexico	Southern Mexico	Western Mexico
Mexican, 1900–1920 (114)[1]	32% (37)	29% (33)	22% (25)	7% (8)	7% (8)	3% (3)
Mexican, 1921–30 (346)[2]	19% (67)	27% (92)	39% (135)	8% (28)	6% (22)	1% (2)
Mexican, 1931–40 (647)[3]	19% (121)	13% (84)	52% (334)	12% (79)	4% (27)	less than 1% (2)
Total Mexican, 1900–1940 (1,127)[4]	20% (228)	19% (213)	45% (504)	10% (115)	5% (59)	1% (8)

Note: This table excludes naturalizers who did not list a state of origin on their naturalization applications and excludes those who included a state of origin but immigrated to the United States before the age of nineteen. Table 4 includes the regional origins of all age groups.

1. This sample includes one Mexican woman.
2. This sample includes twenty Mexican women.
3. This sample includes seventy-one Mexican women. Percentages exceed 100 percent because of rounding.
4. This sample includes ninety-eight Mexican women and twenty-nine Mexicans who applied for naturalization in Chicago but whose specific year of application between 1900 and 1940 could not be determined.

Table 6   Comparison of regional origins of Mexican naturalizers in Chicago and Los Angeles who first crossed into the United States as adults

Nationality (sample size)	Border states and northwestern Mexico	Central Mexico	Bajío	North-central Mexico	Southern Mexico	Western Mexico
Mexicans to Chicago, 1900–1940 (1,127)	20% (228)	19% (213)	45% (504)	10% (115)	5% (59)	1% (8)
Mexicans to Los Angeles before 1940 (1,111)	44% (494)	11% (124)	26% (289)	12% (137)	4% (48)	2% (19)

Note: The Los Angeles table includes 1,111 adult male Mexican naturalizers and was adapted from data in Sanchez, *Becoming Mexican American*, table 5, 46. The Chicago table includes ninety-eight Mexican women, and for comparative purposes it includes only those Mexican naturalizers who immigrated to the United States as adults (after the age of nineteen). Percentages may not sum to 100 percent because of rounding.

Table 7   Regional origins of non-Mexican Hispanic naturalizers in Chicago, 1900–1940

Nationality (sample size)	State, province, or department				
Spanish (377)	Asturias 29% (109)	Madrid 8% (30)	Barcelona 7% (27)	A Coruna 6% (24)	Lugo 5% (17)
Cuban (131)	Havana 44% (56)	Matanzas 14% (18)	Villa Clara 12% (16)	Cienfuegos 9% (12)	Guantánamo 5% (7)
Argentine (115)	Buenos Aires 66% (76)	Santa Fe 15% (17)	Entre Ríos 4% (5)	Misiones 3% (4)	Mendoza 3% (3)
Nicaraguan (49)	León 27% (13)	Granada 24% (12)	Managua 12% (6)	Río San Juan 8% (4)	Jinotega 8% (4)

Note: This table includes only the top five regions of origin of non-Mexican Hispanic naturalizers and excludes the immigrants who did not list a region of origin on their naturalization applications. This table also includes 186 Spanish-speaking women (158 Mexican, 5 Spanish, 6 Cuban, 14 Argentine, and 3 Nicaraguan).

Table 8   Age of Mexican migrants at time of first crossing to Chicago, 1900–1940

Age	Male migrants	Female migrants	Total
Child under 13	9%	19%	10%
	149	30	179
Adolescent	21%	18%	21%
13–15	101	10	111
16–18	261	19	280
Young adult	42%	24%	40%
19–21	396	19	415
22–24	319	18	337
Adult	29%	39%	30%
25–29	253	26	279
30–39	195	25	220
40–49	37	4	41
Over 49	8	6	14
Total	1,719	157	1,876

Note: This table includes 1,876 Mexican naturalizers in Chicago whose age could be determined. Percentages may exceed 100 percent due to rounding.

Table 9   Complexion of Mexican naturalizers in Chicago, 1900–1940

Nationality (sample size)	Dark	Medium	Fair
Mexican, 1900–1930 (304)[1]	69% (209)	9% (27)	22% (68)
Mexican, 1931–40 (1,012)[2]	80% (809)	6% (60)	14% (143)
Total Mexican, 1900–1940 (1,321)[3]	77% (1,023)	7% (87)	16% (211)

Note: This table excludes Mexican immigrants whose complexions could not be ascertained from their naturalization applications. The dark category includes 1,023 Mexicans classified as "dark" by immigration officials. The medium category includes Mexicans classified as "medium" (62), "ruddy" (13), "olive" (8), "swarthy" (2), "brunette" (1), and "brown" (1). The fair category includes Mexicans classified as "fair" (188), "light" (12), and "white" (11). This sample also includes 127 Mexican women.

1. This sample also includes eleven Mexican women.

2. This sample includes 118 Mexican women.

3. This sample includes 128 Mexican women and data on five Mexicans whose complexion was listed on their naturalization applications but whose specific year of application between 1900 and 1940 could not be determined.

Table 10   Complexion of Hispanic naturalizers in Chicago, 1900–1940

Hispanic group (sample size)	Dark	Medium	Fair
Mexican (1,321)[1]	77% (1,023)	7% (87)	16% (211)
Central American (80)[2]	75% (60)	5% (4)	20% (16)
Caribbean (111)[3]	67% (74)	9% (10)	24% (27)
South American (222)[4]	55% (121)	11% (25)	34% (76)
Spaniard (193)[5]	50% (96)	9% (17)	41% (80)

1. The dark category includes the 1,023 Mexicans classified as "dark" by immigration officials. The medium category includes Mexicans classified as "medium" (62), "ruddy" (13), "olive" (8), swarthy (2), "brunette" (1), and "brown" (1). The fair category includes Mexicans classified as "fair" (188), "light" (12), and "white" (11). This sample also includes 127 Mexican women.

2. The dark category includes sixty Central Americans classified as "dark." The medium category includes one "brown," one "ruddy," and two "medium" classified Central Americans. The fair category includes all those classified as "fair." This sample includes thirteen Central American women.

3. The dark category includes one "mulatto" classified Caribbean person and seventy-two "dark" classified persons. The medium category includes one "brown" and nine "medium" classified persons. The fair category includes one "light" and twenty-six "fair" classified persons. This sample includes seven women from the Caribbean.

4. The fair category includes two "light" and seventy-four "fair" classified South Americans. The medium category includes one "brown," one "olive," one "sallow," four "ruddy," and eighteen "medium" classified South Americans. The sample includes twenty-two South American women.

5. The fair category includes one "white," four "light," and seventy-five "fair" classified Spaniards. This sample also includes four Spanish women.

Table 11 Occupational structure for Mexican naturalizers in Chicago

	High white collar	Low white collar	Total white collar	Skilled blue collar	Semiskilled blue collar	Total skilled and semiskilled blue collar	Unskilled blue collar
Mexican, 1900–1930 (793)[1]	8% (66)	9% (69)	17% (135)	16% (124)	14% (109)	29% (233)[2]	54% (425)
Mexican, 1931–40 (802)[3]	5% (44)	6% (46)	11% (90)	13% (103)	19% (153)	32% (256)	57% (456)
Total Mexican, 1900–1940 (1,645)[4]	7% (116)	7% (119)	14% (235)	14% (234)	16% (271)	31% (505)[5]	55% (905)

Note: All occupational tables exclude immigrants who did not list an occupation on their naturalization applications. All occupations were classified in relation to the criteria suggested by Sobek, "Occupations," http://dx.doi.org/10.1017/ISBN-9780511113297Ba.ESS.03.1.

1. This sample includes twenty-seven Mexican women.

2. Percentage is drawn from the raw number.

3. This sample includes 117 Mexican women.

4. This sample includes 137 Mexican women and 50 Mexicans who applied for naturalization in Chicago but whose specific year of application between 1900 and 1940 could not be definitively determined.

5. Percentage is drawn from the raw number.

Table 12   Occupational structure for Hispanic naturalizers in Chicago, 1900–1940

Hispanic group (sample size)	White collar	Skilled and semiskilled blue collar	Unskilled blue collar
Mexican (1,645)	14% (235)	31% (505)	55% (905)
Spanish (401)	28% (114)	40% (161)	31% (126)
South American (446)	28% (124)	41% (184)	31% (138)
Central American (138)	37% (51)	35% (48)	28% (39)
Caribbean (147)	35% (52)	41% (61)	23% (34)

Note: What follows is a list of the nationalities and the number of women included within each of the sections of the table: Mexicans (137 women in sample); Spaniards (6 women); South Americans: 172 Brazilians (2 women), 152 Argentines (13 women), 32 Peruvians (0 women), 25 Chileans (3 women), 27 Colombians (1 woman), 4 Ecuadorians (0 women), 12 Uruguayans (0 women), 12 Venezuelans (2 women), 9 Bolivians (1 woman), 1 Paraguayan (0 women); Central Americans: 46 Nicaraguans (3 women), 32 Guatemalans (4 women), 20 Costa Ricans (2 women), 18 Hondurans (1 woman), 15 Panamanians (2 women), 7 Salvadorans (0 women); and Caribbean origin: 137 Cubans (5 women) and 10 Dominicans (3 women). Percentages may not sum to 100 percent because of rounding.

Table 13   Background of spouse of Mexican migrants, 1900–1940

Background of spouse	Percent (number)
Mexican born	77 (662)
American born	17 (144)
European born	5 (46)
Latin American born (non-Mexican)	1 (10)
Other	Less than 1 (1)
Total	863

Note: This table excludes married and formally married Mexican naturalizers whose naturalization applications omitted the place of birth of their spouses. Percentages may exceed 100 percent because of rounding.

Table 14 Family size of various types of Mexican marriages, 1900–1940

Type of marriage	No children	One or two children	Three to five children	Six to eight children	More than eight children
Mexican-born spouse	158	178	218	96	12
American-born spouse	63	64	14	3	—
European-born spouse	22	15	9	—	—
Latin American–born spouse (non-Mexican)	6	3	—	1	—
Other	—	—	1	—	—
Total	249	260	242	100	12

Note: This table is based on a sample of 863 married Mexican naturalizers in Chicago between the years 1900 and 1940.

Table 15   Place of birth of Mexican children in Chicago, 1900–1940

Place of birth	Before 1910	Decade of birth 1910–20	Decade of birth 1921–30	Decade of birth 1931–40	Number (percentage)
Illinois	1	16	178	105	300 (48.2)
Texas	3	20	20	3	46 (7.4)
Kansas	1	7	9	1	18 (2.9)
Iowa	—	3	2	1	6 (1.0)
Missouri	—	2	2	2	6 (1.0)
New Mexico	1	5	—	—	6 (1.0)
Oklahoma	—	4	1	—	5 (0.8)
Colorado	—	1	3	—	4 (0.6)
Michigan	—	—	3	1	4 (0.6)
Nebraska	—	2	2	—	4 (0.6)
California	—	2	1	—	3 (0.5)
Wyoming	—	—	3	—	3 (0.5)
Arizona	—	—	2	—	2 (0.3)
Wisconsin	—	—	1	1	2 (0.3)
Alabama	—	1	—	—	1 (0.2)
Montana	—	—	1	—	1 (0.2)
New York	—	—	1	—	1 (0.2)
Ohio	—	1	—	—	1 (0.2)
Oregon	—	—	1	—	1 (0.2)
Pennsylvania	—	—	1	—	1 (0.2)
Mexico	31	96	59	1	187 (30.0)
Unknown	—	10	9	2	21 (3.4)
Total	37	170	299	117	623

Note: A dash indicates an empty cell. Percentages may exceed 100 percent because of rounding.

Table 16 Spanish-speaking immigrant societies in metropolitan Chicago, 1900–1940

Name of immigrant society	Community area	Active participants	Affiliated press
Lux en Umbra	Near West Side	Luis Álvares del Castillo, Ruben Flores, Lisando Díaz, Malesio Espinoza, Ignacio Guerrero, Jose Reyes, Enrique Rincon, Ernesto Uribe, Salvador Galvaz, Julio Oliva de Armas, Carlos Gurrola, Carlos Palacios Roji, Carlo Morales	México: El Semario de la Patria
La Cruz Azul Mexicana of Chicago	Near West Side and South Chicago	Oscar G. Carrera, Jana R. de Pena, Carlos Roberts, Carlota Gonzalez, Eva A. de Carrera, Mr. J. Pena, Maria Luisa Sanchez, Mercedes Rios, Juana Pena, Guadalupe Urrola, Carlos Roberts, Ana Maria Gonzalez, Eloisa de la Paz, Milla Dominguez, Gertrudis Galindo, Carolina Lona	—
Sociedad Feminil Mexicana	Near West Side	F. G. de Barron, Maria Jimenez, Virjinia Chavez, Antonia Aquilar, Elena Flores de Lovera, Maria de Jesus Morales, Maria Cervantes, Lala Vilareal, Lala Morales, Maria de la Luz Morales	—
Feminil Excelsior Club	—	P. M. de Cornejo, H. R. de Corneȯ, Elvira Ramirez, Felipe de la Rosa	—
La Alianza Fraternal Mexicana	Near West Side	Julian X. Mordragon, Alfredo Miranda, Guillermo Baquero O'Neill, Leon Lira, Jesus Maldonado, Manuel Aguilar, Joaquin Aguilar, Fernando Moreno	La Alianza
Feminine Club IBIS	South Chicago	Josefina Cerda, Concepcion Jasquez, Maria Barragan, Alfredo R. Quintero	—
El Circulo de Obreros Católicos San José	East Chicago, Indiana	Benjamin Figueroa, Francisco Figueroa, Carlos Figueroa, Pedro Pacheco, J. Jesus Cortez, Ignacio Gonzalez, Luis Zuniga Sanchez, Juan de la Rosa, and Jose Gonzalez	El Amigo del Hogar
Miguel Hidalgo y Costilla Society	South Chicago	Bernardo Pastor, Salvador Trejo, Francisco Avilez, Louis A. Acosta, Jose B. Flores	La Voz de México[1]
Josefa Ortiz de Dominguez Club	Douglas Park	Refugio Alaniz, Maria G. de Mejia, Maria del Rosario, Maria Mariscal, Guadalupe Guerrero	—
Caballeros de Guadalupe	South Chicago (based out of Our Lady of Guadalupe Church)	Gumaro Ortiz, Pedro Luna, E. Aragon	—

(continued)

Organization	Location	Members	Source
Las Hijas de Maria	South Chicago (based out of Our Lady of Guadalupe Church)	—	—
Frente Popular Mexicano of Chicago	Near West Side, Back of the Yards & South Chicago	Nicholas M. Hernandez, Henrique Venegas, Jesus Flores, Fidencio Moreno, A. Escamilla, Refugio Roman Martinez, Lupe Marshall, Jose Lazaro, and Venustiano Rodriquez	La Defensa
La Sociedad Española of Chicago and La Sociedad Española of Gary, Indiana (Society of Spaniards)	Near West Side of Chicago and Gary, Indiana	Miguel Garriga, Faustino Arias, Jose Gonzalez Perez, Jesus Fernandez, Manuel Vega, Jose Arguelles, Alfonso Barcena, Edelmiro Rodriguez Jose Gonzalez, Antonio Perez, Alfonso Bouzo, Luciano Garcia, Miguel Puig, Arturo Garcia, Jose Montos, Frank Rodriguez, Manuel Rodriguez	—
Unión Benéfica Española	—	Jose Amigo, Francisco Abeldua, Pedro Ballesteros, Juan Serrano, Francisco Garcia, Alfredo Quintana, Jose Varela, Jose Cendon	—
Spanish Society	—	Faustino Arias, E. Rodriguez, A. Bouzo, J. Aguilar	—
American-Spanish League	—	Enrique de Luna, Tiburcio Vela, Cruz Vasque Otilio Velasquez	—
Club Cultural Latino Americano	Near West Side	R. Gonzalez, Julio Velez, Francisco Zuniga, J. Jesus Flores, Mr. Cornello, Abraham Gomez, Lupe Plaza, Mr. Santiago, Maria Louisa Garilay, Fidel Paramo, Rosario A. de Flores	—
Committee Against Alcohol, affiliated with the Great National Committee Against Alcoholism	South Chicago	Rafael Aveleyra, F. Gonzalez, Rafael G. Guardado, Eliud Garcia Trevino, Ruben Valasco, Manuel Garcia, Miguel Nieto, Carlos M. Gurrola	—
Mexican Fraternal Society	South Chicago	Enrique Garcia, Sabino B. Hernandez, P. Negrete, M. Sifuentes, Francisco Arias, J. M. Mireles, Sabino B. Hernandez	—
Mexican Confederation of Societies	—	Jose Valdez, J. V. Herrera, Louis Acosta, Francisco Cabrera, Epigmenio Prado Mrs. B. de Blanquete	—
Young Boys Methodist League	—	Pedro Gogora, Jose Cardenas, Samuel Ramirez, Dionisio Munoz, Jeronimo Vaca, Robert Garcia	—

Table 16 (*continued*)

Name of immigrant society	Community area	Active participants	Affiliated press
Sociedad Mutualista Fraternal Mexicana	Lincoln Park	Aureliano Guerra, Catarino Moren, Refugio Moreno, Octaviano Hernandez, Pedro Cuellar, Graciano Carrillo, Sabino Hernandez, Pedro Blanco	—
Sociedad Plutarco Elias Calles	South Chicago	Agustin Arteaga, Ramon Silva, Jesus Gonzalez, Antonio G. Garcia, Leopoldo Escobarete, Jesus Garcia	—
Alas Rojas Sports and Social Club	Near West Side	Pepe Rivera, Cuquita Delago, Rosita Herrera, Margot Maldonado, Laurita Lopez, Beatriz Ibarra, Francis Garces, Lacha Lopez	*El Mexicano*
Club Deportivo Yaquis	South Chicago	Eduardo Peralta, Manuel Garcia, Miguel Hernandez, Lindro Areas, Jose Diaz, Salvador Vallos, Carlos Maravilla	—
Club Deportivo Excelsior	South Chicago	Luis Cornejo, Fernando Cornejo, Manuel Garay	—
Sportive Club Monterrey	South Chicago	Isabel Castro, Alberto Cueller, Justo M. Alvarado, Rafael Cueller, Nicolas Barbosa, Antonio Maravilla	—

Note: A dash indicates an empty cell. Spanish-speaking immigrants also formed the Association Panamericana, Latin American Club, Club Cultural Latino Americano, Sociedad Fraternal Mexicana Logia 170 of the Alianza Hispano-América, United Mexican Clubs, Pro-Mexico Society, Pro–Fiesta Patrias Committee, Fraternal Educational Melchor Ocampo Club, Ignacio Altamirano Educational Club, El Club Educativo de Trabajadores, Benito Juárez Educational Club, Club Mamerto, Cuauhtemoc Club, Anahuac Club, Comité Pro Vasconcelos, Vicente Lombardo Toledono Club, Lázaro Cárdenas Club, Club of Mexican Workers Local 32, Camp Emilio Carranza No. 448 of the Woodmen of the World, Spanish American Anti-alcoholic Committee, La Sociedad Fraternal Mexicana of South Deering, Enterprise Corona, Club 333, Club Oro y Sol, Club Ideal, Club Recreativor 33, Necaxa, Fraternal Evolution, Obreros Guadalupanos Club, Asociación Cristinana de Jovenes Mexicanos (ACJM), Esfuerzo Cristinano, Security and Benefit Association Latin Council No. 4045, Mexican Cooperative, Flechas del Sur y San Antonio, Flechas Azules, Atlas Sports Club, Club of United Spaniards, Committee for the Defense of Spanish Liberties, Chicago Cuban Association, Atlas Feminine Club, Feminine Social Club Venus, Club de Madres Mexicanas, Ladies Society of the Mexican Methodist Church, Union Bautiste de Jovenes, Damas Mexicanas, Mexican Women's Club, and Recreational Mexican Club.

1. This newspaper should not be confused with the PCM newspaper by the same name (see Carr, *Marxism and Communism*, 51).

Notes

Introduction

1. *La Noticia Mundial*, August 28, 1927; and The Weather, *Chicago Daily Tribune*, August 26, 1927. Throughout this book, I use the terms "Mexican," "immigrant," and "migrant" to refer to Mexican nationals. I use "immigrant" when referring to Mexicans who crossed the U.S.-Mexico border and "migrant" for those who migrated within the United States after their first crossing. When needed, I use "Mexican national" for those who held Mexican citizenship and "Mexican American" for those who held U.S. citizenship. When referring to Mexican nationals and Mexican Americans as a group, I use the term "ethnic Mexicans" in place of the more cumbersome "Mexican-origin people" or "people of Mexican descent." I do not use the phrase "ethnic Mexicans" to negate the racialization of the Mexican people in the United States or their long history of experiencing racial discrimination. Regarding my interchanging use of the terms "Mexican" and "immigrant," based on census and Catholic parish records, Francisco Rosales estimated that 97 percent of the Mexican population of Chicago in 1930 had been born in Mexico ("Mexican Immigration," 106).

2. I use the phrase "white ethnics" to refer to persons who were described as "white Americans" by city and federal authorities and yet retained a European ethnic identity. On white ethnics, see Barrett and Roediger, "The Irish."

3. Slayton, *Back of the Yards*, 22, 130, 147, 180–85.

4. *La Noticia Mundial*, December 4, 1927; "Quell Riot as Woman Slays Former Deputy," *Chicago Daily Tribune*, August 26, 1927.

5. Ibid., and on the significance of honor among Mexicans in these years, see Piccato, *The Tyranny of Opinion*, 1–21 and chap. 6. At times, I use the term "Hispanic(s)" because Mexican and Latin American immigrants in Chicago in the 1920s used this term and others like it to describe groups and coalitions of Spanish-speaking people; for example, see *La Noticia Mundial*, January 29, 1928.

6. *México*, February 2, 1929, box 52, Chicago Foreign Language Press Survey, Special Collections, Regenstein Library, University of Chicago. Throughout this book, I use a combination of Chicagoland Spanish-language newspapers and translated excerpts found in the Chicago Foreign Language Press Survey (hereafter cited as CFLPS).

7. *El Heraldo de las Américas*, November 15, 1924; *México*, March 21, 1925; *El Amigo del Hogar*, July 17, 1927, July 24, 1927, July 31, 1927.

8. *La Noticia Mundial*, December 8, 1927.

9. On these characteristics of social movements, see Tilly and Wood, *Social Movements*.

10. Basch, Schiller, and Blanc, *Nations Unbound*, 6.

11. Levitt, *The Transnational Villagers*, 7–15, 180–98.

12. Ibid., 21; Wyman, *Round-Trip to America*, 4; Foner, *In a New Land*, 65–69; Foner, "Engagements," 2486; Roediger, *Working towards Whiteness*, 151–54.

13. Wyman, *Round-Trip to America*, 17.

14. Guglielmo, *Living the Revolution*; Top, *Those without a Country*; and Cannistaro and Meyer, *The Lost World*. For more on migrants as sojourners as opposed to naturalizing settlers, see Harzig and Hoerder, *What Is Migration History?* For a critical evaluation of the political and racial ideologies the immigrants assimilated while in the United States, see Roediger, *The Wages of Whiteness*; Roediger, *Working towards Whiteness*; Jacobson, *Whiteness of a Different Color*; and Spickard, *Almost All Aliens*. For a criticism of the literature on whiteness, see Arnesen, "Whiteness."

15. This literature typically focuses on other important themes; see, for example, Smith, "Diasporic Memberships"; Perlmann, *Italians Then, Mexicans Now*.

16. On the long history of expelling Mexicans from the United States, see Hernández, "Contemporary Deportation Raids"; Hernández, *Mexican American Colonization*, 68–80; Cardoso, "La repatriación"; Balderrama and Rodriguez, *Decade of Betrayal*; García, *Operation Wetback*; Genova and Peutz, *The Deportation Regime*.

17. On the recruitment of Mexican labor into the United States, see Reisler, *By the Sweat of Their Brow*; Calavita, *Inside the State*; Massey, Durand, and Malone, *Beyond Smoke and Mirrors*; Cohen, *Braceros*.

18. While the term "Americanization" may seem problematic to some scholars, Mexican immigrants (and many European immigrants) used the phrase and understood it to mean the process by which immigrants would become U.S. citizens and, broadly defined, culturally American people. See Treviño, "Prensa y patria," 466.

19. Zamora, *The World*, 3–9, 198.

20. On examples of Mexican immigrant transnationalism in the Southwest, see Gomez-Quiñones, "The First Steps," 20. On the "sin fronteras" politics of immigrant laborers, see Weber, *Dark Sweat*, 5–12, 79–111, 182–99; see also Guerin-Gonzalez, *Mexican Workers*, 111–38; Milkman, *L.A. Story*.

21. The phrase "México de afuera" was used by Mexican nationals who helped create new Mexican communities in the United States after the revolution. See Monroy,

Rebirth, 4, 38–40. F. Arturo Rosales (*Dictionary*, 429–30) found that Rodolfo Uranga, a columnist for *La Opinión* in Los Angeles, may have coined the phrase, and John Skirius (*Vasconcelos*, 488) adds that Uranga, the influential Mexican intellectual José Vasconcelos, and other Mexican writers were also using the term in the 1920s.

22. Monroy, *Rebirth*, 32–33, 62–63, 85.

23. Vargas, *Proletarians of the North*, 75–76; Valdes, *Barrios Norteños*, 100–104. On the politics of the middle-class Mexican immigrants who became Mexican Americans in San Antonio, see Garcia, *Rise of the Mexican American Middle Class*; and on a similar process in Houston, see De Leon, *Ethnicity in the Sunbelt*; and Rosales, "Shifting Self Perceptions."

24. Garcia, *Mexicans in the Midwest*, 76–79.

25. All studies of Mexican Chicago acknowledge the presence of middle-class Mexicans, but they do not examine this class in any detail. For example, Gabriella Arredondo (*Mexican Chicago*, 15, 139) notes that middle-class Mexican doctors, engineers, and small business owners lived in Chicago, but she does not tell us much about their beliefs or activities. Michael Innis-Jiménez carefully assesses the predominantly working-class Mexican neighborhood of South Chicago and also points to the presence of middle-class Mexicans, but when addressing the intellectuals within this class, he argues that although a "very small Mexican intelligentsia" existed in Chicago, "these elite Mexicans had, for the most part, lighter complexions and sought to maintain an identity separate from working-class Mexicans" (*Steel Barrio*, 9, 189n21).

26. *El Heraldo de las Américas*, November 22, 1924.

27. Sánchez, *Becoming Mexican American*, 12.

28. Vargas, *Labor Rights*, 4–6.

29. Sánchez, *Becoming Mexican American*, 237, 273.

30. Vargas, *Labor Rights*, 6.

31. On the significance of the CIO, see Zieger, *The CIO*.

32. Vargas, *Labor Rights*, 7–8, 286, 287.

33. For example, while some seven thousand Mexicans lived in Detroit in 1930, more than twenty thousand Mexicans lived in Chicago in this year, and if we combine the Mexican populations of East Chicago, Indiana, and Gary, Indiana, with that of Chicago, we can approximate that more than thirty thousand Mexicans lived in metropolitan Chicago in 1930. See U.S. Bureau of the Census, *Fifteenth Census*; Taylor, *Mexican Labor*.

34. Pallares, "The Chicago Context," 37.

35. On the complex relationship between Mexican Americans and Mexican immigrants, see Gutiérrez, *Walls and Mirrors*.

36. García, "Political Integration," 608. For more on Mexican naturalization, see Grebler, "The Naturalization," 17–31; Sanchez, *Becoming Mexican American*, chap. 10, 275–76; Balderrama and Rodriguez, *Decade of Betrayal*, 20, chap. 1.

37. Kerr, "State of the Discipline," 147. On Kerr's foundational work on Mexican Chicago, see her dissertation, "The Chicano Experience."

38. Knight, *Counter-revolution and Reconstruction*, x, emphasis in the original.

39. Brading, *The First America*; Hart, *Revolutionary Mexico*; Lomnitz, *Deep Mexico*; Meyer, *The Cristero Rebellion*. On the "consciousness" of the Mexicans who participated in the rebellion, see Purnell, *Popular Movements*.

40. On these cultural productions and their meanings in Mexican history, see Vaughan and Lewis, *The Eagle and the Virgin*.

Chapter 1. The Mexican Revolution Migrates to Chicago

1. Knight, *The Mexican Revolution*, 1:40–42, 68–69, 499n27; Lomnitz, *The Return*, 83; Vaughan, "Primary Education," 58n55; Vaughan, *Cultural Politics*, 52; Alba, *The Population of Mexico*, 61.

2. Knight, *The Mexican Revolution*, 1:43–44.

3. Lomnitz, *The Return*, 20, 82–99.

4. Leininger Pycior, *Democratic Renewal*, 14–15; Zamora, *The World*, 104–6, 114, 144; Knight, *The Mexican Revolution*, 1:39.

5. Hart, *Revolutionary Mexico*, 237–42; Lomnitz, *The Return*, 99–103; Knight, *The Mexican Revolution*, 1:55–77; Leininger Pycior, *Democratic Renewal*, 15.

6. Hart, *Revolutionary Mexico*, 245–47; Knight, *The Mexican Revolution*, 1:175.

7. Lomnitz, *The Return*, 90–92.

8. Quotes drawn from Quirk, *The Mexican Revolution*, 71, 90–91. On the complexities of Mexican liberalism, see Hale, *Mexican Liberalism*; Hale, *The Transformation*; and Hale, *Emilio Rabasa*.

9. Flower, "The Mexican Revolt," 119–22; Romanell, "Bergson in Mexico," 502–3; Innes, "The Universidad Popular Mexicana"; Haddox, *Vasconcelos of Mexico*, 3–9; Vasconcelos, *Ulises Criollo*.

10. Jones and Wilson, *The Mexican in Chicago*, 23; untitled newspaper excerpt, 1928–31, box 53, CFLPS.

11. On the U.S. government's "temporary admissions" program of 1917–21, which facilitated the entry of tens of thousands of Mexicans into the United States, see Reisler, *By the Sweat*.

12. U.S. Bureau of the Census, *Fourteenth Census*; U.S. Bureau of the Census, *Fifteenth Census*; Jones, "Conditions Surrounding Mexicans," 92; Taylor, *Mexican Labor*, 28, 32, 36–38; Rosales, "Mexican Immigration," 56–82, 98–99, 108–68; Gutierrez, *Walls and Mirrors*, 44–51.

13. Declarations of Intention and Petitions for Naturalization, 1900–1940, RG 21, National Archives—Great Lakes Region, Chicago (hereafter cited as Naturalization Records, 1900–1940); Cook County Clerk of the Circuit Court, Naturalization Declarations of Intention (1906–29), http://www.cookcountyclerkofcourt.org/NR/ (hereafter cited as Declarations of Intention).

14. Gamio, *Mexican Immigration*, 71–74; Hughes, *Living Conditions*, 10; Jones, "Conditions Surrounding Mexicans," 42, 53; Kerr, "The Chicano Experience," 23; Rosales, "Mexican Immigration," 107, 128; Taylor, *Mexican Labor*, 49.

15. Felter, "Social Adaptations," 11.

16. Arredondo, *Mexican Chicago*, 7–8. Rick A. Lopez also suggests that Mexican immigrants became Mexican in Chicago and emphasizes the roles of postrevolutionary Mexican "elite" academics and statesmen in shaping immigrant identities; see "Forging a Mexican National Identity."

17. Guglielmo, *White on Arrival*, 18, 21.

18. Ibid.; and Vecoli, "The Formation." On "Italy's many village-based diasporas," see Gabaccia, *Italy's Many Diasporas*, 175.

19. Mexicans did not publish newspapers in indigenous languages or in regional dialects of the Spanish language. Out of a sample of 863 Mexican marriages in Chicago, I found little evidence to suggest that Mexican men were choosing their spouses based on a similar region of origin. See table 13 in the appendix for my data on marriages.

20. On examples of city blocks in Chicago that reflected a regional culture, see Innis-Jimenez, *Steel Barrio*, 130–31.

21. Starting in the late 1960s and early 1970s, Mexican immigrants would form hometown associations (HTAs) in Chicago named after particular states in Mexico, but these groups are a consequence of the consolidation and then fractionalization of the PRI. On these HTAs, see Bada, *Mexican Hometown Associations*; Bada, "Mexican Hometown Associations"; Ramirez, Perales-Ramos, and Arellano, "Marchando al Futuro," 127; and Leininger Pycior, *Democratic Renewal* 5.

22. Quoted in Innis-Jimenez, *Steel Barrio*, 47; see also Arredondo, *Mexican Chicago*, 18–20.

23. On the significance of community for Latin American immigrants, see Hamilton and Chinchilla, *Seeking Community*, 11–13, 229–31; Levitt, *The Transnational Villagers*.

24. Simpson, *Many Mexicos*.

25. Naturalization Records, 1900–1940.

26. Ibid.; U.S. Bureau of the Census, *Fourteenth Census*, 730–31.

27. Naturalization Records, 1900–1940. When I reduce the sample size to the Mexican immigrants who were raised in Mexico and immigrated to the United States as adults, I find that their proportions remain relatively consistent with this interpretation. See table 5 in the appendix.

28. Naturalization Records, 1900–1940.

29. Sanchez, *Becoming Mexican American*, table 5, 46.

30. *México*, November 10, 1928, December 19, 1928, box 52, CFLPS.

31. *México*, November 3, 1928, box 52, CFLPS; *México*, January 1925, trans. Robert Redfield, box 59, subseries 12, Redfield Papers.

32. The Mexicans in Chicago Journal, 73, 79–80, box 59, subseries 12, Redfield Papers (hereafter cited as Journal).

33. *El Heraldo de las Américas*, November 11, 1924.

34. *La Noticia Mundial*, September 16, 1927; *El Heraldo de las Américas*, November 15, 1924, my translation; Journal, 1–2, 73.

35. *México*, January 18, 1925, my translation; Journal, 73; *Correo Mexicano*, November 18, 1926, my translation, carton 11, folder 54, Taylor Papers.

36. Journal, 64; scrapbook of Robert C. Jones, 1927, box 52, CFLPS; *México*, February 25, 1930, box 53, CFLPS; *El Nacional*, March 4, 1931, box 52, CFLPS; *México*, October 13, 1928, box 53, CFLPS.

37. Cockcroft, *Intellectual Precursors*, 101n22; Lomnitz, *The Return*, 97, 539n16.

38. *La Noticia Mundial*, September 16, 1927; field notes, societies, p. 123, folder 64, carton 11, Taylor Papers; *México*, November 3, 1928, November 24, 1928, January 5, 1929, February 20, 1929, June 29, 1929, November 9, 1929, box 53, CFLPS.

39. Leininger Pycior, *Democratic Renewal*, 18–19.

40. *México*, January 18, 1925, my translation; *La Noticia Mundial*, August 21, 1927, my translation; *México*, June 2, 1928, November 12, 1929, April 12, 1930, April 29, 1930, May 6, 1930, May 15, 1930; *El Nacional*, June 20, 1931; and scrapbook of Robert C. Jones, 1927, all in box 52, CFLPS; scrapbook of Robert C. Jones, 1927, box 53, CFLPS; Robert C. Jones's field notes, 1928, and interview with Dr. Francisca Luna, both in folder 49, carton 11, Taylor Papers; "Las Sociedades Contestan a la Cruz Azul Mexicana," folder 68, carton 11, Taylor Papers; Integración de la Junta Patriótica de Aquel Lugar, Chicago, IL, Fondo 2006-20, SRE.

41. Ibid.; and see Beito, *From Mutual Aid*, for an examination of the significance of fraternal societies and mutualistas in the years before the New Deal.

42. *México*, November 11, 1928, November 28, 1928, December 5, 1928, December 15, 1928, December 29, 1928, March 15, 1930, April 5, 1930, April 12, 1930, May 1, 1930; and *El Nacional*, December 17, 1930, all in box 52, CFLPS.

43. *México*, April 24, 1930, May 6, 1930, May 8, 1930, May 20, 1930, box 52, CFLPS.

44. On this culture of mutualism, see Hernandez, *Mutual Aid for Survival*.

45. *México*, May 8, 1930; and *El Nacional*, May 2, 1931, May 9, 1931, September 19, 1931, all in box 52, CFLPS.

46. Quoted in Innis-Jimenez, *Steel Barrio*, 121.

47. Scrapbook notes of Miss Elena San Martin and interview with Mr. Jesus Herrera, editor of *La Voz de México*, November 10, 1936, box 52, CFLPS.

48. *El Liberal*, August 5, 1933, August 19, 1933, box 53, CFLPS; *El Mexicano*, May 2, 1934; and *El Nacional*, February 2, February 17, 1934, all in box 52, CFLPS.

49. Baldwin, *Protestants*, 11–26.

50. Rembao, *Outlook in Mexico*; Rembao, *Lecciones*; Rembao, *The Growing Church*; text quotes from *México*, May 20, 1930, box 52, CFLPS.

51. Kerr, "The Chicano Experience," 33.

52. Sanchez, *Becoming Mexican American*, table 2, 34.

53. *México*, December 5, 1928; *El Nacional*, July 18, 1931, March 12, 1932, all in box 52, CFLPS; *El Nacional*, October 24, 1931, May 7, 1932, June 4, 1932, November 19, 1932; *El Mexicano*, May 2, 1934, all in box 53, CFLPS; *Chicago Daily Tribune*, December 14, 1923, December 15, 1923, December 12, 1923, December 24, 1923, January 14, 1924, July 10, 1930, June 6, 1932, April 9, 1939; interview with Dr. Luna, p. 17.

54. Quoted in *Chicago Daily Tribune*, December 12, 1923, and reprinted in part in *Chicago Daily Tribune*, December 14, 1923, December 15, 1923, December 24, 1923.

55. Quoted in *Chicago Daily Tribune*, January 14, 1924 and addressed in interview with Dr. Luna, p. 17.

56. McCarthy, "Which Christ," 175n140.

57. *Chicago Daily Tribune*, July 10, 1930.

58. *Chicago Daily Tribune*, April 9, 1939.

59. *Chicago Daily Tribune*, June 6, 1932; *El Mexicano*, May 2, 1934, box 53, CFLPS.

60. *El Nacional*, July 18, 1931, box 52, CFLPS.

61. *El Nacional*, March 12, 1932, box 52, CFLPS; *El Nacional*, October 24, 1931, May 7, 1932, June 4, 1932, November 19, 1932, all in box 53, CFLPS.

62. *México*, November 3, 1928, box 52, CFLPS; *México*, January 1925, trans. Robert Redfield, Redfield Papers, emphasis in original.

63. *México*, November 10, 1928, December 19, 1928, box 52, CFLPS.

64. Jones, "Conditions Surrounding Mexicans," 100–103; *México*, June 6, 1928, December 15, 1928; *El Nacional*, December 23, 1933, all in box 52, CFLPS; Adena Miller Rich, "The Administrative Organization and Extent of Naturalization in the Chicago District," June 1928, p. 51, folder 3, box 1, IPL; "Aliens Naturalized in the Chicago District, 1922–28," folder 1, box 1, IPL.

65. *México*, December 15, 1928, box 52, CFLPS; Journal, 1–2, 18, 42–57, 101.

66. *México*, December 5, 1928, box 52, CFLPS.

67. Innis-Jimenez, *Steel Barrio*, 53, 68–69.

68. Journal of Robert Redfield, 42–57, 81–83, 96, folder 2, box 59, subseries 12, Redfield Papers; and "Conflict between Mexicans and Poles," box 143, folder 3, Burgess Papers.

69. *México*, June 8, 1929 (Italian assault, Mexican casualty), box 52, CFLPS; "Notes on Newspapers," *La Noticia Mundial*, November 1, 1925 (Polish assault); *México*, October 16, 1926 (Polish assault), November 27, 1926 (Polish and Italian assault), January 8, 1927 (Polish assault, Mexican casualty), April 30, 1927 (white ethnic assault); and *La Noticia Mundial*, August 7, 1927 (Polish assault), all in folder 63, carton 11, Taylor Papers.

70. "Asalto a los mexicanos Ruiz y esposa," SRE 2040-37; "Notes on Mexican Newspapers (September 3, 1929)," folder 63, carton 11, Taylor Papers; *El Nacional*, May 27, 1931; and *La Lucha*, April 28, 1934, both in box 52, CFLPS; *La Noticia Mundial*, August 28, 1927 (Polish assault, thirty Poles attack five Mexicans), folder 63, carton 11, Taylor Papers.

71. *México*, January 18, 1925.

72. *El Heraldo de las Américas*, November 15, 1924.

73. Balderrama, *In Defense of La Raza*, 6–7.

74. "Los cunsules mexicanos no cumplen con su deber," *México*, January 18, 1925.

75. Gonzalez, *Mexican Consuls*.

76. "Cuestionario que deberan contestar los funcionarios," part 1, pp. 2–4, IV-1165-1, SRE.

77. "Marciono Caldern Protección," IV-313-12, SRE; *México*, May 6, 1930, May 8, 1930, box 52, CFLPS.

78. *El Heraldo de las Américas*, November 22, 1924.

79. Innis-Jimenez, *Steel Barrio*, 83, 162–64.

80. *El Nacional*, August 13, 1932.

81. *El Heraldo de las Américas*, November 1, 1924, November 15, 1924; *La Raza*, April 28, 1928.

82. *El Nacional*, July 11, 1931, box 52, CFLPS.

83. Innis-Jimenez, *Steel Barrio*, 140.

84. Quoted in Mendieta, "Celebrating," 335.

85. *México*, April 1, 1930; *El Nacional*, April 4, 1931, May 6, 1931, June 11, 1931, all in box 52, CFLPS; Balderrama, *In Defense of La Raza*, 38.

86. A more inclusive method to determine the naturalization rate of Mexican immigrants might add the number of Mexicans who applied for U.S. citizenship in a given decade in Chicago to the total number of foreign-born Mexicans living in Chicago in the same decade. In other words, in 1920 the Mexican population of Chicago stood at 1,224, and in the years up to and including 1920, 218 Mexicans applied for naturalization. This more inclusive calculation would suggest that Mexicans had a rate of application for naturalization of 18 percent in 1920, 4 percent in 1930, and 14 percent in 1940.

87. Balderrama, *In Defense of La Raza*, 8.

88. Naturalization Records, 1900–1940.

89. Rich, "The Administrative Organization," 51; "Aliens Naturalized."

90. U.S. Bureau of the Census, *Sixteenth Census*, 642.

91. *La Lucha*, April 7, 1934, box 52, CFLPS.

92. *El Nacional*, August 13, 1932, box 53, CFLPS; Innis-Jimenez, *Steel Barrio*, 139, 143; and Valdes, *Barrios Norteños*, 96–97.

93. *México*, January 23, 1929, March 29, 1930; *El Nacional*, May 14, 1932, May 28, 1932; *El Liberal*, August 12, 1933; and interview with Mr. Antonio L. Schmidt, May 19, 1937, all in box 52, CFLPS; *El Nacional*, August 13, 1932; and *La Defensa*, January 18, 1936, both in box 53, CFLPS; field notes, societies, p. 123; and Kerr, "The Chicano Experience," 70.

94. *El Liberal*, May 13, 1933, June 17, 1933, box 52, CFLPS.

95. *El Liberal*, June 17, 1933, July 22, 1933, September 16, 1933; *Sunday Times*, May 26, 1935, all in box 52, CFLPS; *El Ideal Mexicano*, September 6, 1936, box 53, CFLPS.

96. On middle-class Mexican immigrants in Los Angeles, see Monroy, *Rebirth*, 32–33, 62–63, 85; and Sanchez, *Becoming Mexican American*, 114, 176–79. On San Antonio, see Garcia, *Rise of the Mexican American Middle Class*. Houston's Mexican population numbers were low before 1920, but far more Mexican elite ricos made their way to Houston than to Chicago during the revolution. Moreover, by the 1920s, when Houston grew tremendously, a Tejano (Texas-born) identifiable presence existed in the Second Ward. On Houston, see De Leon, *Ethnicity in the Sunbelt*, 18–25; and Rosales, "Shifting Self-Perceptions." Benjamin Johnson finds Mexicans developing a Mexican American identity before 1915 in southern Texas, a sense of identity that was solidified in the aftermath of the "Plan de San Diego" uprising; see Johnson, *Revolution in Texas*.

97. While some ninety-seven thousand Mexicans lived in Los Angeles in 1930, roughly twenty thousand lived in Chicago in this same year. See Sanchez, *Becoming Mexican American*, 90.

Chapter 2. The Counterrevolution Migrates to Chicago and Northwest Indiana

1. "Church of St. Francis D'Assisi—Chicago, June 3, 1926," folder 46, carton 11, Taylor Papers.

2. This chapter builds on and contrasts with an essay on the Círculo by Juan R. Garcia and Angel Cal that frames the Círculo as a largely middle-class organization (see "El Círculo de Obreros Católicos 'San José'"). I argue that the majority of the Círculo's members were actually working class. Most Mexican business owners in East Chicago who advertised in *El Amigo del Hogar* (the Círculo's press) did not serve as leaders of the Círculo. See *El Amigo del Hogar*, November 22, 1925, December 20, 1925, May 16, 1926, June 27, 1926, April 17, 1927, July 10, 1927, May 5, 1927, February 5, 1928, July 7, 1929. *El Amigo del Hogar* frequently reported on members who were injured at the Youngstown Sheet and Tube foundry and others who worked at Inland Steel (see *El Amigo del Hogar*, January 3, 1926, April 8, 1928). When the Círculo listed the occupations of its donors, it named Inland Steel workers as its primary contributors (see *El Amigo del Hogar*, January 31, 1926). And when discussing its educational program, the Círculo emphasized how it would benefit the group's largely blue-collar membership (see *El Amigo del Hogar*, February 7, 1926, April 10, 1927).

3. *El Amigo del Hogar*, April 17, 1927, April 15, 1928.

4. Buchenau, *Plutarco Elias Calles*, 126–30.

5. For more on the rebellion, see Meyer, *The Cristero Rebellion*; and his illustrated history, *La Cristiada*; Butler, *Popular Piety*; Boyer, *Becoming Campesinos*; Purnell, *Popular Movements*; David C. Bailey, *¡Viva Cristo Rey!*

6. Quoted in Meyer, *The Cristero Rebellion*, 31.

7. Buchenau, *Plutarco Elias Calles*, 128; Meyer, *The Cristero Rebellion*, 20–26.

8. Cockcroft, *Intellectual Precursors*, 5, 85–86, 130, 233–34.

9. Quoted in Meyer, *The Cristero Rebellion*, 44.

10. Meyer, *La Cristiada*; Meyer, *The Cristero Rebellion*.

11. Rosales, "Mexican Immigration"; and Young, "Cristero Diaspora," 275.

12. U.S. Bureau of the Census, *Abstract*, 61; Taylor, *Mexican Labor*, 27; U.S. Bureau of the Census, *Fifteenth Census*, 683; U.S. Bureau of the Census, *Sixteenth Census*, 809. Rosales cites 3,662 Mexicans hired by Inland Steel between 1918 and 1930 ("Mexican Immigration," 171–74).

13. In all, Mexicans represented about 65 percent of the total workforce of the Indiana Harbor Railway, 57 percent of Western Indiana, and 6 percent of the Chicago, Milwaukee and Gary Railroad. Mexicans also represented 30 percent of Inland Steel's total workforce and roughly 6 percent of the steelworkers in Gary, Indiana, and 13 percent of the G. H. Hammond meat company's labor force. See Taylor, *Mexican Labor*, 31, 36–37; and Samora and Lamanna, *Mexican-Americans*.

14. McGreevy, *Parish Boundaries*, 9–12.

15. McCarthy, "Which Christ," 127–28, 208–9, 241–42.

16. Young, "Cristero Diaspora," 292.

17. Ibid., 286–92.

18. Innis-Jimenez, *Steel Barrio,* 92.

19. Young, "Cristero Diaspora," 278, 281.

20. Meyer, *La Cristiada,* 146–47; McCarthy, "Which Christ," 151–52, 198–99, 202, 212–13.

21. Miller, *Emigrants and Exiles*; and Barrett, *The Irish Way.*

22. McCarthy, "Which Christ," 202–3, 210–19; Young, "Cristero Diaspora," 295.

23. Ibid.

24. Ibid.; Orsi, *Thank You, St. Jude.*

25. Grannan, "'Here Comes Everybody'"; McCarthy, "Which Christ," 242–45.

26. McCarthy, "Which Christ," 213, 276n116.

27. Ibid., 214–15.

28. Innis-Jimenez, *Steel Barrio,* 120.

29. *El Amigo del Hogar,* November 22, 1925. Other Mexican immigrants, such as Luis Zuñiga Sánchez, Juan de la Rosa, and José González, also were instrumental in founding the Círculo. See Rosales, "Mexican Immigration," 189. I highlight the role of the Figueroas because they were the circle's intellectual leaders and helped found *El Amigo del Hogar.*

30. *El Amigo del Hogar,* January 3, 1926, January 31, 1926.

31. *El Amigo del Hogar,* November 22, 1925.

32. Ibid.

33. *El Amigo del Hogar,* December 2, 1928.

34. *El Amigo del Hogar,* January 19, 1926, January 24, 1926, May 2, 1926.

35. *El Amigo del Hogar,* June 26, 1927, August 28, 1927, October 23, 1927, September 9, 1928.

36. *El Amigo del Hogar,* July 7, 1929.

37. *El Amigo del Hogar,* March 20, 1927.

38. *El Amigo del Hogar,* December 6, 1925, March 20, 1927, May 15, 1927, April 8, 1928, April 15, 1928.

39. Examples would include Perpetua Pacheco, the wife of the circle's Pedro Pacheco, and María L. Pena, daughter of Luis Pena, the head of Benefit Society Benito Juárez. See *El Amigo del Hogar,* May 29, 1927, July 10, 1927.

40. A festival could raise about $100. See *El Amigo del Hogar,* May 19, 1928, November 24, 1929. This is the equivalent of about $1,300 in 2012 (see www.measuringworth.com). The circle also sponsored plays presented by Mexican women, which could generate roughly fifty dollars per play. Both Perpetua Pacheco and María L. Peña performed in these plays. See *El Amigo del Hogar,* January 17, 1926, March 14, 1926, March 6, 1927, March 27, 1927, April 10, 1927, November 6, 1927, November 27, 1927, November 20, 1927.

41. On the role of religion and transnational migration, see Levitt, "'You Know.'"

42. *El Amigo del Hogar,* February 7, 1926, April 10, 1927.

43. *El Amigo del Hogar,* January 29, 1928.

44. *El Amigo del Hogar,* May 22, 1927.

45. Quoted in Meyer, "An Idea," 283–84.

46. *El Amigo del Hogar*, August 12, 1928. Given that some Mexicans were illiterate, the Círculo offered these migrants public reading sessions during their events. See *El Amigo del Hogar*, June 10, 1928, July 15, 1928.

47. Meyer, "An Idea of Mexico," 281.

48. *El Amigo del Hogar*, December 27, 1925, April 18, 1926, May 26, 1929.

49. *El Amigo del Hogar*, November 10, 1929.

50. *El Amigo del Hogar*, October 9, 1927, April 22, 1928.

51. *El Amigo del Hogar*, April 6, 1930.

52. *El Amigo del Hogar*, February 16, 1930.

53. *El Amigo del Hogar*, October 30, 1927.

54. *El Amigo del Hogar*, October 2, 1927, October 16, 1927, October 23, 1927, October 30, 1927, January 15, 1928, September 9, 1928, May 26, 1929, January 16, 1930, April 6, 1930.

55. Sánchez, "'Go After the Women.'"

56. *El Amigo del Hogar*, July 10, 1927.

57. *El Amigo del Hogar*, October 2, 1927, October 16, 1927, October 23, 1927.

58. *El Amigo del Hogar*, October 16, 1927.

59. *El Amigo del Hogar*, January 29, 1928.

60. *El Amigo del Hogar*, October 23, 1927.

61. While many Bajío immigrants supported the Cristeros, some criticized them, accusing them of unjustly commandeering horses and equipment during the rebellion. See untitled notes, folder 4, box 134, Burgess Papers.

62. A few of the other societies that were formed in East Chicago included Benefit Society Miguel Hidalgo y Costilla, Benefit Society Cuauhtémoc, and the Mexican Union. See "Las sociedades mexicanas locales," Fondo 2006-19, SRE.

63. *El Amigo del Hogar*, June 27, 1926, April 17, 1927, June 10, 1928, August 12, 1928.

64. *El Amigo del Hogar*, November 22, 1925, January 3, 1926, January 31, 1926, May 2, 1926, May 16, 1926, March 13, 1927, May 15, 1927.

65. *El Amigo del Hogar*, March 17, 1928, January 27, 1929. In December 1925, the circle was invited to Chicago to join the developing Confederation of Mexican Societies of North America (see *El Amigo del Hogar*, December 13, 1925, December 20, 1925, December 27, 1925). In Chicago, the circle attended Masses at St. Francis of Assisi on the Near West Side and at Our Lady of Guadalupe in South Chicago. Circle members also worked with the Chicago-based Knights of Guadalupe (see *El Amigo del Hogar*, June 12, 1927, February 12, 1928, April 1, 1928, June 10, 1928, September 30, 1928, December 23, 1928). In Detroit, circle members joined with exiled Mexican priests (see *El Amigo del Hogar*, July 8, 1928, November 11, 1928, November 25, 1928, January 27, 1929).

66. *El Amigo del Hogar*, January 3, 1926, May 16, 1926, April 10, 1927, June 27, 1926.

67. *El Amigo del Hogar*, December 13, 1925, December 27, 1925, January 17, 1926, March 20, 1927, June 12, 1927, August 21, 1927, October 9, 1927, December 25, 1927, November 18, 1928, May 5, 1929, June 2, 1929, September 22, 1929, November 17, 1929, February 23, 1930.

68. When the Garden Theater began segregating Mexicans, the Círculo boycotted it under pressure from other migrants, but it explained that Mexicans needed to admit to themselves that some migrants may have "behaved shamefully" at the theater, and this behavior may have prompted the new policy (*El Amigo del Hogar*, July 17, 1927, July 24, 1927, July 31, 1927). Although the Garden Theater attempted to segregate Mexicans from their white customers, most white-owned businesses in East Chicago did not engage in such practices. Many white-owned businesses rented Mexican groups equipment and spaces for their events and advertised their products and services in *El Amigo* (see April 10, 1927, April 8, 1928, April 15, 1928).

69. *El Amigo del Hogar*, July 10, 1927, September 11, 1927, October 21, 1928, November 4, 1928, December 9, 1928, January 20, 1929.

70. *El Amigo del Hogar*, November 25, 1928.

71. *El Amigo del Hogar* reported that it had approximately fifteen hundred subscribers and was sold in Mexican-owned shops in East Chicago. See *El Amigo del Hogar*, April 24, 1927.

72. *El Amigo del Hogar*, May 15, 1927.

73. *El Amigo del Hogar*, June 5, 1927, February 12, 1928, May 19, 1928.

74. *El Amigo del Hogar*, April 24, 1927.

75. *El Amigo del Hogar*, April 24, 1927, May 15, 1927, July 31, 1927, August 7, 1927.

76. *El Amigo del Hogar*, February 1928. This issue of *El Amigo* did not include a day of publication.

77. *El Liberal*, June 17, 1933, July 22, 1933, September 16, 1933, box 52, CFLPS.

78. *El Amigo del Hogar*, April 15, 1928.

79. *El Amigo del Hogar*, October 21, 1928, December 2, 1928.

80. *El Amigo del Hogar*, February 26, 1930.

81. *México*, June 12, 1929, May 20, 1938, box 52, CFLPS; *El Amigo del Hogar*, January 5, 1930, February 16, 1930.

82. *El Amigo del Hogar*, February 16, 1929, March 30, 1930.

83. *El Amigo del Hogar*, June 9, 1929.

84. *El Amigo del Hogar*, July 7, 1929.

85. Untitled report, American Legion of East Chicago, Kelly Files.

86. Untitled report and "Mexicans Residing in East Chicago Receiving Aid from North Township," Kelly Files.

87. W. M. Fenwick, General Passenger Agent, Missouri-Kansas-Texas Railroad Company, to Paul E. Kelly, April 28, 1932; J. V. Lanigan, Passenger Traffic Manager, to Paul E. Kelly, March 2, 1933; and Paul E. Kelly to Congressman Arthur R. Robinson, March 10, 1932, all in Kelly Files.

88. R.R.F. of Inland Steel Company to Paul Kelly, June 1, 1932, Kelly Files.

89. Paul Kelly to Consul Rafael Avelyra, September 15, 1932, Kelly Files. See also Innis-Jimenez, *Steel Barrio*, 145–46.

90. "List of Mexicans Returned to Mexico from Indiana Harbor on June 9, 1932," "List of Mexicans Returned to Mexico from Indiana Harbor on July 27, 1932," "Mexicans to Be Sent to Their Homes in Mexico, August 23, 1932," "List of Mexicans Re-

turned to Mexico from Indiana Harbor on September 27, 1932," "List of Mexicans Returned to Mexico from Indiana Harbor on October 15, 1932," all in Kelly Files.

91. Concepción González, March 27, 1989, interviewed by Ruth Needleman, CRA.

92. Traditionalists in East Chicago attended Masses and participated in Catholic cultural events in Chicago, and they received support from priests from Chicago, but they technically did not fall under the actual purview of the Chicago archdiocese. They were actually living in the diocese of Fort Wayne, Indiana, under the leadership of Bishop John F. Noll, but it does not appear that they received much attention from Bishop Noll.

Chapter 3. Mexican Immigrant Understandings of Empire, Race, and Gender

1. *El Heraldo de las Américas*, November 22, 1924.

2. Meyer, Sherman, and Deeds, *The Course*, 327–35, 364–67; Hart, *Empire and Revolution*; Ansell, *Oil Baron*; Ocasio Melendez, *Capitalism and Development*; Monroy, *Rebirth*, 40.

3. Quoted in Cockcroft, *Intellectual Precursors*, 161.

4. Britton, "Redefining Intervention," 41.

5. Fabela, *Los Estados Unidos*.

6. Quoted in Hodges, *Intellectual*, 123–24. See also Gobat, *Confronting the American Dream*.

7. *El Heraldo de las Américas*, November 1, 1924; *La Noticia Mundial*, January 29, 1928.

8. *El Heraldo de las Américas*, November 1, 1924; *La Noticia Mundial*, January 29, 1928; *México*, April 11, 1925; *El Heraldo de las Américas*, November 15, 1924; *México*, March 21, 1925, April 11, 1925.

9. U.S. Bureau of the Census, *Fourteenth Census*, 730–31; U.S. Bureau of the Census, *Fifteenth Census*, 249–50; U.S. Bureau of the Census, *Sixteenth Census*, 642.

10. U.S. Bureau of the Census, *Fourteenth Census*, 730–31; and U.S. Bureau of the Census, *Sixteenth Census*, 642.

11. Naturalization Records, 1900–1940.

12. Ibid.

13. "Border Crossings: From Mexico to U.S., 1895–1964," manifest, U.S. Department of Labor, Immigration Service, Mexican Border District, 12044, November 28, 1924, Ancestry.com. Original data from "Nonstatistical Manifests and Statistical Index Cards of Aliens Arriving at Laredo, Texas, May 1903–November 1929," RG 85, Records of the Immigration and Naturalization Service, microfilm serial A3379, microfilm roll 64, National Archives and Records Administration, Washington, DC.

14. While it is quite common for scholars to say that Mexicans were white and aspired to be considered white before the 1960s, an emerging literature is challenging this claim. See Gomez, *Manifest Destinies*; Orozco, *No Mexicans*; and Johnson, "The Cosmic Race."

15. Naturalization Records, 1900–1940; and Declarations of Intention.

16. To accurately compare George Sanchez's findings on Los Angeles in *Becoming Mexican American* to my own on Chicago, here I adhere to his classification choices and fold the twenty-five Mexicans who were classified as brown, brunette, olive, ruddy, and swarthy in Chicago into the "dark" category. By doing so, I have raised the proportion of dark-skinned Mexican immigrants to 79 percent in Chicago. On the complexions of Mexican naturalizers to Los Angeles, see Sanchez, *Becoming Mexican American*, table 1, 30.

17. On the "preliteracy" of Irish immigrants, see Miller, *Emigrants and Exiles*, 71.

18. See, for example, "Volunteer Worker," October 10, 1935, folder 30, box 3, Rich Papers; and Jones, "Conditions Surrounding Mexicans," 40.

19. *México*, January 18, 1925, February 7, 1925, March 7, 1925, January 4, 1928; *El Amigo del Hogar*, November 1, 1924, May 22, 1927, June 5, 1927, January 29, 1928, August 12, 1928, November 4, 1928; Redfield journal, November 19, 1924, April 7, 1925, box 59, subseries 12, Redfield Papers.

20. *El Heraldo de las Américas*, November 22, 1924.

21. *El Heraldo de las Américas*, November 1, 1924; *La Noticia Mundial*, August 28, 1927, September 4, 1927, October 16, 1927, February 5, 1928; *México*, January 18, 1928, January 25, 1928, January 28, 1928, February 13, 1928, December 19, 1928, box 52, CFLPS. On U.S. government perceptions and practices in Latin America, see Schoultz, *Beneath the United States*.

22. Quoted in Caban, *Constructing*, 1, 41–42.

23. Quoted in Nieto-Phillips, "Citizenship and Empire," 60.

24. Quoted in Caban, *Constructing*, 45, 107–12.

25. Quoted in Guerra, *Popular Expression*, 29; and Guerra, "The Promise," 16.

26. Guerra, "The Promise," 15.

27. Quoted in Thomas, *Puerto Rican Citizen*, 9, emphasis in the original; see also Briggs, *Reproducing Empire*, 54–55, 84–86; Iglesias, *Memoirs of Bernardo Vega*, 114–15, 127–31, 144.

28. *La Noticia Mundial*, August 7, 1927, August 28, 1927, August 30, 1927, September 25, 1927, October 6, 1927, October 30, 1927, November 6, 1927, November 13, 1927, November 30, 1927.

29. *New York Times*, July 13, 1927.

30. *La Noticia Mundial*, January 8, 1928, January 22, 1928; *México*, January 25, 1928, January 28, 1928; *La Noticia Mundial*, February 12, 1928.

31. *La Noticia Mundial*, January 29, 1928; *México*, January 11, 1928. On Villa's politics, see Katz, *The Life and Times*.

32. *México*, January 25, 1928, January 28, 1928.

33. *El Amigo del Hogar*, September 4, 1927.

34. Quoted in McCarthy, "Which Christ," 185, 189, 193, 197.

35. *El Amigo del Hogar*, October 21, 1928, December 2, 1928.

36. On the understandings of mestizaje by influential Mexican theorists and artists in the 1920s, see Vasconcelos, *The Cosmic Race*; Gamio, *Forjando Patria*, 74–75, 12–16,

99–101; and the brief but informative commentaries of Orozco, *An Autobiography*, 19–21, 108, and Siqueiros, *No hay mas ruta*, 15–18.

37. Foley, *Quest for Equality*, 8.

38. Kevles, *In the Name of Eugenics*, in particular chaps. 5–7; and Barkan, *The Retreat of Scientific Racism*.

39. Vasconcelos, *The Cosmic Race*, 9.

40. On mestizaje, the oppression of Africans in Mexico, and the erasure of Afro-Mexicans from the Mexican national imaginary, see Fabregat, *Mestizaje in Ibero-America*; Knight, "Racism, Revolution, and Indigenismo"; Miller, *Rise and Fall*; Vaughn, "Afro-Mexico"; Martinez, *Genealogical Fictions*; Vinson and Vaughn, *Afromexico*; Vinson and Restall, *Black Mexico*; and Katzew and Deans-Smith, *Race and Classification*.

41. On the "in-between" ambiguous racial place of southern and eastern European immigrants in the United States, see Barrett and Roediger, "Inbetween Peoples."

42. For references to Netzahualcoyotl, see *El Nacional*, July 15, 1933, box 52, CFLPS; and *México*, January 5, 1929, box 53, CFLPS. For a reference to the "Bronze Cuauhtémoc," see *México*, January 25, 1928. On Juárez, see *México*, March 21, 1925.

43. *México*, March 21, 1925.

44. Nervo, *Antología poética*; *El Nacional*, July 15, 1933, box 52, CFLPS; *México*, January 5, 1929, box 53, CFLPS. For an interpretation of race relations in Chicago that emphasizes the ways that Mexicans distanced themselves from African Americans and the idea of "blackness," see Arredondo, "Navigating Ethno-Racial Currents."

45. *México*, January 1925, box 59, subseries 12, Redfield Papers.

46. *La Noticia Mundial*, August 14, 1927; *México*, February 1, 1928.

47. *El Amigo del Hogar*, June 5, 1927, August 14, 1927, October 13, 1929.

48. *El Amigo del Hogar*, September 1, 1929, September 16, 1928.

49. *México*, January 5, 1929, box 53, CFLPS; *El Amigo del Hogar*, October 2, 1927.

50. *El Amigo del Hogar*, May 15, 1927.

51. *El Amigo del Hogar*, November 20, 1927.

52. Here I draw on the title of an insightful anthology on African American–Latina/o relations: Dzidzienyo and Oboler, *Neither Enemies nor Friends*.

53. Innis-Jimenez, *Steel Barrio*, 70.

54. "Conflict between Mexicans and Poles," folder 3, box 143, Burgess Papers; Redfield journal, 81–83, 96, folder 2, box 59, subseries 12, Redfield Papers. For a contrary interpretation of all of this evidence, see Arredondo, "Navigating Ethno-Racial Currents," 399–427.

55. "Melting Pot," folder 5, box 155, Burgess Papers.

56. Innis-Jimenez, *Steel Barrio*, 94.

57. The Burgess, Taylor, and Redfield papers all include examples of Mexican and African American marriages. See, for example, footnote 53 and "Notes," 62, 1928, folder 49, carton 11, Taylor Papers; and Redfield journal, 67, folder 2, box 59, subseries 12, Redfield Papers.

58. While 17 percent of the Mexican men in our sample married an American-born spouse, these American spouses included white, black, and Mexican American women.

59. As I describe in more detail in the following pages, Mexican men not only preferred to date Mexican women but could offer harsh criticisms of white American women.

60. Redfield journal, 96, folder 2, box 59, subseries 12, Redfield Papers.

61. I thank Joey Lipari for bringing these sources to my attention. City of Chicago Billiard Commission, March 27, 1924, folder 25, box 3, Dever Collection.

62. Ibid.

63. Quoted in Arredondo, "Navigating Ethno-Racial Currents," 417.

64. See, for example, ibid.; and Arredondo, *Mexican Chicago*, chap. 2; Foley, "Becoming Hispanic," 53–70; and Foley, *Quest for Equality*.

65. Innis-Jimenez, *Steel Barrio*, 78; Varas, *Proletarians*, 48–49; Hernandez-Fujigaki, "Mexican Steelworkers," 30–34.

66. Quoted in Shankman, "The Image of Mexico," 48–50.

67. Fuchs, "The Reactions," 293–313. For a sociological analysis that compares the perceptions of African American politicians to those of the African American electorate, see Diamond, "African-American Attitudes," 451–70.

68. Reisler, *By the Sweat*, 193n114.

69. Ibid., 51–52.

70. Taylor, *Mexican Labor*, 111n45. On the nativism of white Americans, see Higham, *Strangers in the Land*.

71. Quoted in Shankman, *Ambivalent Friends*, 74.

72. Innis-Jimenez, *Steel Barrio*, 138–39.

73. *El Liberal*, August 12, 1933, box 52, CFLPS; "Repatriación de colonos mexicanos," IV-354-4, SRE.

74. Mexican Consul Ernesto Laveaga to Basilio Pacheco, September 30, 1950, Mexican American Folder 1, East Chicago Room.

75. *La Defensa*, August 22, 1936, box 52, CFLPS, emphasis added. For a contrary use of this quote, see Arredondo, "Navigating Ethno-Racial Currents," 417.

76. On Mexican patriarchy, see Mirande, *Hombres y Machos*, chap. 2. For more on the revolution and patriarchy, see Smith, *Gender and the Mexican Revolution*.

77. *El Heraldo de las Américas*, November 1, 1924, November 15, 1924, November 22, 1924; *La Noticia Mundial*, October 16, 1927.

78. *El Heraldo de las Américas*, November 1, 1924, November 15, 1924.

79. *El Heraldo de las Américas*, November 15, 1924.

80. For more on the Mexican New Woman, see Ruiz, *From out of the Shadows*, chap. 3.

81. Monroy, *Rebirth*, 175–78; Vargas, *Proletarians of the North*, 165–66.

82. *El Heraldo de las Américas*, November 1, 1924; *México*, March 21, 1925; *La Noticia Mundial*, October 9, 1927; *México*, December 15, 1928, box 52, CFLPS.

83. Octavio Paz used this phrase to capture how patriarchal Mexican men defined Mexican women who challenged their patriarchy. See Paz, *The Labyrinth of Solitude*, 29–46.

84. *La Noticia Mundial,* October 23, 1927.

85. *El Heraldo de las Américas,* February 13, 1928.

86. *El Nacional,* December 19, 1931, box 52, CFLPS, emphasis added.

87. *El Amigo del Hogar,* May 26, 1929.

88. Ibid.

89. *El Amigo del Hogar,* October 30, 1927, November 11, 1928.

90. *El Amigo del Hogar,* October 30, 1927, November 11, 1928.

91. *El Amigo del Hogar,* November 11, 1928, November 25, 1928.

92. *El Amigo del Hogar,* May 16, 1926, January 3, 1926, June 27, 1926, April 10, 1927, August 21, 1927, October 2, 1927, October 9, 1927, October 16, 1927, October 23, 1927, December 25, 1927, November 18, 1928.

93. Lopez, *Racism on Trial,* 2.

94. For "racial project," see Omi and Winant, *Racial Formation,* 56, 80–84. The second quote is from Lopez, *Racism on Trial,* 2.

95. Gramsci, *Prison Notebooks,* 3:109, 168; Omi and Winant, *Racial Formation,* 80–88. On the U.S. white racial state, see Jung, Vargas, and Bonilla-Silva, *State of White Supremacy.*

Chapter 4. The Rise of the Postrevolution Mexican Left in Chicago

1. On the concept of organic intellectuals, see Hoare and Smith, *Selections,* 5–23.

2. Carr, *Marxism and Communism,* 52–57; Olcott, *Revolutionary Women,* 129.

3. While a few historians have mentioned the Frente Popular Mexicano in Chicago, to my knowledge no one has reconstructed the organization's transnational history. See Acuña, *Occupied America,* 246; Kerr, "The Chicano Experience," 85–89; Halpern, *Down on the Killing Floor,* 102; Horowitz, "Negro and White," 68.

4. The CMM was formed in 1932 but would merge with the Sonoran Federación de Maestros Socialistas, the Federación Mexicana de Trabajadores de le Ensenanza, and the Confederación Nacional de Trabajadores de Educación to form the Sindicato de Trabajadores de la Ensenanza de la República Mexicana (STERM) in 1938. See Vaughan, *Cultural Politics,* 69.

5. For more on the process of state incorporation in Latin America, see Collier and Collier, *Shaping the Political Arena.* On cardenismo, see Córdova, *La política de masas;* Knight, "Cardenismo"; and Joseph and Buchenau, *Mexico's Once and Future Revolution,* 126–40.

6. Ibid.

7. Primer Congreso Nacional del Frente Popular Antiimperialista (hereafter cited as PCNFPA), February 27 and 28, 1936, AGN; Benjamin Erosa Peniche to Luis I. Rodríguez, undated, and Lic. Esteban García de Alba to Gobernador Constl. del Estado, February 11, 1936, both in Lázaro Cárdenas del Río (hereafter cited as LCR), 433/121, AGN.

8. PCNFPA.

9. *México,* January 24, 1925, January 31, 1925, February 7, 1925, translated by the author; *México,* January 23, 1929; *La Defensa,* February 8, 1936, box 52, CFLPS; *El Nacional,* August 13, 1932, box 53, CFLPS; Dr. C. S. Shuman to Adena Miller Rich,

December 4, 1936, and "Lista de clubs y sociedades mexicanas," April 1937, both in box 1, folder 11, Rich Papers; Secretario de Propaganda, Gran Junta Popular flyer, in Anderson, Book No. 310, May 20, 1936, folder Mexican Work, box 25, University of Chicago Settlement House Collection. Anderson was a social worker at the University of Chicago Settlement House who attended the Frente's meetings and took notes on their activities.

10. Anderson, Book No. 310, February 2, 1936.

11. PCNFPA, p. 8, AGN; LCR, 433/121, AGN; Anderson, Book No. 310, February 2, 1936.

12. Quoted in Anderson, Book No. 310, March 1, 1936, and see February 9, 1936, February 16, 1936.

13. Mexican Adult Grays (May 5, 1936), Mexican Adult Group Report (Dorothy Anderson Report for June 1936), folder Mexican Work, box 25, University of Chicago Settlement House Collection; Anderson, Book No. 310, February 9, 1936, February 17, 1936, March 2, 1936, April 26, 1936, June 29, 1936.

14. Innis-Jimenez, *Steel Barrio*, 51–52.

15. Anderson, Book No. 310, February 23, 1936, June 14, 1936, June 24, 1936.

16. Olcott, *Revolutionary Women*, 96–98; Vaughan, *Cultural Politics*, 65.

17. Quote drawn from "Mrs. De la Mora Requests," Mexican Group, March 3, 1936, folder 11, box 1, Rich Papers. See also *La Alianza*, May 1936, July 1936; *La Defensa*, October 31, 1936, box 52, CFLPS; *La Defensa*, May 30, 1936, box 53, CFLPS; Anderson, Book No. 310, February 2, 1936, February 17, 1936, February 21, 1936, March 8, 1936, March 21, 1936, April 19, 1936, April 26, 1936, July 1, 1936, August 12, 1936.

18. *La Defensa*, April 11, 1936, box 52, CFLPS; "Mrs. Rich" (note), March 31, 1936, folder 11, box 1, Rich Papers; "ASAMBLEA GENERAL, Angélica Arenal and Consuelo García Morán, Domingo 5 de abril," flyer, in Anderson, Book No. 310, March 21, 1936, April 5, 1936; Arenal, *Páginas sueltas*, 111.

19. Olcott, *Revolutionary Women*, 89–90, 120.

20. See note 18.

21. On the civil war, see Graham, *The Spanish Republic*; and on the international and American support for the Republicans, see Carroll, *The Odyssey*.

22. Hernández quote in meeting of the Frente Popular, November 1, 1936; see also meeting on November 22, 1936; Anderson, Book No. 310, June 3, 1936, August 26, 1936; "In Support of Spanish Democracy" flyer, all in folder Mexican Work, box 25, University of Chicago Settlement House Collection; *Milwaukee Journal*, December 1, 1936.

23. See the commentaries of Reynolds, "The Spanish Wave"; and Fernandez and Argeo, "Invisible Immigrants."

24. "Country of Birth of the Foreign Born," in U.S. Bureau of the Census, *Fifteenth Census*, 249–50; and U.S. Bureau of the Census, *Sixteenth Census*, 693.

25. *El Nacional*, March 12, 1932, September 16, 1932, July 8, 1933, box 52, CFLPS.

26. See, for example, the naturalization applications of Faustino Arias, José González Pérez, Manuel Vega, José Arguelles, Edelmiro Rodríguez, Frank Rodríguez,

and Manuel Rodríguez, all in "Declarations of Intention and Petitions for Naturalization, 1900–1940," RG 21, National Archives—Great Lakes Region, Chicago.

27. On Maximilian Olay, see his "Declarations of Intention"; see also interview with Mr. Maximilian Olay, December 22, 1936, box 52, CFLPS.

28. Esenwein and Shubert, *Spain at War*.

29. Quoted in Payne, *Spain's First Democracy*, 218–28; and see Shubert, *The Road to Revolution*.

30. Spears, "Rehabilitating the Workers."

31. Anderson, Book No. 310, June 3, 1936.

32. Braga, "To Relieve the Misery."

33. Ibid.; Farber, *Revolution and Reaction*; Aguilar, *Cuba*; Fernandez, *Cuban Anarchism*.

34. Quoted in Braga, "To Relieve the Misery," 33.

35. Ibid.

36. Anderson, Book No. 310, 1936, June 3, 1936.

37. *La Defensa*, May 30, 1936, box 52, CFLPS; Anderson, Book No. 310, May 20, 1936, August 5, 1936.

38. Quoted in Kirkwood, *The History of Mexico*, 164.

39. *Daily Illini*, May 19, 1936; Hamilton, *The Limits of State Autonomy*, 148–55; Kirkwood, *The History of Mexico*, 162–67.

40. Levenstein, *Labor Organizations*, 146–60; Alexander and Parker, *International Labor Organizations*, 82–84; Millon, *Vicente Lombardo Toledano*.

41. *La Defensa*, May 30, 1936, box 52, CFLPS; Anderson, Book No. 310, May 20, 1936, August 5, 1936.

42. Hamilton, *The Limits of State Autonomy*, 148–55; Kirkwood, *The History of Mexico*, 162–67.

43. Hamilton, *The Limits of State Autonomy*, 220–32; Kirkwood, *The History of Mexico*, 165–66.

44. *La Defensa*, May 30, 1936, box 52, CFLPS; Anderson, Book No. 310, May 20, 1936, August 5, 1936.

45. Meeting of the Frente Popular note, October 25, 1936, folder Mexican Work, box 25, University of Chicago Settlement House Collection.

46. "The Unemployed and W.P.A. Workers Must Organize," flyer, folder Mexican Work, box 25, University of Chicago Settlement House Collection; meeting of the Frente Popular, October 25, 1936; Anderson, Book No. 310, May 20, 1936; March, interview transcript; Arredondo, "Navigating Ethno-Racial Currents," 418, 427n158. In these instances Mexicans were resisting the process of assimilation that James R. Barrett describes in "Americanization from the Bottom Up." Additionally, while white ethnics and African Americans may have been drawn to the CIO as part of a broad New Deal coalition, as Lizabeth Cohen shows, Mexicans were largely noncitizens and were encouraged to participate in CIO activities by radical Mexican nationalists. See Cohen, *Making a New Deal*.

47. Quoted in Anderson, Book No. 310, February 16, 1936.

48. Anderson, Book No. 310, February 21, 1936.

49. Meyer, *El sinarquismo*, 47.

50. Olcott, *Revolutionary Women*, 107–11.

51. *El Ideal Mexicano*, November 8, 1936, January 3, 1937, box 52, CFLPS; *El Ideal Mexicano*, October 25, 1936, box 53, CFLPS; "Mrs. De la Mora Requests."

52. Meeting of the Frente Popular, October 25, 1936; "Mrs. De la Mora Requests."

53. Klehr, Haynes, and Anderson, *The Soviet World*, 71.

54. Meetings of the Frente Popular, January 10, 1937, January 24, 1937.

55. Meeting of the Frente Popular, January 31, 1937; report of the meeting of the study group, May 7, 1937, folder Mexican Work, box 25, University of Chicago Settlement House Collection.

Chapter 5. Mexican Radicals and Traditionalists Unionize Workers in the United States

1. See Arredondo, *Mexican Chicago*, 59–61; Sanchez, *Becoming Mexican American*, 12, 228–29; Vargas, *Labor Rights*, 6, 14–15, 254, 277–79, 286–87. For monographs that emphasize the prounion attitudes of Mexican immigrants, see Zamora, *The World of the Mexican Worker*, 198; Weber, *Dark Sweat, White Gold*, 5–12, 79–111, 182–99; and Milkman, *L.A. Story*.

2. On the history of the relatively small but influential "militant minority" of European American "men and women who endeavored to weld their workmates and neighbors into a self-aware and purposeful working class," see Montgomery, *The Fall of the House of Labor*, 2.

3. Ruth Needleman argues that African American steel workers also had organized themselves prior to the arrival of the CIO (see *Black Freedom Fighters*).

4. Hart, *Anarchism*; Raat, *Revoltosos*; Cockcroft, *Intellectual Precursors*, 68–70, 161, 175; MacLachlan, *Anarchism and the Mexican Revolution*; Lomnitz, *The Return*, 243–49.

5. See the works listed in the previous note.

6. Quoted in Monroy, *Rebirth*, 223.

7. See Guerin-Gonzales, *Mexican Workers*; Reisler, *By the Sweat of Their Brow*, 234–48; Balderrama and Rodriguez, *Decade of Betrayal*, 63–88; and Dinwoodie, "Deportation," 193–203.

8. The literature on the relationship between the CPUSA and the CIO is extensive. For a partial list of these monographs, see Halpern, *Down on the Killing Floor*; Kelley, *Hammer and Hoe*; Honey, *Southern Labor*; Korstad, *Civil Rights Unionism*; Biondi, *To Stand and Fight*. For a series of essays that focus on the CIO unions heavily influenced by Communists, see Rosswurm, *The CIO's Left-Led Unions*.

9. Zieger, *The CIO*.

10. Cohen, *Making a New Deal*, 338; Halpern, *Down on the Killing Floor*, 186; Horowitz, "Negro and White," 68; Acuña, *Occupied America*, 246.

11. On the power of *testimonios* in reconstructing the history of ethnic Mexicans in the United States, see Garcia and Castro, *Blowout!*, 19–23.

12. Statement of Refugio Martínez, August 9, 1938, U.S. Department of Labor, Immigration, and Naturalization Service, Chicago, file 4001/3627, Chicago Metro History Education Center (hereafter cited as CMHEC), Newberry Library, Chicago, Illinois; and statement of Refugio Martínez, October 16, 1946, U.S. Department of Justice, Immigration, and Naturalization Service, Chicago, file 4001/3627, and Central Office file 55984/495, A.R. #3407165, CMHEC.

13. Ocasio Melendez, *Capitalism and Development*.

14. Quoted in ibid., 55.

15. Ansell, *Oil Baron*; Santiago, *The Ecology of Oil*.

16. Ocasio Melendez, *Capitalism and Development*, 145.

17. Ibid., chap. 3.

18. Kondracke, *Saving Milly*, 8–9.

19. Report, June 24, 1941, folder 5, box 4, United Packinghouse, Food, and Allied Workers Records (hereafter UPWA), Wisconsin Historical Society.

20. *El Heraldo de las Américas*, November 1, 1924, November 22, 1924; *La Noticia Mundial*, August 28, 1927, September 4, 1927, October 16, 1927, November 6, 1927, and February 5, 1928, box 52, CFLPS; *México*, April 4, 1925, April 11, 1925, October 23, 1927, January 18, 1928, January 25, 1928, January 28, 1928, and February 13, 1928, translated by the author; *México*, December 5, 1928. For more on the political culture of radical Mexicans, see Monroy, "Fence Cutters."

21. Anderson, Book No. 310, February 16, 1936.

22. *El Heraldo de las Américas*, November 22, 1924.

23. Innis-Jimenez, *Steel Barrio*, 152.

24. Martínez statement, October 16, 1946.

25. Vargas, *Labor Rights*, chap. 2.

26. Balderrama and Rodriguez, *Decade of Betrayal*, 53–54.

27. Storch, *Red Chicago*, 25–40; Halpern, *Down on the Killing Floor*, 101–2, 111–12; Horowitz, "Negro and White," 68.

28. All of the INS hearings cited in this chapter address events that occurred before the date of the hearing in question. For the quotes used in this paragraph, see Martínez statement, August 9, 1938. See also statement of Refugio Martínez, October 20, 1948, U.S. Department of Justice, Immigration, and Naturalization Service, Chicago, file 4001/3627, and Central Office file 55984/495, A.R. #3407165, CMHEC.

29. "Mexicans on Relief in Chicago," box 52, folder 2, Burgess Papers.

30. Martínez statement, October 20, 1948.

31. Storch, *Red Chicago*, 115–20.

32. Ibid., 138.

33. Draper, *American Communism*, 272–75.

34. Ottanelli, *The Communist Party*, 101.

35. Statement of Refugio Martínez, January 15, 1947, U.S. Department of Justice, Immigration and Naturalization Service, Chicago, file 55984/495, and Central Office file 55984/495, A.R. #3407165, CMHEC.

36. "Programme of the Communist International," box 344, Pamphlet Collection, Special Collections, Richard J. Daley Library. See also Martínez statement, August 9, 1938.

37. Martínez statement, January 15, 1947; and March interview, November 16, 1977.

38. "Primer Congreso Nacional del Frente Popular Antiimperialista," February 27 and 28, 1936, LCR, 433/121, AGN.

39. The liberals addressed poverty, inequality, and unionization, but they never discussed these social problems through radical theoretical frameworks and were, in fact, often critical of Mexican radicals. See *El Heraldo de las Américas*, November 1, 1924, November 22, 1924; *La Noticia Mundial*, August 28, 1927, September 4, 1927, October 16, 1927, February 5, 1928; *México*, January 18, 1928, January 25, 1928, January 28, 1928, February 13, 1928, translated by the author.

40. Denning, *The Cultural Front*, 425–34.

41. Recollections of Herbert March, Packinghouse Workers Organizing Committee, November 16, 1970, Orear Files; March interview, November 16, 1977; report, June 24, 1941, UPWA; Starr interview, November 5, 2003.

42. Ibid.

43. *CIO News*, April 3, 1939.

44. Martínez statement, January 15, 1947; Martinez Defense Committee, undated, and Fourth Constitutional Convention of UPWA, January 14, 1947, folder 11, box 51, UPWA.

45. *Packinghouse Worker*, November 26, 1943, March 30, 1945.

46. Sub-Committee of the Latin American Committee to President Lewis J. Clark, March 13, 1946, folder 3, box 37, UPWA.

47. "Education of Our Membership" section in press release, March 15, 1948, folder 14, box 51, UPWA.

48. *CIO News—PWOC Edition*, June 10, 1940, October 13, 1944.

49. *Packinghouse Worker*, July–August 1953, February 1954, September 1954, May 1955, June 1955, July 1955, August 1955, November 1955, December 1955.

50. Barrett, "Americanization."

51. March interview, November 16, 1977.

52. Ibid.

53. For this analysis, I excluded the 482 Mexicans who also applied for U.S. citizenship in these years but worked in white-collar positions, owned small businesses, or did not list an occupation on their naturalization papers.

54. On Europeans, see Foner, *In a New Land*, 65–69; Foner, "Engagements," 2486; Roediger, *Working towards Whiteness*, 152–54.

55. Naturalization Records, 1900–1940.

56. Olcott, *Revolutionary Women*, 107. On the radical labor culture of Mexico City, see Lear, *Workers, Neighbors, and Citizens*.

57. Innis-Jimenez, *Steel Barrio*.

58. Innis-Jimenez, *Steel Barrio*, 125.

59. On Alfredo de Ávila and Manual García, see Naturalization Records, 1900–1940. Also, on Ávila, see U.S. Naturalization Record Indexes, 11-205278, reproduced

in Innis-Jimenez, *Steel Barrio,* 126, which suggest that he was under investigation for possible Communist activities. Biographical information on George A. Patterson can be found in the Patterson Papers. On Mexican steelworkers in this early era, see Rosales and Simon, "Chicano Steel Workers." Throughout this chapter, I will typically refer to a steel mill by what it was called in the year that I reference it. U.S. Steel's subsidiary, the Illinois Steel Company, operated South Works and Gary Works until 1935, when U.S. Steel combined the Illinois Steel Company with the Carnegie Steel Company, thereafter known as the Carnegie-Illinois Steel Corporation. For more on the SWOC in this early period, see Brody, "The Origins of Modern Steel Unionism"; and Zieger, *The CIO,* 34–41.

60. Kornblum, *Blue Collar Community.*

61. Cohen, *Making a New Deal,* 254, 309, 500n30.

62. "Membership of Lodge #65" and "Notes on Envelope," both in folder 6, box 6, Patterson Papers; and "SWOC Mexican Committee 1937" and "Postcard Mailing List," both in folder 7, box 6, Patterson Papers.

63. Rosales and Simon, "Chicano Steel Workers," 271.

64. Clark, Gottlieb, and Kennedy, *Forging a Union of Steel.*

65. Villalpando interview, June 3, 1986; and Flores interview, November 22, 1988.

66. Hull House Educational Events in Chicago, May 1937, folder 11, "Halstead's Mexican Community and Hull House," October 1934–May 1937, Rich Papers; meeting of the Frente Popular, October 18, 1936, folder Mexican Work, box 25, University of Chicago Settlement House Collection; and Senate Committee on Education and Labor, *The Chicago Memorial Day Incident,* part 14, 4945.

67. Senate Committee on Education and Labor, *The Chicago Memorial Day Incident,* part 14, 4659–61, 4941–57.

68. Rosales, "Mexican Immigration," 44, 106.

69. *El Amigo del Hogar,* March 13, 1927, translated by the author.

70. *El Amigo del Hogar,* November 18, 1928, and December 23, 1928, translated by the author.

71. Mendieta, "Celebrating Mexican Culture," 339n89.

72. Villalpando interview, June 3, 1986.

73. Maria G. Vásquez and Ignacia G. Dávila to José M. Fernández, November 3, 1940, Unión Benéfica Mexicana Records, CRA; and Rosales and Simon, "Chicano Steel Workers," 267–75.

74. Mendieta, "Celebrating Mexican Culture," 326–27.

75. "Mexicans Residing in East Chicago, Receiving Aid from North Township," February 23, 1933, Mexican American Folder 1 (hereafter cited as MF1), East Chicago Room.

76. Evett Oral History Interview, 1971, box 12, CRA.

77. Consul Ernesto Laveaga to Basilio Pacheco, September 30, 1950, MF1.

78. The membership cards of Benito Juárez can be found in box 1, Unión Benéfica Mexicana Records, CRA. For more on the Benefit Society, see Mendieta, "Celebrating Mexican Culture."

79. Rosales, "Mexican Immigration," 241n6.

80. Naturalization Records, 1900–1940.

81. Vargas, *Labor Rights*, chap. 2.

82. Claude G. Spraker, Recording Secretary, to Pacheco, March 7, 1942, MF1.

83. Lester H. Thorton to Basil V. Pacheco, November 29, 1944, MF1.

84. Alex B. Levee to Basil Pacheco, April 20, 1942; Congressman Ray J. Madden to Basil Pacheco, March 25, 1948; Senator Homer E. Capehart to Basil Pacheco, March 25, 1949; Senator William E. Jenner to Basil Pacheco, March 26, 1949, all in MF1.

85. Basil Pacheco to Twin City Council of Boy Scouts of America, August 17, 1955; Basil Pacheco to Sheriff of Crown Point, Indiana, April 5, 1956; Comité Patriótico Mexicano de East Chicago, Indiana, April 14, 1956, all in MF1.

86. *The Union Benefica Mexicana: A Brief History*, UBM booklet in possession of the author.

87. For more on the antidiscrimination and educational programs of the immigrant societies of East Chicago, see chapter 2. See also Basil Pacheco to Congressman Ray J. Madden, August 2, 1971, MF1; and "From the Desk of the President" and "The Union Benefica Mexicana: A Brief History," both in the possession of the author.

88. Vargas, *Labor Rights*, 3–15.

89. Sanchez, *Becoming Mexican American*, 11–12.

90. Naturalization Records, 1900–1940.

Chapter 6. The Cold War and the Decline of the Revolutionary Generation

1. The epigraph quote is from Judge Campbell, Memorandum and Order, in the United States District Court (Caption-49-C-1318), October 1, 1951, copy in a bound tutorial by Esther R. Lopez, "Learning History through Biography: The Life of a Mexican Immigrant, Refugio Roman Martinez," A-3 4007 165 (#13) (CMHEC and Chicago Community Trust and the Lloyd A. Fry Foundation, 1995), Files on Mexican Americans, CMHEC; alien card number A3407165, U.S. Citizenship and Immigration Services, U.S. Department of Homeland Security, Freedom of Information Act file number 11292006, in the possession of the author; Marcus T. Neelly to Refugio Martinez, April 27, 1953, copy in Lopez, "Learning History"; Esther R. Lopez, telephone conversation with the author, December 2010.

2. Eugene Cotton to Marcus T. Neely, January 27, 1953, 40013627 (#33), CMHEC.

3. Eugene Cotton to Marcus T. Neely, May 12, 1953, 40013627 (#33), CMHEC.

4. Garcia, *Memories of Chicano History*, 117; see the biography of Luisa Moreno in the *Encyclopedia Britannica*, www.britannica.com/biography/Luisa-Moreno.

5. Ruiz, *Cannery Women*, 36, 42–65, 77–101; *Encyclopedia Britannica*, www.britannica.com/biography/Luisa-Moreno.

6. Garcia, *Mexican Americans*, 147–51.

7. Quoted in Gutierrez, *Walls and Mirrors*, 113.

8. Quoted in Ruiz, *From out of the Shadows*, 96.

9. Garcia, *Mexican Americans*, 155–56.

10. Flores, "Corona, Bert."

11. Quoted in Arnold, "Humberto Silex," 3–5.

12. Quoted in ibid.

13. Vargas, *Labor Rights*, 174, 256–57.

14. Ibid., 174.

15. Quoted in Garcia, *Mexican Americans*, 186.

16. Ibid., 201.

17. Ibid., 203–8.

18. Ibid., 210, 212, 215, 220–21.

19. Ibid., 213.

20. Larralde and Griswold del Castillo, "Luisa Moreno."

21. Garcia, *Mexican Americans*, 145–227; Garcia, *Memories of Chicano History*, 106–19, 249–71; Vargas, *Labor Rights*, 123–50.

22. Garcia, *Memories of Chicano History*, 119.

23. Martínez statement, January 15, 1947. The discussion of Martinez's interrogation by the INS in 1938 is compiled from testimony given in INS hearings in 1938, 1947, and 1948; those statements are at the CMHEC.

24. Martínez statement, October 20, 1948.

25. Ngai, *Impossible Subjects*, 55.

26. Martínez statement, August 9, 1938.

27. Ngai, *Impossible Subjects*, 77.

28. Martínez statement, October 20, 1948.

29. Ibid.

30. Martínez statement, August 9, 1938; and "Programme of the Communist International," box 344, Pamphlet Collection.

31. Ibid.

32. Dunbar, "We Wear the Mask."

33. Ngai, *Impossible Subjects*, 59, 87–89.

34. Martinez Defense Committee, undated, and Fourth Constitutional Convention of UPWA, January 14, 1947, folder 11, box 51, UPWA.

35. Sam Sponseller to Refugio Martínez, January 13, 1943; Sponseller to Martínez March 3, 1943; Sponseller to Martínez, April 10, 1943; and Sponseller to Martínez, April 20, 1943, folder 6, box 4, UPWA Records.

36. Warrant for Arrest of Alien, April 8, 1941, U.S. Department of Justice, Washington, DC, 4001-3627, no. 55984/495, CMHEC.

37. This section of the chapter is compiled from testimony given in Martínez's INS hearings in 1946, 1947, and 1948.

38. Martínez statement, October 20, 1948.

39. Ibid.

40. Martínez statement, October 16, 1946; Martínez statement, January 15, 1947.

41. Ibid.

42. Martínez statement, October 16, 1946.

43. "Opinion of the Presiding Inspector," COF 4001/3627, COF 55984/495, A.R. #3407165, January 20, 1947, CMHEC.

44. "It Can Happen to You" (flyer); and Lewis J. Clark to Jack Freeman, August 4, 1947, both in folder 11, box 51, UPWA.

45. Garcia, *Mexican Americans*, chapter 2; Kaplowitz, *LULAC*, 54–59.

46. Flores interview, November 22, 1988.

47. Villalpando interview, June 3, 1986.

48. Gutierrez interview, November 30, 1988.

49. "Origin and Purpose of the Mexican Civic Committee," folder 4, box 89, Chicago Area Project Papers, Chicago History Museum. On nativism, see Zolberg, *A Nation by Design*.

50. Longtime labor activist Bert Corona maintained that progressive American community groups and the CIO did not adequately defend Mexicans who were investigated during the McCarthy witch hunts of the 1950s. See Garcia, *Memories of Chicano History*, 119.

51. "Stop the Deportation Menace!" (flyer), January 30, 1948, CMHEC.

52. Ibid.; and "It Can Happen to You," folder 11, box 51, UPWA.

53. Program for National Conference for Protection of Foreign Born, October 1947, and "It Can Happen to You," both in folder 11, box 51, UPWA.

54. Cotton, videocassette interview, 1995; amended complaint, November 1, 1949, in "Learning History through Biography" tutorial, CMHEC.

55. Cohen, *Braceros*, 2, 232n4.

56. Garcia, *Operation Wetback*, 37, 42.

57. Cohen, *Braceros*, 1–5, 106, 192–98.

58. Ngai, *Impossible Subjects*, 143–52.

59. Samora, *Los Mojados*, 43–48.

60. Garcia, *Operation Wetback*, 36–39, 109–11, 126–27; Calavita, *Inside the State*, 18–46.

61. Garcia, *Operation Wetback*, 158.

62. Quoted in ibid., 171.

63. Ibid., 172.

64. Ibid., 111, 172–74, 220, 224; Calavita, *Inside the State*, 46–72, 106–12.

65. "Subject Operation Cloudburst" and Department of Justice report, RG 56363/299, National Archives and Records Administration, Washington, DC.

66. Garcia, *Operation Wetback*, 189, 236; Calavita, *Inside the State*, 53–82.

67. Tom Littlewood, "Mexicans Are Chicago's Least Understood Group," *Chicago Sun-Times*, October 19, 1953.

68. Fernandez, *Brown in the Windy City*, 34–37, 49–55.

69. Martinez v. Neelly, 344 U.S. 916 (1953). The United States Court of Appeals had earlier affirmed the district court's ruling; see Martinez v. Neelly, 197 F.2d 462 (1952).

70. *Chicago Sun Times*, October 19, 1953; and *Chicago Tribune*, January 13, 1953.

71. Villarreal, videocassette interview, 1995.

72. I borrow Sanchez's phrase "ambivalent American" from *Becoming Mexican American*, 210, and see part 4.

Conclusion

1. On contemporary Mexican social movements advancing these politics, see Bacon, *The Right to Stay Home.*

2. On a "we are here because you are there" paradigm of Latin American immigration to the United States, see Gonzalez, *Harvest of Empire.* On the uses and meanings of this immigrant rights slogan in Britain, see Weber, "Borderline Justice"; and Kundnani, *The End of Tolerance.* On subaltern nationalism as an anti-imperialist ideology, see Hardt and Negri, *Empire,* 105–9.

3. Garcia, *Mexican Americans,* 1–3, 18–22. For an interpretation that suggests that the Mexican American generation was conservative, see Benjamin Marquez's early work, *The Evolution of a Mexican American Political Organization*; and for a perspective that emphasizes Mexican Americans' antiblack racism, see Foley, "Becoming Hispanic"; and Foley, *Quest for Equality.* On works that point to the progressive dimensions of the Mexican American generation, see Garcia, *Mexican Americans*; Orozco, *No Mexicans*; Zamora, *Claiming Rights*; and Johnson, "The Cosmic Race."

4. In the 1950s, new Mexican American groups in Chicago like the Mexican American Council (MAC) came to argue that undocumented immigrants complicated the lives of Mexican Americans and legally residing Mexican nationals, but they too did not advocate extreme xenophobic arguments. On these new groups, see Fernandez, *Brown in the Windy City,* 39, 51–53, 67–68, 79, 82.

5. MacLean, *Freedom Is Not Enough,* 158.

6. Thomas, *Puerto Rican Citizen,* 227.

7. On the revolution's influence on the Chicano movement and on its international dimensions, see Perez, *The Decolonial Imaginary,* chaps. 2 and 3; and Mariscal, *Brown-Eyed Children,* chaps. 2 and 3. On the Chicano movement in Chicago, see Fernandez, *Brown in the Windy City,* chap. 6; and Ramirez, *Chicanas of 18th Street.*

8. Fink, "Labor Joins La Marcha," 117; and Pallares, "The Chicago Context," 44.

9. "Activists Say It's No Surprise Chicago Immigration Rally Set Tone for the Nation," *Chicago Independent Media Center,* http://chicago.indymedia.org/archive/newswire/display/71593/index.php; and "'Socialist' 25th Ward Candidate Jorge Mujica Brings Breakfast to the Unemployment Line," *Chicago Reader,* http://www.chicagoreader.com/Bleader/archives/2014/12/31/socialist-25th-ward-candidate-jorge-mujica-brings-breakfast-to-the-unemployment-line.

10. Vaughan and Lewis, *The Eagle and the Virgin,* back cover.

Appendix

1. Sanchez, *Becoming Mexican American,* 275.

2. Aguila, "Mexican/U.S. Immigration Policy," 211.

Bibliography

Archives

Archivo General de la Nación (AGN), Distrito Federal, Mexico
Archivo Histórico de la Secretaria de Relaciones Exteriores (SRE), Distrito Federal, Mexico
Bancroft Library, University of California, Berkeley
    Paul S. Taylor Papers
Calumet Regional Archives (CRA), Indiana University Northwest, Gary, Indiana
    Unión Benéfica Mexicana Records
Chicago History Museum, Chicago, Illinois
    Chicago Area Project Papers
    William E. Dever Collection
    George A. Patterson Papers
    University of Chicago Settlement House Collection
Chicago Metro History Education Center (CMHEC), Newberry Library, Chicago, Illinois
Cook County Clerk of the Circuit Court, Naturalization Declarations of Intention (1906–29), http://www.cookcountyclerkofcourt.org/NR/
East Chicago Room, East Chicago Public Library, East Chicago, Indiana
    Paul E. Kelly Files
Illinois Labor History Society, Chicago, Illinois
    Les Orear Files
Special Collections, Regenstein Library, University of Chicago
    Ernest W. Burgess Papers
    Chicago Foreign Language Press Survey (CFLPS)
    Robert Redfield Papers

Special Collections, Richard J. Daley Library, University of Illinois at Chicago
    Immigrants' Protective League Collection (IPL)
    Pamphlet Collection
    Adena Miller Rich Papers
National Archives and Records Administration, College Park, Maryland
National Archives and Records Administration, Great Lakes Region, Chicago
    Declarations of Intention and Petitions for Naturalization, 1900–1940, RG 21
National Archives and Records Administration, Washington, DC
    Records of the Immigration and Naturalization Service
Wisconsin Historical Society, Madison
    United Packinghouse, Food, and Allied Workers Records (UPWA)

Interviews

Cotton, Eugene. Interview on videocassette, 1995. Chicago Metropolitan History Education Center.
Flores, Bob. Interview by Ruth Needleman, November 22, 1988. CRA.
González, Concepción. Interview by Ruth Needleman, March 27, 1989. CRA.
March, Herbert. Interview by Elizabeth Ballanoff, November 16, 1977, transcript. Roosevelt University, Chicago.
Orear, Les. Interview on videocassette, 1995. Chicago Metropolitan History Education Center.
———. Interview by the author, November 5, 2003.
Starr, Vicky. Interview by the author, November 12, 2003.
Villalpando, Jesse. Interview by Ruth Needleman, June 3, 1986. CRA.
Villarreal, Anita. Interview on videocassette, 1995. Chicago Metropolitan History Education Center.

Published Government Records

U.S. Bureau of the Census. *Abstract of the Twelfth Census of the United States 1900.* 3rd ed. Washington, DC: Government Printing Office, 1904.
———. *Fifteenth Census of the United States: 1930.* Vol. 3, pt. 1, Population. Washington, DC: Government Printing Office, 1930.
———. *Fourteenth Census of the United States 1920.* Vol. 3, Composition and Characteristics of the Population by States. Washington, DC: Government Printing Office, 1922.
———. *Sixteenth Census of the United States: 1940.* Reports on Population. Washington, DC: Government Printing Office, 1940.
U.S. House of Representatives. Committee on Immigration and Naturalization. *Temporary Admission of Illiterate Mexican Laborers.* 66th Cong., 2nd sess. Washington, DC: U.S. Government Printing Office 1920.
U.S. Senate. Committee on Education and Labor. *The Chicago Memorial Day Incident Part 14.* Washington, DC: U.S. Government Printing Office, 1937.

Periodicals

Chicago Daily Tribune, 1923–39
CIO News—PWOC Edition, 1940–44
Correo Mexicano, 1926
Daily Illini, 1936
El Amigo del Hogar, 1924–30
El Heraldo de las Américas, 1924, 1928
El Ideal Mexicano, 1936–37
El Indicador, 1933
El Liberal, 1933
El Mexicano, 1934
El Nacional, 1931–34
La Alianza, 1936
La Defensa, 1936
La Lucha, 1934
La Noticia Mundial, 1925–31
La Raza, 1928
México, 1925, 1927–31, 1938
Milwaukee Journal, 1936
New York Times, 1927
Packinghouse Worker, 1945, 1953–55
Sunday Times, 1935

Dissertations and Master's Theses

Felter, Eunice. "Social Adaptations of the Mexican Churches in the Chicago Area." M.A. thesis, University of Chicago, 1941.

Hernandez-Fujigaki, Jorge. "Mexican Steelworkers and the United Steelworkers of America in the Midwest: The Inland Steel Experience, 1936–1976." Ph.D. dissertation, University of Chicago, 1991.

Jones, Anita Edgar. "Conditions Surrounding Mexicans in Chicago." M.A. thesis, University of Chicago, 1928.

Kerr, Louise Año Nuevo. "The Chicano Experience in Chicago: 1920–1970." Ph.D. dissertation, University of Illinois at Chicago, 1976.

McCarthy, Malachy Richard. "Which Christ Came to Chicago: Catholic and Protestant Programs to Evangelize, Socialize and Americanize the Mexican Immigrant, 1900–1940." Ph.D. dissertation, Loyola University of Chicago, 2002.

Rosales, Francisco Arturo. "Mexican Immigration to the Urban Midwest during the 1920s." Ph.D. dissertation, Indiana University, 1978.

Weber, David Stafford. "Anglo Views of Mexican Immigrants: Popular Perceptions and Neighborhood Realities in Chicago, 1900–1940." Ph.D. dissertation, Ohio State University, 1982.

Articles, Essays in Anthologies, Encyclopedia Entries, and Websites

Aguila, Jaime R. "Mexican/U.S. Immigration Policy prior to the Great Depression." *Diplomatic History* 31, no. 2 (April 2007): 207–25.

Arnesen, Eric. "Whiteness and the Historians' Imagination." *International Labor and Working-Class History* 60 (October 2001): 3–32.

Arnold, Frank. "Humberto Silex: CIO Organizer from Nicaragua." *Southwest Economy and Society* 4 (Fall 1978): 3–18.

Arredondo, Gabriela F. "Navigating Ethno-Racial Currents: Mexicans in Chicago, 1919–1939." *Journal of Urban History* 30, no. 4 (March 2004): 399–427.

Bada, Xóchitl. "Mexican Hometown Associations in Chicago: The Newest Agents of Civic Participation." In *¡Marcha! Latino Chicago and the Immigrant Rights Movement*, edited by Amalia Pallares and Nilda Flores-Gonzalez, 146–62. Urbana: University of Illinois Press, 2010.

Barrett, James R. "Americanization from the Bottom Up: Immigration and the Remaking of the Working Class in the United States, 1880–1930." *Journal of American History* 79, no. 3 (December 1992): 996–1020.

Barrett, James R., and David R. Roediger. "Inbetween Peoples: Race, Nationality and the 'New Immigrant' Working Class." *Journal of American Ethnic History* 16, no. 3 (1997): 3–44.

———. "The Irish and the 'Americanization' of the 'New Immigrants' in the Streets and in the Churches of the Urban United States, 1900–1930." *Journal of American Ethnic History* 24, no. 4 (2005): 3–33.

Braga, Michael Marconi. "To Relieve the Misery: Sugar Mill Workers and the 1933 Cuban Revolution." In *Workers' Control in Latin America*, edited by Jonathan C. Brown, 16–44. Chapel Hill: University of North Carolina Press, 1997.

Britton, John A. "Redefining Intervention: Mexico's Contribution to Anti-Americanism." In *Anti-Americanism in Latin America and the Caribbean*, edited by Alan L. McPherson, 37–60. New York: Berghahn Books, 2006.

Brody, David. "The Origins of Modern Steel Unionism." In *Forging a Union of Steel: Philip Murray, SWOC, and the United Steelworkers*, edited by Paul F. Clark, Peter Gottlieb, and Donald Kennedy, 13–29. Ithaca, NY: ILR Press, 1987.

Cardoso, Lawrence A. "La repatriación de braceros en época de Obregón: 1920–1923." *Historia Mexicana* 26, no. 4 (April–June 1977): 576–95.

Diamond, Jeff. "African-American Attitudes towards United States Immigration Policy." *International Migration Review* 32, no. 2 (Summer 1998): 451–70.

Dinwoodie, D. H. "Deportation: The Immigration Service and the Chicano Labor Movement in the 1930s." *New Mexico Historical Review* 52, no. 3 (July 1977): 193–206.

Dunbar, Paul Laurence. "We Wear the Mask." In *The Complete Poems of Paul Laurence Dunbar*. New York: Fili-Quarian Classics, 2010.

Fernandez, James D., and Luis Argeo. "Invisible Immigrants: Spaniards in the U.S., 1868–1945." http://invisibleimmigrants.com.

Fink, Leon. "Labor Joins La Marcha: How New Immigrant Activists Restored the Meaning of May Day." In *¡Marcha! Latino Chicago and the Immigrant Rights Movement*, edited by Amalia Pallares and Nilda Flores-Gonzalez, 109–22. Urbana: University of Illinois Press, 2010.

Flores, John H. "Corona, Bert (May 29, 1918-February 15, 2001), Activist for Mexican and Mexican-American Rights." In *Encyclopedia of U.S. Labor and Working-Class History*, edited by Eric Arnesen, 324–26. New York: Routledge, 2007.

———. "A Migrating Revolution: Mexican Political Organizers and Their Rejection of American Assimilation, 1920–1940." In *Workers across the Americas: The Transnational Turn in Labor History*, edited by Leon Fink, 329–52. New York: Oxford University Press, 2011.

Flower, Elizabeth. "The Mexican Revolt against Positivism." *Journal of the History of Ideas* 10, no. 1 (January 1949): 115–29.

Foley, Neil. "Becoming Hispanic: Mexican Americans and the Faustian Pact with Whiteness." In *Reflexiones 1997: New Directions in Mexican American Studies*, edited by Neil Foley, 53–70. Austin: University of Texas Press, 1998.

Foner, Nancy. "Engagements across National Borders, Then and Now." *Fordham Law Review* 75, no. 5 (2007): 2483–92.

Fuchs, Lawrence H. "The Reactions of Black Americans to Immigration." In *Immigration Reconsidered: History, Sociology, and Politics*, edited by Virginia Yans-McLaughlin, 293–314. New York: Oxford University Press, 1990.

Garcia, John A. "Political Integration of Mexican Immigrants: Explorations into the Naturalization Process." *International Migration Review* 15, no. 4 (Winter 1981): 608–25.

Garcia, Juan R., and Angel Cal. "El Círculo de Obreros Católicos 'San José,' 1925 to 1930." In *Forging a Community: The Latino Experience in Northwest Indiana, 1919–1975*, edited by James B. Lane and Edward J. Escobar, 95–114. Bloomington: Indiana University Press, 1987.

Gómez-Quiñones, Juan. "The First Steps: Chicano Labor Conflict and Organizing, 1900–1920." *Aztlan* 3, no. 1 (Spring 1972): 13–49.

Grannan, Jill Thomas. "'Here Comes Everybody': The 28th International Eucharistic Congress." *Chicago History*, Spring 2009, 20–45.

Grebler, Leo. "The Naturalization of Mexican Immigrants in the United States." *International Migration Review* 1, no. 1 (Autumn 1966): 17–32.

Guerra, Lillian. "The Promise and Disillusion of Americanization: Surveying the Socioeconomic Terrain of Early-Twentieth-Century Puerto Rico." *Centro Journal* 11, no. 1 (1999): 9–32.

Hernández, José Angel. "Contemporary Deportation Raids and Historical Memory: Mexican Expulsions in the Nineteenth Century." *Aztlan: A Journal of Chicano Studies* 35, no. 2 (Fall 2010): 115–42.

Innes, John S. "The Universidad Popular Mexicana." *Americas* 30, no. 1 (July 1973): 110–22.

214 *Bibliography*

Johnson, Benjamin. "The Cosmic Race in Texas: Racial Fusion, White Supremacy, and Civil Rights." *Journal of American History* 98, no. 2 (September 2011): 404–19.

Kerr, Louise Año Nuevo. "State of the Discipline: Chicano History." In *Voices of a New Chicano History*, edited by Refugio I. Rochin and Dennis N. Valdes, 14–165. East Lansing: Michigan State University Press, 2000.

Knight, Alan. "Cardenismo: Juggernaut or Jalopy?" *Journal of Latin American Studies* 26, no. 1 (February 1994): 73–107.

———. "Racism, Revolution, and Indigenismo: Mexico, 1910–1940." In *The Idea of Race in Latin America, 1870–1940*, edited by Richard Graham, 71–113. Austin: University of Texas Press, 1990.

Larralde, Carlos M., and Richard Griswold del Castillo. "Luisa Moreno and the Beginnings of the Mexican American Civil Rights Movement in San Diego." *Journal of San Diego History* 43, no. 3 (Summer 1997): 158–75.

Levitt, Peggy. "'You Know, Abraham Was Really the First Immigrant': Religion and Transnational Migration." *International Migration Review* 37, no. 3 (Fall 2003): 847–73.

Lopez, Rick A. "Forging a Mexican National Identity in Chicago: Mexican Migrants and Hull-House." In *Pots of Promise: Mexicans and Pottery at Hull-House, 1920–40*, edited by Cheryl R. Ganz and Margaret Strobel, 89–93. Urbana: University of Illinois Press, 2004.

Mendieta, Eva. "Celebrating Mexican Culture and Lending a Helping Hand: Indiana Harbor's Sociedad Mutualista Benito Juárez, 1924–1957." *Indiana Magazine* 108, no. 4 (December 2012): 311–44.

Meyer, Jean. "An Idea of Mexico: Catholics in the Revolution." In *The Eagle and the Virgin: Nation and Cultural Revolution in Mexico*, edited by Mary Kay Vaughan and Stephen E. Lewis, 281–96. Durham, NC: Duke University Press, 2006.

Monroy, Douglas. "Fence Cutters, *Sedicioso*, and First-Class Citizens: Mexican Radicalism in America." In *The Immigrant Left in the United States*, edited by Paul Buhle and Dan Georgakas, 11–44. Albany: State University of New York Press, 1996.

Nieto-Phillips, John. "Citizenship and Empire: Race, Language, and Self-Government in New Mexico and Puerto Rico, 1898–1917." *Centro Journal* 11, no. 1 (1999): 51–74.

Pallares, Amalia. "The Chicago Context." In *¡Marcha! Latino Chicago and the Immigrant Rights Movement*, edited by Amalia Pallares and Nilda Flores-Gonzalez, 37–61. Urbana: University of Illinois Press, 2010.

Ramirez, Leonard G., Jose Perales-Ramos, and Jose Antonio Arellano. "Marchando al Futuro: Latino Immigrant Rights Leadership in Chicago." In *¡Marcha! Latino Chicago and the Immigrant Rights Movement*, edited by Amalia Pallares and Nilda Flores-Gonzalez, 123–145. Urbana: University of Illinois Press, 2010.

Reynolds, Eileen. "The Spanish Wave: America's Forgotten Immigrants." http://www.nyu.edu/about/news-publications/nyu-stories/james-fernandez-on-the-spaniards-in-the-us.html.

Romanell, Patrick. "Bergson in Mexico: A Tribute to José Vasconcelos." *Philosophy and Phenomenological Research* 21, no. 4 (June 1961): 501–13.

Rosales, Francisco Arturo. "Shifting Self-Perceptions and Ethnic Consciousness among Mexicans in Houston, 1908–1946." *Aztlan* 16, no. 1–2 (1985): 71–94.

Rosales, Francisco A., and Daniel T. Simon. "Chicano Steel Workers and Unionism in the Midwest, 1919–1945." *Aztlan* 6, no. 2 (Summer 1975): 266–75.

Sánchez, George J. "'Go After the Women': Americanization and the Mexican Immigrant Woman, 1915–1929." In *Unequal Sisters: A Multicultural Reader in U.S. Women's History*, edited by Vicki L. Ruiz and Ellen Carol Dubois, 250–63. New York: Routledge, 1994.

Shankman, Arnold. "The Image of Mexico and the Mexican American in the Black Press, 1890–1935." *Journal of Ethnic Studies* 3, no. 2 (Summer 1975): 43–56.

Skirius, John. "Vasconcelos and México de afuera (1928)." *Aztlan: A Journal of Chicano Studies* 7, no. 3 (1976): 479–97.

Smith, Robert C. "Diasporic Memberships in Historical Perspective: Comparative Insights from the Mexican, Italian, and Polish Cases." *International Migration Review* 37, no. 3 (Fall 2003): 724–59.

Sobek, Matthew. "Occupations." In *Historical Statistics of the United States, Earliest Times to the Present: Millennial Edition*, edited by Susan B. Carter, Scott Sigmund Gartner, Michael R. Haines, Alan L. Olmstead, Richard Sutch, and Gavin Wright, tables Ba1159–1439. New York: Cambridge University Press, 2006.

Spears, Andrea. "Rehabilitating the Workers: The U.S. Railway Mission to Mexico." In *Workers Control in Latin America*, edited by Jonathan C. Brown, 72–97. Chapel Hill: University of North Carolina Press, 1997.

Treviño, Roberto R. "Prensa y patria: The Spanish-Language Press and the Biculturation of the Tejano Middle Class, 1920–1940." *Western Historical Quarterly* 22, no. 4 (November 1991): 454–72.

Vaughan, Mary Kay. "Primary Education and Literacy in Nineteenth-Century Mexico: Research Trends, 1968–1988." *Latin American Research Review* 25, no. 1 (1990): 31–66.

Vecoli, Rudolf J. "The Formation of Chicago's 'Little Italies.'" *Journal of American Ethnic History* 2, no. 2 (Spring 1983): 5–20.

Weber, France. "Borderline Justice." *Race & Class* 54, no. 2 (2012): 39–54.

Young, Julia G. "Cristero Diaspora: Mexican Immigrants, the U.S. Catholic Church, and Mexico's Cristero War, 1926–1929." *Catholic Historical Review* 98, no. 2 (April 2012): 271–300.

Books

Acuña, Rodolfo F. *Occupied America: A History of Chicanos*. 6th ed. 1972; New York: Pearson Longman, 2007.

Aguilar, Luis E. *Cuba: Prologue to Revolution*. Ithaca, NY: Cornell University Press, 1972.

Alba, Francisco. *The Population of Mexico: Trends, Issues, and Policies*. Translated by Marjory Mattingly Urquidi. 1977; New Brunswick, NJ: Transaction, Inc., 1982.

Alexander, Robert J., and Eldon M. Parker. *International Labor Organizations and Organized Labor in Latin America and the Caribbean: A History*. Santa Barbara, CA: Praeger, 2009.

Ansell, Martin R. *Oil Baron of the Southwest: Edward L. Doheny and the Development of the Petroleum Industry in California and Mexico*. Columbus: Ohio State University Press, 1998.

Arenal, Angélica. *Páginas sueltas con Siqueiros*. Mexico City: Editorial Grijalbo, S.A., 1979.

Arredondo, Gabriela F. *Mexican Chicago: Race, Identity, and Nation, 1916–39*. Urbana: University of Illinois Press, 2008.

Bacon, David. *The Right to Stay Home: How U.S. Policy Drives Mexican Migration*. Boston: Beacon Press, 2013.

Bada, Xóchitl. *Mexican Hometown Associations in Chicagoacán: From Local to Transnational Civic Engagement*. New Brunswick, NJ: Rutgers University Press, 2014.

Bailey, David C. *¡Viva Cristo Rey! The Cristero Rebellion and the Church-State Conflict in Mexico*. Austin: University of Texas Press, 1974.

Balderrama, Francisco E. *In Defense of La Raza: The Los Angeles Mexican Consulate and the Mexican Community, 1929 to 1936*. Tucson: University of Arizona Press, 1982.

Balderrama, Francisco E., and Raymond Rodriguez. *Decade of Betrayal: Mexican Repatriation in the 1930s*. Rev. ed. Albuquerque: University of New Mexico Press, 2006.

Baldwin, Deborah J. *Protestants and the Mexican Revolution: Missionaries, Ministers, and Social Change*. Urbana: University of Illinois Press, 1990.

Barkan, Elazar. *The Retreat of Scientific Racism: Changing Concepts of Race in Britain and the United States between the World Wars*. New York: Cambridge University Press, 1992.

Barrett, James R. *The Irish Way: Becoming American in the Multiethnic City*. London: Penguin Press, 2012.

Basch, Linda, Nina Glick Schiller, and Cristina Szanton Blanc, eds. *Nations Unbound: Transnational Projects, Postcolonial Predicaments, and Deterritorialized Nation-States*. Amsterdam: Gordon and Breach Science Publishers, 1994.

Beito, David T. *From Mutual Aid to the Welfare State: Fraternal Societies and Social Services, 1890–1967*. Chapel Hill: University of North Carolina Press, 2000.

Berlin, Ira. *Generations of Captivity: A History of African-American Slaves*. Cambridge, MA: Belknap Press of Harvard University Press, 2003.

Biondi, Martha. *To Stand and Fight: The Struggle for Civil Rights in Postwar New York City*. Cambridge, MA: Harvard University Press, 2006.

Boyer, Christopher R. *Becoming Campesinos: Politics, Identity, and Agrarian Struggle in Postrevolutionary Michoacán, 1920–1935*. Stanford, CA: Stanford University Press, 2003.

Brading, D. A. *The First America: The Spanish Monarchy, Creole Patriots, and the Liberal State, 1492–1867*. Cambridge: Cambridge University Press, 1991.

Briggs, Laura. *Reproducing Empire: Race, Sex, Science, and U.S. Imperialism in Puerto Rico*. Berkeley: University of California Press, 2002.

Brown, Jonathan C., ed. *Workers' Control in Latin America*. Chapel Hill: University of North Carolina Press, 1997.

Buchenau, Jürgen. *Plutarco Elías Calles and the Mexican Revolution*. Lanham, MD: Rowman and Littlefield Publishers, 2007.

Butler, Mathew. *Popular Piety and Political Identity in Mexico's Cristero Rebellion: Michoacán, 1927–29*. New York: Oxford University Press, 2004.

Caban, Pedro A. *Constructing a Colonial People: Puerto Rico and the United States, 1898–1932.* Boulder, CO: Westview Press, 1999.

Calavita, Kitty. *Inside the State: The Bracero Program, Immigration, and the I.N.S.* New York: Routledge, 1992.

Cannistaro, Philip, and Gerald Meyer, eds. *The Lost World of Italian-American Radicalism.* Westport, CT: Praeger, 2003.

Carr, Barry. *Marxism and Communism in Twentieth-Century Mexico.* Lincoln: University of Nebraska Press, 1992.

Carroll, Peter N. *The Odyssey of the Abraham Lincoln Brigade: Americans in the Spanish Civil War.* Stanford, CA: Stanford University Press, 1994.

Clark, Paul F., Peter Gottlieb, and Donald Kennedy, eds. *Forging a Union of Steel: Philip Murray, SWOC, and the United Steelworkers.* Ithaca, NY: ILR Press, 1987.

Cockcroft, James D. *Intellectual Precursors of the Mexican Revolution, 1900–1913.* Austin: University of Texas Press, 1968.

Cohen, Deborah. *Braceros: Migrant Citizens and Transnational Subjects in the Postwar United States and Mexico.* Chapel Hill: University of North Carolina Press, 2011.

Cohen, Lizabeth. *Making a New Deal: Industrial Workers in Chicago, 1919–1939.* New York: Cambridge University Press, 1990.

Collier, Ruth Berins, and David Collier. *Shaping the Political Arena: Critical Junctures, the Labor Movement, and Regime Dynamics in Latin America.* Notre Dame, IN: University of Notre Dame Press, 2002.

Córdova, Arnaldo. *La política de masas del cardenismo.* Mexico City: Ediciones ERA, 1974.

Deans-Smith, Susan, and Ilona Katzew, eds. *Race and Classification: The Case of Mexican America.* Stanford, CA: Stanford University Press, 2009.

De Leon, Arnoldo. *Ethnicity in the Sunbelt: Mexican Americans in Houston.* Rev. ed. College Station: Texas A&M University Press, 2001.

Denning, Michael. *The Cultural Front: The Laboring of American Culture in the Twentieth Century.* New York: Verso, 2011.

Draper, Theodore. *American Communism and Soviet Russia: The Formative Period.* New York: Viking Press, 1960.

Dzidzienyo, Anani, and Suzanne Oboler, eds. *Neither Enemies nor Friends: Latinos, Blacks, Afro-Latinos.* New York: Palgrave Macmillan, 2005.

Esenwein, George, and Adrian Shubert. *Spain at War: The Spanish Civil War in Context, 1931–1939.* London: Longman, 1995.

Fabela, Isidro. *Los Estados Unidos contra la libertad: Estudios de historia diplomática americana; Cuba, Filipinas, Panamá, Nicaragua, República Dominicana.* Barcelona: Talleres Gráficos Lux, 1920.

Fabregat, Claudio Esteva. *Mestizaje in Ibero-America.* Translated by John Wheat. Tucson: University of Arizona Press, 1995.

Farber, Samuel. *Revolution and Reaction in Cuba, 1933–1960: A Political Sociology from Machado to Castro.* Middletown, CT: Wesleyan University Press, 1976.

Fernandez, Frank. *Cuban Anarchism: The History of a Movement.* Tucson, AZ: Sharp Press, 2001.

Fernandez, Lilia. *Brown in the Windy City: Mexicans and Puerto Ricans in Postwar Chicago*. Chicago: University of Chicago Press, 2010.

Fink, Leon. *The Maya of Morganton: Work and Community in the Nuevo New South*. Chapel Hill: University of North Carolina Press, 2003.

Foley, Neil. *Quest for Equality: The Failed Promise of Black-Brown Solidarity*. Cambridge, MA: Harvard University Press, 2010.

Foner, Nancy. *In a New Land: A Comparative View of Immigration*. New York: New York University Press, 2005.

Gabaccia, Donna R. *Italy's Many Diasporas*. New York: Routledge, 2003.

Gamio, Manuel. *Forjando patria*. 1916; Mexico City: Editorial Porrua, 1982.

———. *Mexican Immigration to the United States: A Study of Human Migration and Adjustment*. Chicago: University of Chicago Press, 1930.

Garcia, Juan Ramon. *Mexicans in the Midwest, 1900–1932*. Tucson: University of Arizona Press, 1996.

———. *Operation Wetback: The Mass Deportation of Mexican Undocumented Workers in 1954*. Westport, CT: Greenwood Press, 1980.

Garcia, Mario T. *Memories of Chicano History: The Life and Narrative of Bert Corona*. Berkeley: University of California Press, 1994.

———. *Mexican Americans: Leadership, Ideology and Identity, 1930–1960*. New Haven, CT: Yale University Press, 1989.

Garcia, Mario T., and Sal Castro. *Blowout! Sal Castro and the Chicano Struggle for Educational Justice*. Chapel Hill: University of North Carolina Press, 2011.

Garcia, Richard A. *Rise of the Mexican American Middle Class: San Antonio, 1929–1941*. College Station: Texas A&M University Press, 1991.

Genova, Nicholas de, and Nathalie Peutz, eds. *The Deportation Regime: Sovereignty, Space, and the Freedom of Movement*. Durham, NC: Duke University Press, 2010.

Glenn, Susan. *Daughters of the Shtetl: Life and Labor in the Immigrant Generation*. Ithaca, NY: Cornell University Press, 1990.

Gobat, Michael. *Confronting the American Dream: Nicaragua under U.S. Imperial Rule*. Durham, NC: Duke University Press, 2005.

Gomez, Laura E. *Manifest Destinies: The Making of the Mexican American Race*. New York: New York University Press, 2007.

Gómez-Quiñones, Juan. *Mexican American Labor: 1790–1990*. Albuquerque: University of New Mexico Press, 1994.

Gonzalez, Gilbert G. *Mexican Consuls and Labor Organizing: Imperial Politics in the American Southwest*. Austin: University of Texas Press, 1999.

Gonzalez, Juan. *Harvest of Empire: A History of Latinos in America*. New York: Penguin Books, 2011.

Graham, Helen. *The Spanish Republic at War, 1936–1939*. New York: Cambridge University Press, 2002.

Gramsci, Antonio. *Prison Notebooks*. 3 vols. Translated by J. A. Buttigieg. 1975; New York: Columbia University Press, 2007.

Guerin-Gonzales, Camille. *Mexican Workers and American Dreams: Immigration, Repatriation, and California Farm Labor, 1900–1939*. New Brunswick, NJ: Rutgers University Press, 1994.

Guerra, Lillian. *Popular Expression and National Identity in Puerto Rico: The Struggle for Self, Community, and Nation*. Gainesville: University Press of Florida, 1998.

Guglielmo, Jennifer. *Living the Revolution: Italian Women's Resistance and Radicalism in New York City, 1880–1945*. Chapel Hill: University of North Carolina Press, 2012.

Guglielmo, Thomas A. *White on Arrival: Italians, Race, Color and Power in Chicago, 1890–1945*. New York: Oxford University Press, 2003.

Gutierrez, David G. *Walls and Mirrors: Mexican Americans, Mexican Immigrants, and the Politics of Ethnicity*. Berkeley: University of California Press, 1995.

Gutman, Herbert G. *Work, Culture, and Society in Industrializing America: Essays in American Working-Class and Social History*. New York: Knopf, distributed by Random House, 1976.

Haddox, John H. *Vasconcelos of Mexico: Philosopher and Prophet*. Austin: University of Texas Press, 1967.

Hale, Charles A. *Emilio Rabasa and the Survival of Porfirian Liberalism: The Man, His Career, and His Ideas, 1856–1930*. Stanford, CA: Stanford University Press, 2008.

———. *Mexican Liberalism in the Age of Mora, 1821–1853*. New Haven, CT: Yale University Press, 1968.

———. *The Transformation of Liberalism in Late Nineteenth-Century Mexico*. Princeton, NJ: Princeton University Press, 1989.

Halpern, Rick. *Down on the Killing Floor: Black and White Workers in Chicago's Packinghouses, 1904–54*. Urbana: University of Illinois Press, 1997.

Hamilton, Nora. *The Limits of State Autonomy: Post-revolutionary Mexico*. Princeton, NJ: Princeton University Press, 1982.

Hamilton, Nora, and Norma Stoltz Chinchilla. *Seeking Community in a Global City: Guatemalans and Salvadorans in Los Angeles*. Philadelphia: Temple University Press, 2001.

Hardt, Michael, and Antonio Negri. *Empire*. Cambridge, MA: Harvard University Press, 2000.

Hart, John Mason. *Anarchism and the Mexican Working Class, 1860–1931*. Austin: University of Texas Press, 1978.

———. *Empire and Revolution: The Americans in Mexico since the Civil War*. Berkeley: University of California Press, 2002.

———. *Revolutionary Mexico: The Coming and Process of the Mexican Revolution*. Berkeley: University of California Press, 1987.

Harzig, Christiane, and Dirk Hoerder. *What Is Migration History?* Cambridge: Polity Press, 2009.

Hernández, José Amaro. *Mutual Aid for Survival: The Case of the Mexican American*. Malabar, FL: Robert E. Krieger Publishing Company, 1983.

Hernández, José Angel. *Mexican American Colonization during the Nineteenth Century: A History of the U.S.-Mexico Borderlands*. New York: Cambridge University Press, 2012.

Higham, John. *Strangers in the Land: Patterns of American Nativism, 1860–1925*. New Brunswick, NJ: Rutgers University Press, 1955.

Hoare, Quintin, and Geoffrey Nowell Smith, eds. *Selections from the Prison Notebooks of Antonio Gramsci*. New York: International Publishers, 1971.

Hodges, Donald C. *Intellectual Foundations of the Nicaraguan Revolution*. Austin: University of Texas Press, 1986.

Honey, Michael K. *Southern Labor and Black Civil Rights: Organizing Memphis Workers*. Urbana: University of Illinois Press, 1993.

Horowitz, Roger. *"Negro and White, Unite and Fight!": A Social History of Industrial Unionism in Meatpacking, 1930–90*. Urbana: University of Illinois Press, 1997.

Hughes, Elizabeth A. *Living Conditions for Small-Wage Earners in Chicago*. Chicago: Department of Public Welfare, 1925.

Hundley, Norris, Jr., ed. *The Chicano: Essays*. Santa Barbara, CA: Clio Books, 1975.

Iglesias, Cesar Andreu, ed. *Memoirs of Bernardo Vega: A Contribution to the History of the Puerto Rican Community in New York*. New York: Monthly Review Press, 1984.

Innis-Jimenez, Michael. *Steel Barrio: The Great Mexican Migration to South Chicago, 1915–1940*. New York: New York University Press, 2013.

Jacobson, Matthew Frye. *Whiteness of a Different Color: European Immigrants and the Alchemy of Race*. Cambridge, MA: Harvard University Press, 1999.

Johnson, Benjamin Heber. *Revolution in Texas: How a Forgotten Rebellion and Its Bloody Suppression Turned Mexicans into Americans*. New Haven, CT: Yale University Press, 2003.

Jones, Robert C., and Louis R. Wilson. *The Mexican in Chicago*. Chicago: Comity Commission of the Chicago Church Federation, 1931.

Joseph, Gilbert M., and Jürgen Buchenau. *Mexico's Once and Future Revolution: Social Upheaval and the Challenge of Rule since the Late Nineteenth Century*. Durham, NC: Duke University Press, 2013.

Jung, Moon-Kie, Joao Costa Vargas, and Eduardo Bonilla-Silva, eds. *State of White Supremacy: Racism, Governance, and the United States*. Stanford, CA: Stanford University Press, 2011.

Kaplowitz, Craig A. *LULAC, Mexican Americans, and National Policy*. College Station: Texas A&M University Press, 2005.

Katz, Friedrich. *The Life and Times of Pancho Villa*. Stanford, CA: Stanford University Press, 1998.

Kelley, Robin D. G. *Hammer and Hoe: Alabama Communists during the Great Depression*. 25th anniversary ed. 1990; Chapel Hill: University of North Carolina Press, 2015.

Kenny, Kevin. *Making Sense of the Molly Maguires*. New York: Oxford University Press, 1998.

Kevles, Daniel J. *In the Name of Eugenics: Genetics and the Uses of Human Heredity.* 1985; Cambridge, MA: Harvard University Press, 1998.

Kiddle, Amelia M., and María L. O. Muñoz, eds. *Populism in Twentieth Century Mexico: The Presidencies of Lázaro Cárdenas and Luis Echeverría.* Tucson: University of Arizona Press, 2010.

Kirkwood, Burton. *The History of Mexico.* 2nd ed. Westport, CT: Greenwood Press, 2000.

Klehr, Harvey, John Earl Haynes, and Kyrill M. Anderson. *The Soviet World of American Communism.* New Haven, CT: Yale University Press, 1998.

Knight, Alan. *Counter-revolution and Reconstruction.* Vol. 2 of *The Mexican Revolution.* Cambridge: Cambridge University Press, 1986.

———. *Porfirians, Liberals, and Peasants.* Vol. 1 of *The Mexican Revolution.* Cambridge: Cambridge University Press, 1986.

Kondracke, Morton. *Saving Milly: Love, Politics, and Parkinson's Disease.* New York: Public Affairs, 2001.

Kornblum, William. *Blue Collar Community.* Chicago: University of Chicago Press, 1975.

Korstad, Robert Rogers. *Civil Rights Unionism: Tobacco Workers and the Struggle for Democracy in the Mid-Twentieth-Century South.* Chapel Hill: University of North Carolina Press, 2003.

Kundnani, Arun. *The End of Tolerance: Racism in 21st Century Britain.* London: Pluto Press, 2007.

Lear, John. *Workers, Neighbors, and Citizens: The Revolution in Mexico City.* Lincoln: University of Nebraska Press, 2001.

Leininger Pycior, Julie. *Democratic Renewal and the Mutual Aid Legacy of U.S. Mexicans.* College Station: Texas A&M University Press, 2014.

Levenstein, Harvey A. *Labor Organizations in the United States and Mexico.* 1971; Westport, CT: Greenwood Press, 1980.

Levitt, Peggy. *The Transnational Villagers.* Berkeley: University of California Press, 2001.

Lichtenstein, Nelson. *Labor's War at Home: The CIO in World War II.* New York: Cambridge University Press, 1982.

Lomnitz, Claudio. *Deep Mexico Silent Mexico: An Anthology of Nationalism.* Minneapolis: University of Minnesota Press, 2001.

———. *The Return of Comrade Ricardo Flores Magón.* New York: Zone Books, 2014.

Lopez, Ian F. Haney. *Racism on Trial: The Chicano Fight for Justice.* Cambridge, MA: Belknap Press of Harvard University Press, 2003.

MacLachlan, Colin M. *Anarchism and the Mexican Revolution: The Political Trials of Ricardo Flores Magón in the United States.* Berkeley: University of California Press, 1991.

MacLean, Nancy. *Freedom Is Not Enough: The Opening of the American Workplace.* Cambridge, MA: Harvard University Press, 2006.

Mariscal, George. *Brown-Eyed Children of the Sun: Lessons from the Chicano Movement, 1965–1975*. Albuquerque: University of New Mexico Press, 2005.

Marquez, Benjamin. *The Evolution of a Mexican American Political Organization*. Austin: University of Texas Press, 1993.

Martínez, María Elena. *Genealogical Fictions: Limpieza de Sangre, Religion, and Gender in Colonial Mexico*. Stanford, CA: Stanford University Press, 2011.

Massey, Douglas S., Jorge Durand, and Nolan J. Malone. *Beyond Smoke and Mirrors: Mexican Immigration in the Era of Economic Integration*. New York: Russell Sage Foundation, 2002.

McGreevy, John T. *Parish Boundaries: The Catholic Encounter with Race in the Twentieth-Century Urban North*. Chicago: University of Chicago Press, 1996.

Meyer, Jean A. *The Cristero Rebellion: The Mexican People between Church and State, 1926–1929*. Cambridge, UK: Cambridge University Press, 1976.

———. *El sinarquismo: ¿Un fascismo mexicano? 1937–1947*. Mexico City: Editorial Joaquín Mortiz, 1979.

———. *La Cristiada: The Mexican People's War for Religious Liberty*. Garden City Park, NY: Square One Publishers, 2013.

Meyer, Michael C., William L. Sherman, and Susan M. Deeds. *The Course of Mexican History*. 9th ed. Oxford: Oxford University Press, 2011.

Milkman, Ruth. *L.A. Story: Immigrant Workers and the Future of the U.S. Labor Movement*. New York: Russell Sage Foundation, 2006.

Miller, Kerby A. *Emigrants and Exiles: Ireland and the Irish Exodus to North America*. New York: Oxford University Press, 1985.

Miller, Marilyn Grace. *Rise and Fall of the Cosmic Race: The Cult of Mestizaje in Latin America*. Austin: University of Texas Press, 2004.

Millon, Robert P. *Vicente Lombardo Toledano, Mexican Marxist*. Chapel Hill: University of North Carolina Press, 1966.

Mirande, Alfredo. *Hombres y Machos: Masculinity and Latino Culture*. Boulder, CO: Westview Press, 1997.

Monroy, Douglas. *Rebirth: Mexican Los Angeles from the Great Migration to the Great Depression*. Berkeley: University of California Press, 1999.

Montgomery, David. *The Fall of the House of Labor: The Workplace, the State, and American Labor Activism, 1865–1925*. New York: Cambridge University Press, 1987.

Mormino, Gary, and George Pozzeta. *The Immigrant World of Ybor City: Italians and Their Latin Neighbors in Tampa, 1885–1985*. Urbana: University of Illinois Press, 1987.

Needleman, Ruth. *Black Freedom Fighters in Steel: The Struggle for Democratic Unionism*. Ithaca, NY: Cornell University Press, 2003.

Nervo, Amado. *Antología poética e ideario ae Amado Nervo. Editores Mexicanos Unidos, Poesia*. Editores Mexicanos Unidos, 1999.

Ngai, Mae M. *Impossible Subjects: Illegal Aliens and the Making of Modern America*. Princeton, NJ: Princeton University Press, 2004.

Ocasio Melendez, Marcial E. *Capitalism and Development: Tampico, Mexico, 1876–1924*. New York: Peter Lang Publishing, 1998.

Olcott, Jocelyn. *Revolutionary Women in Postrevolutionary Mexico*. Durham, NC: Duke University Press, 2005.

Omi, Michael, and Howard Winant. *Racial Formation in the United States: From the 1960s to the 1990s*. 1986; New York: Routledge, 1994.

Orozco, Cynthia. *No Mexicans, Women, or Dogs Allowed: The Rise of the Mexican American Civil Rights Movement*. Austin: University of Texas Press, 2009.

Orozco, José Clemente. *An Autobiography*. Translated by Robert C. Stephenson. 1942; Austin: University of Texas Press, 1962.

Orsi, Robert. *Thank You, St. Jude: Women's Devotion to the Patron Saint of Hopeless Causes*. New Haven, CT: Yale University Press, 1996.

Ottanelli, Fraser M. *The Communist Party of the United States: From the Depression to World War II*. New Brunswick, NJ: Rutgers University Press, 1991.

Pallares, Amalia, and Nilda Flores-Gonzalez, eds. *¡Marcha! Latino Chicago and the Immigrant Rights Movement*. Urbana: University of Illinois Press, 2010.

Park, Robert E., and Herbert A. Miller. *Old World Traits Transplanted*. New York: Harper, 1921.

Payne, Stanley G. *Spain's First Democracy: The Second Republic, 1931–1936*. Madison: University of Wisconsin Press, 1993.

Paz, Octavio. *The Labyrinth of Solitude and Other Writings*. Translated by Lysander Kemp. 1961; New York: Grove Press, 1985.

Perez, Emma. *The Decolonial Imaginary: Writing Chicanas into History*. Bloomington: Indiana University Press, 1999.

Perlmann, Joel. *Italians Then, Mexicans Now: Immigrant Origins and Second-Generation Progress, 1890 to 2000*. New York: Russell Sage Foundation, 2005.

Piccato, Pablo. *The Tyranny of Opinion: Honor in the Construction of the Mexican Public Sphere*. Durham, NC: Duke University Press, 2010.

Purnell, Jennie. *Popular Movements and State Formation in Revolutionary Mexico: The Agraristas and Cristeros of Michoacán*. Durham, NC: Duke University Press, 1999.

Quirk, Robert. *The Mexican Revolution and the Catholic Church, 1910–1929*. Bloomington: Indiana University Press, 1973.

Raat, W. Dirk. *Revoltosos: Mexico's Rebels in the United States, 1903–1923*. College Station: Texas A&M University Press, 1981.

Ramirez, Leonard G. *Chicanas of 18th Street: Narratives of a Movement from Latino Chicago*. Champaign: University of Illinois Press, 2011.

Reisler, Mark. *By the Sweat of Their Brow: Mexican Immigrant Labor in the United States, 1900–1940*. Westport, CT: Greenwood Press, 1976.

Rembao, Alberto. *The Growing Church and Its Changing Environment in Latin America: From Missions to Mission in Latin America*. New York: Committee, 1958.

———. *Lecciones de filosofía de la religión*. Matanzas: Publicaciones del Seminario Evangélico de Teología, 1958.

———. *Outlook in Mexico*. New York: Friendship Press, 1942.

Roediger, David R. *The Wages of Whiteness: Race and the Making of the American Working Class*. Rev. ed. New York: Verso, 2007.

———. *Working towards Whiteness: How America's Immigrants Became White*. New York: Basic Books, 2006.

Rosales, F. Arturo. *Dictionary of Latino Civil Rights History*. Houston: Arte Público Press, 2006.

Rosswurm, Steve, ed. *The CIO's Left-Led Unions*. New Brunswick, NJ: Rutgers University Press, 1992.

Ruiz, Vicki L. *Cannery Women, Cannery Lives: Mexican Women, Unionization, and the California Food Processing Industry, 1930–1950*. Albuquerque: University of New Mexico Press, 1987.

———. *From out of the Shadows: Mexican Women in Twentieth-Century America*. New York: Oxford University Press, 1998.

Samora, Julian. *Los Mojados: The Wetback Story*. Notre Dame, IN: University of Notre Dame Press, 1971.

Samora, Julian, and Richard A. Lamanna. *Mexican-Americans in a Midwest Metropolis: A Study of East Chicago*. Mexican American Study Project, Advance Report 8. Los Angeles: University of California Press, 1967.

Sanchez, George J. *Becoming Mexican American: Ethnicity, Culture and Identity in Chicano Los Angeles, 1900–1945*. Oxford: Oxford University Press, 1993.

Santiago, Myrna I. *The Ecology of Oil: Environment, Labor, and the Mexican Revolution, 1900–1938*. New York: Cambridge University Press, 2006.

Schoultz, Lars. *Beneath the United States: A History of U.S. Policy toward Latin America*. Cambridge, MA: Harvard University Press, 1998.

Shankman, Arnold. *Ambivalent Friends: Afro-Americans View the Immigrant*. Westport, CT: Greenwood Press, 1982.

Shubert, Adrian. *The Road to Revolution in Spain: Coal Miners of Asturias, 1860–1934*. Urbana: University of Illinois Press, 1987.

Simpson, Lesley Byrd. *Many Mexicos*. 4th ed. Berkeley: University of California Press, 1966.

Siqueiros, David Alfaro. *No hay más ruta que la nuestra*. Mexico City: Talleres Gráficos, 1945.

Slayton, Robert A. *Back of the Yards: The Making of a Local Democracy*. Chicago: University of Chicago Press, 1988.

Smith, Stephanie J. *Gender and the Mexican Revolution: Yucatan Women and the Realities of Patriarchy*. Chapel Hill: University of North Carolina Press, 2009.

Spickard, Paul. *Almost All Aliens: Immigration, Race, and Colonialism in American History and Identity*. New York: Routledge, 2007.

Storch, Randi. *Red Chicago: American Communism at Its Grassroots, 1928–35*. Urbana: University of Illinois Press, 2008.

Taylor, Paul S. *Mexican Labor in the United States: Chicago and the Calumet Region*. University of California Publications in Economics, vol. 7, no. 2. Berkeley: University of California Press, 1932.

Thomas, Lorrin. *Puerto Rican Citizen: History and Political Identity in Twentieth-Century New York City*. Chicago: University of Chicago Press, 2010.

Tilly, Charles, and Lesley J. Wood. *Social Movements, 1768-2008*. Boulder, CO: Paradigm Publishers, 2009.

Top, Michael Miller. *Those without a Country: The Political Culture of Italian American Syndicalists*. Minneapolis: University of Minnesota Press, 2001.

Valdes, Dionicio Nodin. *Al Norte: Agricultural Workers in the Great Lakes Region, 1917-1970*. Austin: University of Texas Press, 1991.

———. *Barrios Norteños: St. Paul and Midwestern Mexican Communities in the Twentieth Century*. Austin: University of Texas Press, 2000.

Vargas, Zaragosa. *Labor Rights Are Civil Rights: Mexican American Workers in Twentieth-Century America*. Princeton, NJ: Princeton University Press, 2005.

———. *Proletarians of the North: A History of Mexican Industrial Workers in Detroit and the Midwest, 1917-1933*. Berkeley: University of California Press, 1993.

Vasconcelos, José. *The Cosmic Race: A Bilingual Edition*. Translated by Didier T. Jaen. 1925; Baltimore, MD: Johns Hopkins University Press, 1997.

———. *Ulises criollo (autobiografía)*. Mexico City: Editorial Jus, S.A., 1969.

Vaughan, Mary Kay. *Cultural Politics in Revolution: Teachers, Peasants, and Schools in Mexico, 1930-1940*. Tucson: University of Arizona Press, 1997.

Vaughan, Mary Kay, and Stephen E. Lewis, eds. *The Eagle and the Virgin: Nation and Cultural Revolution in Mexico, 1920-1940*. Durham, NC: Duke University Press, 2006.

Vinson, Ben, III, and Matthew Restall, eds. *Black Mexico: Race and Society from Colonial to Modern Times*. Albuquerque: University of New Mexico Press, 2009.

Vinson, Ben, III, and Bobby Vaughn. *Afroméxico: El pulso de la población negra en México; Una historia recordada, olvidada y vuelta a recordar*. Mexico City: CIDE—Fondo de Cultura Económica, 2004.

Weber, Devra. *Dark Sweat, White Gold: California Farm Workers, Cotton, and the New Deal*. Berkeley: University of California Press, 1994.

Wyman, Mark. *Round-Trip to America: The Immigrants Return to Europe, 1880-1930*. Ithaca, NY: Cornell University Press, 1993.

Zamora, Emilio. *Claiming Rights and Righting Wrongs in Texas: Mexican Workers and Job Politics during World War II*. College Station: Texas A&M University Press, 2009.

———. *The World of the Mexican Worker in Texas*. College Station: Texas A&M University Press, 1993.

Zieger, Robert H. *The CIO, 1935-1955*. Chapel Hill: University of North Carolina Press, 1995.

Zolberg, Aristide R. *A Nation by Design: Immigration Policy in the Fashioning of America*. Cambridge, MA: Harvard University Press, 2006.

Index

JOHN H. FLORES is an assistant professor of history at Case Western Reserve University.

Latinos in Chicago and the Midwest

The University of Illinois Press
is a founding member of the
Association of American University Presses.

Composed in 10.5/13 Minion Pro
by Lisa Connery
at the University of Illinois Press
Cover designed by Dustin J. Hubbart
Cover illustration: Diego Rivera, *Man, Controller of the Universe*
© 2017 Banco de México Diego Rivera Frida Kahlo Museums Trust,
Mexico, D.F. / Artists Rights Society (ARS), New York.

University of Illinois Press
1325 South Oak Street
Champaign, IL 61820-6903
www.press.uillinois.edu